# RURAL DEVELOPMENT: TOWARDS SUSTAINABILITY

# RURAL DEVELOPMENT: TOWARDS SUSTAINABILITY

## (In 3 Volumes)

## (Rural Empowerment)
## Volume 1

*Editor*
**B.K. Pandey**

ISHA

**ISHA BOOKS**
**Delhi-110033**

**Rural Development: Towards Sustainability**
*(Rural Empowerment)*

Rs. 2500 (Set)
Rs. 835 (Each Volume)

ISBN : 81-8205-209-2 (Set)
ISBN : 81-8205-310-2 (Vol. 1)



Published in 2005 in India by
Isha Books
D-43, Prithviraj Road,
Adarsh Nagar, Delhi - 110033
e-mail : ishabooks@hotmail.com

Laser Typesetting at : Global Printers, New Delhi
Printed at : Chawla Offset Press, Delhi

# Contents

# Preface

Rural development is the process of helping rural people to set the priorities in their own communities through effective and democratic bodies, by providing the local capacity; investment in basic infrastructure and social services; justice, equity and security; dealing with the injustices of the past and ensuring safety and security of the rural population.

In recent years, rural development is getting increased attention in countries around the world. It is one of the most important item in the development agenda of all countries. It contributes greatly to the development of disadvantaged (rural) regions through its various structural funds. A reason for the heightened attention is the deep structural change in rural areas, which includes not only changes in the rural economy, but also serious demographic, social and cultural transitions.

The sustainability of rural development initiatives depends greatly on the capacities of the stake-holders involved, the relationships among them and their relative power. A strategy to foster pluralistic approaches to rural development should focus on building the capacities of those who have been marginalised by development strategies as well as on developing relationships that allow more effective, efficient and equal interactions and greater accountability among all participants. Therefore, the types of changes that are needed to promote substantive and sustainable community-based development are closely associated with more general processes of promoting pluralism and democratisation. Without political space it is exceedingly difficult for local people to organise or have an impact on policy-making processes.

*Rural Development: Towards Sustainability* is a compilation of three volumes: *Rural Empowerment, Rural Sustainable Development* and *Rural Diversity and Community Development*. Each volume describes the issues and concerns related to its title. It is hoped that this work will address the needs of a wide range of audiences like students, teachers, researchers, policymakers, governmental and non-governamental organisations and all who are directly or indirectly related with rural development.

***Editor***

# 1

# Poverty Alleviation in Rural India

India is home to 22 percent of the world's poor. Such a high incidence of poverty is a matter of concern in view of the fact that poverty eradication has been one of the major objectives of the development planning process. Indeed, poverty is a global issue. Its eradication is considered integral to humanity's quest for sustainable development. Reduction of poverty in India, is, therefore, vital for the attainment of international goals.

Agricultural wage earners, small and marginal farmers and casual workers engaged in non-agricultural activities, constitute the bulk of the rural poor. Small land holdings and their low productivity are the cause of poverty among households dependent on land-based activities for their livelihood. Poor educational base and lack of other vocational skills also perpetuate poverty.

Due to the poor physical and social capital base, a large proportion of the people are forced to seek employment in vocations with extremely low levels of productivity and wages. The creation of employment opportunities for the unskilled workforce has been a major challenge for development planners and administrators. Poverty alleviation has been one of the guiding principles of the planning process in India. The role of economic growth in providing more employment avenues to the population has been clearly recognised.

The growth-oriented approach has been reinforced by focusing on specific sectors which provide greater opportunities to the people to participate in the growth process. The various dimensions of poverty relating to health, education and other basic services have been progressively internalised in the planning process. Central and state governments have considerably enhanced allocations for the provision of education, health, sanitation and other facilities which promote capacity-building and well-being of the poor.

Investments in agriculture, area development programmes and afforestation provide avenues for employment and income. Special programmes have been taken up for the welfare of scheduled castes (SCs) and scheduled tribes (STs), minorities, the disabled and other vulnerable groups.

Anti-poverty programmes that seek to transfer assets and skills to people for self-employment, coupled with public works programmes that enable people to cope with transient poverty, are the third strand of the larger anti-poverty strategy. The targetted public distribution system (TPDS) protects the poor from the adverse effects of a rise in prices and ensures food and nutrition security at affordable prices.

The success of the anti-poverty strategy can be gauged from the decline in poverty levels from 37.27 per cent in 1993-94 to 27.09 per cent in 1999-2000 in the rural areas. In absolute terms, the number of rural poor fell below the 200 million mark for the first time since 1973-74. However, this achievement falls short of the Ninth Plan projections.

At the beginning of the Plan, it was projected that, with a growth target of 6.5 per cent per annum during the Plan period, only 18.61 per cent of the population would be below the poverty line by 2001. This shortfall can be attributed largely to the uneven performance of states in poverty alleviation.

The distribution of poor across states is also disparate, with Uttar Pradesh, Bihar, Madhya Pradesh, West Bengal and Orissa accounting for 69 per cent of the poor in 1999-2000. Kerala, Haryana, Bihar, Himachal Pradesh, Karnataka and Rajasthan experienced a sharp reduction in poverty levels.Uttar Pradesh, West Bengal and Tamil Nadu also registered significant reduction in poverty (8-12 percentage points).

However, Orissa and Madhya Pradesh have shown virtually no reduction in poverty levels. In fact, these are the states where the absolute number of poor has actually gone up between 1993-94 and 1999-2000.

## Anti-Poverty Programmes in the Ninth Plan

### Integrated Rural Development Programme/ Swarnajayanti Gram Swarozgar Yojana

The Integrated Rural Development Programme (IRDP), introduced in selected blocks in 1978-79 and universalised from 2 October 1980 has provided assistance to rural poor in the form of subsidy and bank credit for productive employment opportunities through successive plan periods.

Subsequently, Training of Rural Youth for Self Employment (TRYSEM), Development of Women and Children in Rural Areas (DWCRA), Supply of Improved Tool Kits to Rural Artisans (SITRA) and Ganga Kalyan Yojana (GKY) were introduced as sub-programmes of IRDP to take care of the specific needs of the rural population.

These schemes were, however, implemented as 'stand alone programmes', an approach which substantially detracted from their effectiveness. The Mid-Term Appraisal of the Ninth Plan had indicated that these sub-programmes "presented a matrix of multiple programmes without desired linkages".

The programme suffered from sub critical investments, lack of bank credit, over-crowding in certain projects, and lack of market linkages. The programme was basically subsidy driven and ignored the processes of social intermediation necessary for the success of self-employment programmes. A one-time provision of credit without follow-up action and lack of a continuing relationship between borrowers and lenders also undermined the programme's objectives.

The marginal impact of self-employment programmes led to the constitution of a committee by the Planning Commission in 1997 to review selfemployment and wage-employment programmes. The committee recommended the merger of all selfemployment programmes for the rural poor and a shift from the individual beneficiary approach to a group-based approach. It emphasised the identification of activity clusters in specific areas and strong training and marketing linkages.

The committee's recommendations were accepted by the Government. On 1 April 1999, the IRDP and allied programmes, including the Million Wells Scheme (MWS), were merged into a single programme known as Swarnajayanti Gram Swarozgar Yojana (SGSY). The SGSY is conceived as a holistic programme of micro enterprise development in rural areas with emphasis on organising the rural poor into self-help groups, capacity-building, planning of activity clusters, infrastructure support, technology, credit and marketing linkages.

It seeks to promote a network of agencies, namely, the District Rural Development Agencies (DRDAs), line departments of state governments, banks, NGOs and panchayati raj Institutions (PRIs) for implementation of the programme. The SGSY recognises the need to focus on key activities and the importance of activity clusters. The programme has in-built safeguards for the weaker sections. It insists that 50 per cent of the self-help groups must be formed exclusively by women and that 50 per cent of the benefits should flow to SCs and STs. There is also a provision for disabled beneficiaries.

The programme is credit driven and subsidy is back-ended. The credit and subsidy ratio is pegged at 3:1. The subsidy is fixed at 30 per cent of the project cost subject to a maximum of Rs. 7,500 per individual beneficiary for those in the general category and 50 per cent of the project cost subject to a maximum of Rs. 10,000 in the case of SC/STs. In the case of group projects, the subsidy is 50 per cent of the project cost subject to a ceiling of Rs. 1.25 lakh.

Funds under the scheme are shared between the Centre and state governments in the ratio of 75:25. The new approach to self-employment has made significant contribution to the empowerment of beneficiaries as evidence from the evaluation of SGSY in Tamil Nadu shows. Implementation of the programme between 1999-2000 and 2001-02 has highlighted many areas of concern. While the IRDP concentrated on individual beneficiaries, the SGSY laid greater emphasis on social mobilisation and group formation.

However, the DRDAs responsible for administering the programme did not have the requisite skills in social mobilisation. Linkages with NGOs, which could have facilitated this process, were also not in place. The programme, therefore, suffered in the initial years. Central releases were substantially lower than the allocation as the field offices were not in a position to organise self-help groups which could be provided financial assistance. Credit mobilisation also suffered in the process.

Against a target of Rs. 9,611 crore of credit, the achievement during the last three years has been only Rs. 3,235 crore, i.e. 33.66 per cent of the target. In the last three years of the Ninth Plan, 7,67,141 self-help groups were formed. While 9,34,000 individuals were assisted in 1999-2000, 10,30,000 individuals were provided support in 2000-01. The coverage was considerably lower than around 2.2 million beneficiaries under IRDP every year during the Eighth Plan period.

**Wage Employment Programmes**

Wage employment programmes, an important component of the anti-poverty strategy, have sought to achieve multiple objectives. They not only provide employment opportunities during lean agricultural seasons but also in times of floods, droughts and other natural calamities. They create rural infrastructure which supports further economic activity. These programmes also put an upward pressure on market wage rates by attracting people to public works programmes, thereby reducing labour supply and pushing up demand for labour.

While public works programmes to provide employment in times of distress have a long history, major thrust to wage employment programmes in the country was provided only after the attainment of self-sufficiency in food grains in the 1970s. The National Rural Employment Programme (NREP) and Rural Landless Employment Guarantee Programmes (RLEGP) were started in the Sixth and Seventh Plans.

**Jawahar Rozgar Yojana/Jawahar Gram Samridhi Yojana**

The NREP and RLEGP were merged in April 1989 under

the Jawahar Rozgar Yojana (JRY). The JRY was meant to generate meaningful employment opportunities for the unemployed and underemployed in rural areas through the creation of economic infrastructure and community and social assets. Initially, the JRY also included the Indira Awas Yojana (IAY) and the MWS. Both these schemes were made into independent schemes in 1996.

Under JRY, 73,764.83 lakh mandays of employment were generated till 1998-99 Employment generation progressively declined over the years, partly due to lower central allocations in the Ninth Plan and partly due to the increasing cost of creating employment. A major proportion of JRY funds was spent on roads and buildings. Over 47 per cent of the employment generated benefited SC/STs.

The share of landless labourers among the beneficiaries was 36 per cent. The village community found the assets created under the programme useful. However, against 40 per cent of population in a village panchayat who sought work, only 15 per cent were actually employed. The JRY was revamped from 1 April 1999 as the Jawahar Gram Samridhi Yojana (JGSY). It now became a programme for the creation of rural economic infrastructure with employment generation as a secondary objective.

The 60:40 wage labour/material ratio in the JRY was relaxed. The programme is implemented by the village panchayats and provides for specific benefits to SC/ STs, the disabled and the maintenance of community assets created in the past. Since inception it has generated 27 crore mandays of employment each year (on an average), a substantial drop from the 103 crore mandays generated under JRY in the year 1993-94.

The works taken up under JGSY have not been comprehensively evaluated for their quality and employment potential. Initial reports from the states, however, indicates that since every village panchayat has to be covered by the scheme, many panchayats get less than Rs. 10,000 per annum. Except for states like Kerala, West Bengal and Orissa, where village panchayats cover large areas and get substantial funds under the scheme, in other states most panchayats get less than Rs. 50,000 per annum.

Benefits to the SC/STs and the disabled have to be earmarked. In addition, the administrative expenses of the panchayat and expenditure on assets already created are to be met from JGSY funds. In effect, panchayats are left with very little money to take up meaningful infrastructure projects.

**Employment Assurance Scheme**

The Employment Assurance Scheme (EAS) was launched on 2 October 1993 covering 1,778 drought-prone, desert, tribal and hill area blocks. It was later extended to all the blocks in 1997-98. The EAS was designed to provide employment in the form of manual work in the lean agricultural season. The works taken up under the programme were expected to lead to the creation of durable economic and social infrastructure and address the felt-needs of the people.

The scheme prohibited construction of buildings for religious purposes, monuments, memorials, welcome gates, panchayat buildings, government office buildings and buildings for higher secondary schools and colleges. It also provided for maintenance of assets created in the past under the scheme. Initially, the scheme was demand-driven but from 1999, resources were allocated to states based on the incidence of poverty.

The EAS is a centrally-sponsored scheme, with the Centre providing 75 per cent of the funds and the states 25 per cent. The zilla parishads and panchayat samitis were the implementing agencies. While 10,719.59 lakh mandays of employment were generated during the Eighth Plan, 4,717.74 lakh mandays of employment were generated in the first year of the Ninth Plan.

Employment generation went down in subsequent years. The allocations between 1999-2000 and 2001-02 were also lower than the first two years of the Ninth Plan because watershed projects taken up for implementation under the EAS before April 1999 were transferred to Integrated Wasteland Development Programme (IWDP). Though the creation of community assets has important spin offs for rural poverty and development, the impact of these programmes on employment and income has been limited.

The universalisation of the scheme severely eroded its basic objective of providing assured employment in areas of extreme poverty and chronic unemployment. Allocations were based on a fixed criterion that did not specifically provide for regionally differentiated needs. This led to a very thin spread of resources across the country. As a result, even in the poorer regions, employment was provided for only 31 days. In many states, the works taken up were not labour-intensive. Cases of bogus reporting and fudged muster rolls have been reported.

The efficacy of the programme was also affected by faulty project selection and the absence of a coherent plan which integrated EAS projects in a long-term development strategy. In spite of their many shortcomings, wage employment schemes have proved beneficial in some respects. They created muchneeded rural infrastructure. The programmes are self-targeting in nature since only the poor come to work at minimum wage rates.

The various works undertaken created demand for unskilled labour and exerted upward pressure on wage rates. The programmes have played a major role in protecting consumption patterns of the rural poor during natural calamities. A study conducted in four drought-affected districts of Rajasthan found that the consumption of foodgrains was higher in the drought years compared to normal years due to the wage employment programmes.

Since PRIs were associated with the implementation of JRY /JGSY and EAS, government financing of panchayats strengthened these institutions and promoted better coordination between the village community and government departments.

### Food for Work Programme

The Food for Work programme was stared in 2000-01 as a component of the EAS in eight notified drought-affected states of Chattisgarh, Gujarat, Himachal Pradesh, Madhya Pradesh, Orissa, Rajasthan, Maharastra and Uttaranchal. The programme aims at augmenting food security through wage employment. Food grains are supplied to states free of cost. However, lifting of food grains for the scheme from Food Corporation of India (FCI) godowns has been slow. Against an allocation of 35.31 lakh tonnes of foodgrains, only 21.26 lakh tonnes were lifted by the target states up to January 2002.

#### *Sampoorna Gramin Rozgar Yojana (SGRY)*

Given the complementarity of the JGSY, EAS and Food for Work Programme, all of which aim at the creation of employment opportunities in the rural areas, they were revamped and merged under the new Sampoorna Gramin Rozgar Yojana (SGRY) scheme from September 2001. The basic aim of the scheme continues to be generation of wage employment, creation of durable economic infrastructure in rural areas and provision of food and nutrition security to the poor. The amalgamation of the earlier schemes has led to an augmentation of resources for this programme.

The works taken up under the programme are labour-intensive and the workers are paid the minimum wages notified by the states. Payment of wages is done partly in cash and partly in kind - 5 kg of foodgrains and the balance in cash. The Centre and the states share the cost of the cash component of the scheme in the ratio of 75:25. An allocation of Rs. 3,780 crore was made for the programme in 2001-02.

A review of various wage employment programmes during the Ninth Plan shows that there has been a considerable reduction in terms of allocation as well as in employment generation. This was largely due to changes in allocation for rural development schemes during the Plan period. The allocation by both the Centre and the states under JRY went down from Rs. 18,691 crore in the Eighth Plan to Rs. 11,688 crore in the Ninth Plan.

As the EAS was launched only in 1993-94 and was intially a demand driven scheme, it would be difficult to compare EAS allocations in the Eighth and Ninth Plan periods. However, even here it is seen that the allocations have fallen in the later half of the Ninth Plan period. The allocation for wage employment programmes, at current prices, in the Ninth Plan was only 88 per cent of what they were in the Eighth Plan. In real terms, the allocations were much lower.

A decline in allocation coupled with the increased cost of providing employment meant that as against 513 crore mandays of employment generated under JRY and EAS in the Eighth Plan, only 286 crore mandays of employment were generated under JRY/JGSY and EAS in the Ninth Plan.

The reduction in allocation for wage employment was compensated by increased allocation for some programmes and initiation of new schemes. For example, there was a substantial increase in allocation for IAY. Many other programmes taken up during the Plan period have generated employment in the rural areas.

The construction of houses under IAY, programmes of rural connectivity and watershed development have fairly high employment elasticities. However, it is difficult to estimate whether these programmes were able to offset the reduction in employment generated through specific wage employment programmes.

### *Rural Housing*

Initiated in 1985-86, the IAY is the core programme for providing free housing to BPL families in rural areas and targets SC/STs households and freed bonded labourers. It was first merged with the JRY in 1989 and then spun off into a separate housing scheme for the rural poor in 1996. The Ninth Plan Housing Programme under IAY was framed in the light of the National Housing and Habitat Policy 1998, which set an ambitious target of providing shelter for all in the rural areas by the end of the Plan period.

The allocations by the central and state governments for the programme during the Ninth Plan were substantially higher than in the Eighth Plan. In spite of this, the housing programme under IAY has not achieved the stated objectives. As against a requirement of 109.53 lakh new and upgraded houses between 1997-98 to 2001-02, the actual construction during the period is estimated at 45 lakh houses. This, however, is a quantum jump over the Eighth Plan achievement of 26 lakh houses.

An evaluation of the IAY shows that while the programme has certainly enabled many BPL families to acquire pucca houses, the coverage of the beneficiaries is limited given the resource constraints. In addition, there have also been high level of leakages with a large number of non-eligible beneficiaries getting houses. The fact that houses are provided free of cost under IAY has meant that there has been virtually no progress in the other sub-schemes of IAY such as credit-cum-subsidy scheme for rural housing.

This scheme, introduced in 1999-2000 to provide assistance for construction of a house to people below double the poverty line income, provides a subsidy of Rs. 10,000 and a construction loan of up to Rs. 40,000 per household. However, it failed to pick up and only 42,000 houses were constructed under the scheme between 1999 and 2001. The Samagra Awas Yojana (SAY) was taken up in 25 blocks to ensure convergence of housing, provision of safe drinking water, sanitation and common drainage facilities. The achievements under this scheme were equally unsatisfactory.

A mere 30 projects have been sanctioned since the inception of the scheme and only Rs. 7.07 crore dispersed. Similarly, progress under various innovative schemes for rural housing and habitat development, which seek to encourage the use of cost-effective, environment-friendly modern designs have been equally dismal.

### *Housing and Urban Development*

Housing and Urban Development Corporation (HUDCO) has extended its activities to the rural areas, providing loans at a concessional rate of interest to economically weaker sections and low-income group households for construction of houses. HUDCO's rural housing programme was given a major boost in the Ninth Plan. The Government provided equity support for the construction of rural houses and a sum of Rs.350 crore was released to the Corporation. In the 1997- 2002 period, HUDCO sanctioned 799 schemes for the construction of 50.97 lakh dwelling units at a total cost of Rs. 3991.73 crore.

The regional spread of HUDCO's sanctions indicates that only Andhra Pradesh, Tamil Nadu, Karnataka, Kerala, Orissa and West Bengal took advantage of the scheme. States like Bihar, Uttar Pradesh, Madhya Pradesh, Rajasthan and Assam were not covered under the programme. One of the reasons for the lukewarm response to the scheme could be the IAY itself, which is a 100 per cent subsidy programme. Besides, HUDCO's rural housing scheme consists of a loan component and a grant component. State governments prefer the grant-based programme to the loan-based programme.

### *Social Security Programmes*

Democratic decentralisation and centrallysupported Social Assistance Programmes were two major initiatives of the government in the 1990s. The National Social Assistance Programme (NSAP), launched in August 1995 marks a significant step towards fulfillment of the Directive Principles of State Policy. The NSAP has three components:

— National Old Age Pension Scheme (NOAPS);

— National Family Benefit Scheme (NFBS);

— National Maternity Benefit Scheme (NMBS).

The NSAP is a centrally-sponsored programme that aims at ensuring a minimum national standard of social assistance over and above the assistance that states provide from their own resources. The NOAPS provides a monthly pension of Rs. 75 to destitute BPL persons above the age of 65. The NFBS is a scheme for BPL families who are given Rs. 10,000 in the event of the death of the breadwinner. The NMBS provides Rs. 500 to support nutritional intake for pregnant women.

The coverage under NSAP is limited due to resource constraints. For example, against the target of 8.71 million eligible beneficiaries for oldage pension in 1999-2000, only about 5 million beneficiaries were provided assistance from central funds. Many states implement the pension scheme from their own resources.

However, in the states that do not have their own scheme, a central pension of Rs. 75 per month is clearly inadequate to provide relief to old, indigent persons. A redeeming feature of the scheme, though, is that the benefits have indeed reached the poor and leakages under the scheme are low compared to many other government programmes.

In addition to NSAP, the Annapurna scheme was launched from I April 2000 to provide food security to senior citizens who were eligible for pension under NOAPS but could not receive it due to budget constraints. The scheme seeks to cover 20 per cent of persons eligible for NOAPS. These beneficiaries are given 10 kg of foodgrains per month free of cost. However, there have been major problems in the implementation of the Annapurna scheme.

Haryana, Karnataka and Tamil Nadu did not agree to implement the scheme in its present form. Many other states wanted modifications before implementing it. During 2000- 01, only 19,000 metric tonnes (mt) of foodgrains was lifted by ten states. As against an allocation of Rs. 99.05 crore in 2000-01, actual expenditure was only Rs. 17.44 crore.

The performance in 2001-02 was equally unsatisfactory. Against a targetted coverage of 1.34 million persons, the actual coverage was only 203,000 -15 per cent of the target.

### *Land Reforms*

In an economy where over 60 per cent of the population is dependent on agriculture, the structure of land ownership is central to the wellbeing of the people. The government has strived to change the ownership pattern of cultivable land, but has had limited success. The abolition of intermediaries immediately after Independence, inspite of its many well-documented shortcomings and lack of implementation in certain parts of the country, was a significant achievement and covered close to 40 per cent of the cultivated area.

These achievements notwithstanding, the lack of progress in the other components of the land reforms programme, viz., implementation of land ceiling laws, security of tenure to tenants and consolidation of land holdings, remains a matter of serious concern. Agricultural workers did not benefit from the abolition of zamindari. The SC/STs, who constitute the bulk of the labour force, do not have either the assets or the skills to participate in the limited but emerging employment opportunities in different sectors of the economy.

The problem is further compounded by the fact that though the contribution of agriculture to GDP has nearly halved from over 50 per cent in 1951 to around 25 per cent in 2000-01, a similar transformation of employment opportunities has not taken place. The number of people dependent on agriculture and allied activities has fallen only 12 percentage points - from 71 per cent of the population in 1951 to 59 per cent in 2001.

Land reforms seem to have been relegated to the background in the 1990s. More recently, initiatives of state governments have related to liberalisation of land laws in order to promote largescale corporate farming. This is in sharp contrast to the policy environment soon after Independence when land reforms were meant to provide ownership rights to small and marginal farmers on equity considerations. Though the pressure of population has led to sub-division and fragmentation of land holdings, thereby considerably weakening the case for further lowering of land ceilings, the need for effective implementation of the existing land ceiling laws cannot be over-emphasised.

The Ninth Plan had laid strong emphasis on agrarian restructuring to make agriculture more efficient leading to increased "output and employment". However, progress on different components of the land reforms package during the Plan has been extremely limited. At the end of the Eighth Plan, 74.9 lakh acres was declared as ceiling surplus and 52.13 lakh acres was distributed among 5.5 million beneficiaries.

By the end of the Ninth Plan, the position was virtually the same. There has been no progress in the detection of concealed land and its distribution to the landless rural poor. The case of tenancy reforms is equally unsatisfactory. Tenancy laws in the states follow different patterns, as land is a state subject. Several states, including Uttar Pradesh, Bihar and Orissa have either banned tenancy completely or have imposed such restrictive conditions that land leases are virtually impossible.

Studies by the Lal Bahadur Shastri National Academy of Administration indicate that this has only resulted in concealed tenancy. It is estimated that over 34 per cent of land is operated under concealed tenancy in Bihar. The ban on tenancy, which was meant to protect tenants, has only ended up hurting the economic interests of the tenants as they are not even recognised as tenants. As a result, they are denied the benefits of laws that provide security of tenure and regulate rent.

The progress on the consolidation of land holdings has also been slow. Consolidation has to be a continuing process, but most states have stopped consolidation proceedings. As on 31 March, 2002, consolidation of holdings has taken place only in an area of 66.10 million hectares against a total cultivable area of 142 million hectares.

Alienation of tribals from their land is a major issue in tribal areas. States have passed legislation to restore alienated land to the tribal landholders. The progress in this regard, however, has been limited. The restoration proceedings have been challenged in courts, thwarting the restoration of land to tribals. During the Ninth Plan period, 1.63 lakh cases were decided by the courts in favour of the tribals and 1,75,286 hectares (ha) was restored as a result of the governmental action. However, as on 31 March 2002, 57,521 cases were still pending in courts with 58,260 ha being under dispute in these cases.

A land record management system is a pre-condition for an effective land reform programme. In 1987-88, a centrally-sponsored scheme for Strengthening of Revenue Administration and Updating of Land Records (SRA & ULR) was introduced in Orissa and Bihar. The scheme was extended to other states in 1989-90. Survey and re-settlement operations, pre-service and in-service training to revenue and settlement staff, facilities for modernisation of survey and settlement operations and strengthening of revenue machinery at the village level are funded under the scheme.

During the Eighth Plan, Rs. 8.23 crore was released to the states under the scheme, while Rs. 92.60 crore was allocated during the Ninth Plan under the Programme of SRA & ULR against which Rs. 85.74 crore were released to states/ Union Territories. In addition to SRA&ULR, a centrallysponsored scheme of Computerisation of Land Records (CLR) provides assistance to states for modernisation of record keeping operations. Activities funded under the programme include the screening and digitalisation of existing cadastral maps, computer processing of agricultural land holdings records for the purpose of consolidation of holdings and preparation of consolidated revenue settlement and installation of computer networks at the headquarters of states/Union Territories for revenue administration.

During the Eighth Plan period, Rs. 9.42 crore was released to the state governments for covering 238 districts. In the Ninth Plan, 333 more districts were brought under the scheme, thus taking the total districts covered under CLR to 571 districts. A total of 2705 talukas/tehsils/ blocks were taken up for computerisation.

Against a total allocation of Rs. 178 crore, a sum of Rs. 167.52 crore was released. The resources provided under SRA & ULR and CLR programmes meet a small part of the total resources required for the modernisation of revenue administration. The states have to undertake modernisation of the land records management system on a much larger scale.

**Strategy for Tenth Plan**

The Approach Paper to the Tenth Plan has set a target for reduction of poverty and creation of high quality gainful employment during the Plan period. The projected GDP growth rate of 8 per cent for the period 2002-07, if achieved, would lead to reduction of incidence of poverty by 5 percentage points by 2007. Compared to 1999-2000, poverty is expected to decline by 15 percentage points by 2011-12.

Effective implementation of anti-poverty programmes would be central to achieving the planned reductions in poverty. The challenge before the State is to provide employment opportunities which provide enhanced incomes. This becomes more important in view of the fact that substantial additions to labour force are expected to take place during the next five years. Enlargement of self and wage-employment programmes and their effective delivery becomes an imperative in such a scenario.

*Self Employment Programmes*

The coverage of beneficiaries in the Ninth Plan was considerably lower than the coverage under SGSY. The formation of self-help groups by itself contributes to the empowerment and economic well-being of the poor by improving their collective bargaining position. The group formation also emphasises social capital and enables the poor to interact with other social groups from a position of strength.

Group formation would continue to be the focus under the SGSY.. The self-help groups move through various stages: social mobilisation and formation of groups (initial phase); savings and internal lending among the members of the group on their own, augmented by revolving fund grants from the government and linkages with banks and other credit agencies (second phase); obtaining micro finance (third phase) and setting up of micro enterprises (fourth phase). This is a long process and groups require time to mature as cohesive units.

Savings by members and internal lending help the group members to improve their economic position. A strong group acts as collateral for banks to provide micro finance to these groups. They get access to credit for a variety of consumption needs, seasonal activities and for undertaking petty production and trading activities. Setting up of a micro enterprise could be the objective of every group.

However, only those groups which possess special skills, technical know-how, establish marketing linkages and have access to the essential infrastructure needed for success of that particular activity can reach the stage of micro enterprise. The IRDP's approach of fixing targets and timeframes was given up under the SGSY in the Ninth Plan itself. This approach would continue in the Tenth Plan too.

The SGSY programme is intended to provide benefits to SCs and STs, disabled and women-headed households form the bulk of the rural poor. However, these sections would be excluded from the ambit of the programme if they are not listed in the below poverty line (BPL) census conducted at the beginning of every Five-Year Plan for inclusion of beneficiaries under different government programmes.

Greater attention would, therefore, be given to identification of BPL families by clearly specifying exclusion and inclusion criteria. These would be published and subjected to periodic social audit in a transparent manner by the gram sabhas. Self-help groups become cohesive in the long run only if they are homogenous. Social mobilisation is an important step in the formation of self-help groups. It requires a high degree of motivation, morale, expertise, management skills, time and pro-poor orientation on the part of the person who acts as a catalyst for group formation.

SGSY is implemented through the DRDAs. These organisations would have to be supported by NGOs, PRIs and other community-based organisations in the formation of the self-help groups. The Small Industries Development Bank of India (SIDBI), National Bank of Agriculture and Rural Development (NABARD), Rashtriya Mahila Kosh (RMK) and many zilla parishads have emerged as important players in the promotion of self-help groups.

Strong networks and linkages would be established with such institutions under SGSY. These organisations would act as self-help promotion institutions and would ensure a continuing relationship with self-help groups. Successful experiments in the promotion of micro finance and micro enterprise have revealed a strong partnership between NGOs and financial institutions.

NGOs have an inherent advantage in reaching the poor due to their proximity, the trust they generate by working in the area, their commitment, flexibility in approach, responsiveness and cost effectiveness. They have played a dynamic role as social animators and organisers in rural areas. Many NGOs have not only been instrumental in the formation of self-help groups but have also nurtured them over the years.

Such NGOs have a strong presence in many states. However, voluntary and non-governmental action is weak in some of the poorer states. These are also the states where the spirit of cooperation and collaboration may be lacking because of poverty itself. Training of social animators would have to be promoted in such states. Departments of social sciences, social work, agriculture and rural development in universities and colleges could be engaged as facilitators in the process of group formation so that every rural habitation has at least one self-help group by the end of 2004.

The institutions which promote self-help groups could be provided remuneration at different stages of the evolution of the groups so that they have an incentive in the formation of cohesive groups and in ensuring their success. Micro enterprises succeed only if they cater to the specific needs of an area. The identification of key activities and planning of activity clusters is an important component of SGSY though it has been a weak link so far.

It is necessary to identify livelihood opportunities, the constraints in the realisation of these opportunities and the investments that would have to be made to remove these constraints. The micro-level planning process would have to be strengthened in the districts for the programme to succeed. In this endeavour, the involvement of PRIs, banks, micro finance institutions, NGOs and district-level officers of different departments would have to be ensured.

They would have to work in close coordination in the preparation of a District Plan for activities under SGSY. Economic activities require high degree of skills. After the identification of key activities, it would be necessary to organise training programmes for upgrading skills of beneficiaries selected under the programme. Skill acquisition is a long-drawn process; this requires not only short-term training in campus-based programmes, but also on-the-job training in existing enterprises.

Campus-based training programmes under SGSY would only be a beginning of the process. The design of the curricula and method of training would have to correspond to the activities chosen. A basic foundation course to expose trainees to accounting procedures, management techniques, banking and marketing would be a part of the training programme.

The training institutions would be expected to arrange for practical on-the-job training programmes and upgrade their syllabi in tune with changing market conditions. They would be continuously appraised to ensure that their faculty is well qualified and imparts training which is relevant and of high quality. They would also be expected to monitor the progress of their trainees in the trades that they pursue.

It would be necessary for training institutions to forge partnerships with technical and management institutes to facilitate greater interaction and learning. In the coming years, the corporate sector is expected to play a larger role in the rural areas. Industry associations have indicated their willingness to adopt villages and regions. The corporate sector could associate itself with training institutes, enabling the latter to keep abreast of the market requirements and revise their curricula.

The trainees could also set up ancillary units to supply components to industry. The SGSY programme would be credit driven. The outreach of the credit delivery system in the country continues to be limited, despite several measures to streamline it. The legitimate demands for credit remain unfulfilled as a vast majority of the poor remain outside the purview of the formal credit system. The mismatch between demand and supply of credit arises out of an inadequate and inefficient delivery system.

The policies of direct lending, administered pricing of credit and lack of freedom in the selection of borrowers have resulted in the high cost of credit delivery for the formal credit institutions and, consequently, to the borrowers. A system would have to be put in place which is flexible and responsive to the financial needs of the poor and is capable of supplying timely and adequate credit. The inadequacies of formal credit institutions could be overcome by combining the strength of commercial banks with the intermediation capabilities of NGOs to effectively link the poor with the commercial banking channels.

This would be a cost-effective alternative for providing credit to the poor as banks would be able to reach a larger number of small borrowers with lower transaction costs. The risk of default on loans would be lower due to group pressure and the groups would also monitor the end use of credit. Access to banks through self-help groups would reduce the transaction cost of the borrowers. In the credit delivery system under SGSY, financial intermediation by NGOs would be encouraged. The experience of Self Employed Women's Association (SEWA) and other organisations would be replicated on a larger scale.

Since the commercial banking network has its limitations in reaching the rural poor in every part of the country, other formal institutions that cater to the specific credit needs of the rural population could be integrated into the credit delivery structure for self-employment programmes. Primary Agriculture Credit Cooperative Societies (PACS) have an extensive network in the country and possess detailed knowledge of the borrowers.

Regional Rural Banks (RRBs) and other credit organisations, presently outside the purview of micro finance activities, could be associated with self-employment programmes. It would be the Government's endeavour to leverage funds under different self-employment programmes to enable the rural poor to diversify into non-agricultural activities. Different government agencies have, in the past, attempted to promote rural non-farm employment.

Khadi and Village Industries Commission (KVIC) and District Industries Centres (DICs) were set up to promote non-farm activities. In spite of this, the rural nonfarm sector continues to lag behind. Only 16 per cent of the rural population is engaged in non-farm activities and that too largely in village or cottage enterprises. Economic census data shows that 77 per cent of rural enterprises are own account enterprises that do not engage hired labour.

These enterprises are unable to attract capital and technology since they are small, family-based enterprises. Many of these enterprises use obsolete technology and are highly vulnerable to market fluctuations and competition from the organised sector. The inadequate availability of micro infrastructure relevant to the service or trade has been a major constraint in the rapid development of the rural non-farm sector. For example, dairy activity was one of the main activities financed under IRDP.

Often the beneficiaries were constrained by the absence of small equipment like milk cans and fat testing machines. Provision of milk collection vans, bulk coolers, chilling plants and pasteurisation facilities were also not a part of the programme. There is, therefore, a need to identify the type of infrastructure required for a particular activity while planning an activity cluster. Provision would have to be made for the creation of infrastructure either under SGSY or by convergence with the other sectoral programmes and to ensure that the missing infrastructure is provided at the planning stage itself.

Marketing strategy is an integral part of every self-employment venture. Market intelligence has to be developed. Survey of local and urban markets to understand product demand is necessary. Rural haats or village markets have to be set up to position the products of self-help groups. Such haats would also be promoted at the taluka level, district centres and other larger towns. The construction of permanent spaces and pucca sheds along with the provision of storage facilities/ godowns would be taken up under SGSY and transport links provided to such centres.

Metropolitan cities and export markets are important from the point of view of higher value realisation. Linkages to these would have to be developed largely through private channels, industrial enterprises and export houses. This model was successfully demonstrated in Andhra Pradesh where Phillips India and Hindustan

Lever had forged links with DWCRA groups for marketing their products. Intermediate aggregate mechanisms like producer cooperatives and marketing agencies could facilitate the transaction between dispersed producers and industrial enterprises/export houses.

Products would be positioned through KVIC outlets, State Emporia and Handlooms and Handicrafts Trade Fairs. SGSY groups from a cluster of villages could also form a federation. Such federations, producing a single product, can take advantage of the economies of scale, undertaking collective purchase of raw materials to reduce the cost of production. They could ensure better marketing, quality control and promote their brand name through aggressive advertisement campaigns.

Greater attention to quality control, standardisation and packaging would be required for products of rural areas to find a market in the urban centres. Efforts would be made to create a market niche for rural products that require specialised skills. Rural enterprises need technology support for product development, quality improvement and standardisation. India has large research and development facilities in national laboratories, universities and other specialised institutions.

Suitable linkages between the rural enterprises and these institutions would be developed so that technological assistance can be extended to the self-help groups. Advances in information technology and communication would be harnessed to benefit the self-help groups. Self-employment programmes are likely to have an uneven regional spread, succeeding in areas that have a tradition of artisanship, developed road and rail infrastructure, banking facilities and a skilled human resource base.

The negative relationship between the incidence of rural poverty and land access is well-established. The landless face the greatest risk of poverty. Access to even small pieces of land which may not be sufficient for providing income to a family for subsistence can significantly reduce poverty and food insecurity by providing an essential component in a diversified livelihood system. Their impact may be less visible in under-developed, backward and tribal regions.

The SGSY programme would continue to promote land-based activities for individual and group beneficiaries in the backward regions. Diversification into other land-based activities such as sericulture, aquaculture, horticulture and floriculture would be encouraged. The programme would, therefore, support the purchase of land and its distribution to the landless rural poor. Women swarozgaris would be sole owners or joint owners of redistributed land. The swarozgaris provided land would be organised to access inputs and credit facilities that enhance productivity of land.

In addition to the provision for purchase and redistribution of land, self-help groups will be encouraged to explore prospects of leasing or purchasing land in joint ownership. Schemes that give subsidised credit for land purchase and leasing would be converged with the SGSY programme in these areas. Convergence would also be attempted with schemes that provide subsidised credit for farm equipment such as tractors, tube-wells, fertilisers, seeds and other inputs.

The Government would make special efforts to provide information and give financial and infrastructural support to SGSY groups engaged in land-based activities in such areas. In the Ninth Plan, both IRDP and SGSY were subsidy-driven programmes. This subsidy itself has become a major obstacle in the promotion of self-employment ventures. The experience of institutions providing micro finance shows that the poor are capable and also willing to pay for the credit and other financial services rendered by NGOs and financial institutions without depending on the government for subsidy.

Financial resources in the Tenth Plan, therefore, would be directed towards providing infrastructure and other support facilities which increase the returns to households and reduce their risks. It would be used in innovative ways to lower the transaction cost for both the swarozgaris and the lenders and to create a strong and viable partnership with NGOs and other organisations working for the economic well-being of the rural poor.

### *Wage Employment Programme*

The SGRY would be the single wage employment programme. Allocations to the programme would be stepped up. The programme would seek to provide productive employment opportunities in employment-intensive sectors. The Government would endeavour to generate a shelf of projects for execution under SGRY that fits into the overall development plan of an area.

The SGRY would have three streams. One to address the need for rural infrastructure in all states; the other to provide focused attention to areas facing endemic poverty while the third would respond to natural calamities. The general stream universalised across states would be for the creation of local infrastructure.

Water tanks, anganwadis, primary school buildings, sanitation facilities, primary health centres, multi-purpose community halls and other projects that are required in the village would be taken up under the universal stream. In agriculturally developed areas, it may be necessary to allow upward adjustments in wages to attract unskilled labour. Village communities could augment the resources under the universal stream by mobilising contributions from within the community.

The second stream would seek to provide an employment guarantee of at least 100 days for areas facing chronic unemployment and poverty. The districts and blocks would be selected on the basis of an objective criterion and efforts would be made to create at least minimum infrastructure in these areas by ensuring convergence of other government programmes.

Thus, the second stream would, in essence, correspond to the EAS, which was started with the objective of providing employment for 100 days in drought-prone, desertprone, hilly and flood-prone blocks of the country. Such an assurance would ensure a minimum level of employment and stability to the incomes of the poor and give them an opportunity to develop their collective strength.

It would improve their economic position, reduce vulnerability and discourage migration to facilitate their continued access to health, education and welfare facilities available in the village. The allocation under this second stream would be enhanced to meet the target of 100 days of employment for every able-bodied person willing and seeking work. The third stream would be an enabling mechanism for the Government to respond to natural calamities such as floods, droughts, earthquakes and other contingencies that require quick response to mitigate the hardships faced by people.

The wage employment programmes provide only short-term relief to the poor. Longterm sustainable poverty reduction in the underdeveloped regions can come about only if other sectors of the economy grow rapidly. It is imperative, therefore, to ensure that the growth process is inclusive and pro-poor. Agricultural growth still holds the key to poverty alleviation in the

Indian context. There is considerable scope for increasing agricultural productivity through expansion of irrigation, better land and water management practices and infrastructure support. The planning of works under the SGRY would be undertaken keeping this in mind.

A large number of rural facilities have been built under various programmes over successive Plan periods. However, they have degenerated either due to their initial faulty design and construction, or lack of maintenance. Therefore, a specific proportion of allocations under SGRY would be used for the maintenance of assets.

PRIs would play a major role in the planning, implementation and monitoring of wage employment programmes and allocations under the SGRY would be routed through them. A rational criterion would have to be evolved for distribution of funds between the three tiers of the PRIs to ensure balanced development of villages, blocks and districts.

The IAY is one of the successful programmes being implemented by the Ministry of Rural Development, it has certain weaknesses. The provision of free houses has meant that other loan-based schemes have not been able to take off. The scheme has also been open to misuse. Public funds have to be utilised for the promotion of economic activity and growth.

The creation of employment opportunities, both selfemployment and wage-employment, has to receive a higher priority than provision of free houses. During the Tenth Plan period, free houses under IAY would be provided largely to SC/ST BPL families. For other BPL families, there would be a gradual shift to a credit-linked housing programme.

There is a need to create institutional capability in the rural housing sector with reference to designing of houses, supply of raw materials and construction. The rural communities have to be involved in the layout and design of the houses. The houses should have provisions for rain water harvesting, water supply and sanitation.

*Social Schemes*

While the NSAP and state-level welfare schemes have provided some succour to the poor in the form of assistance to the old and the bereaved, a large section of people have not been covered under the schemes because of limited resources. The NSAP needs to be enlarged in scope to cover all eligible beneficiaries. The content and coverage of the social welfare scheme would have to be strengthened during the Plan period to provide meaningful protection to the poor.

There are a plethora of welfare schemes in both the central and state sectors. They lead to avoidable overlap and confusion and need to rationalised. Since welfare is basically a state subject, these schemes are best administered by state governments. The NSAP has been transferred to states with earmarked funds in the Tenth Plan.

Successive Five-Year Plans have addressed the issue of secure rights in land for increased agricultural productivity under the land reforms programme. Land reform legislations, besides abolishing intermediaries and providing ownership rights to farmers, also provided for security of tenure to tenants and regulation of rent. Actual cultivators were brought into a direct relationship with the State. The abolition of intermediaries succeeded in providing ownership rights to a large number of tenants.

The advent of the green revolution technology coupled with schemes of asset transfer under IRDP have contributed significantly to the increased incomes not only from agricultural operations but also on account of diversification into animal husbandry. Agricultural workers, however, did not gain from zamindari abolition. Scheduled Castes and Scheduled Tribes constitute bulk of the agricultural labour force. These people have neither assets nor skills to participate in the limited but emerging employment opportunities in different sectors of the economy.

The problem is further compounded by the fact that employment opportunities in non-farm sector have not increased over time to absorb the rural labour force. Ownership of even a small plot of land enables a family to raise its income, improve its nutritional status, have access to credit facilities and lead a more dignified life. Studies of economies of scale in farm operations show that modern agricultural technology is scale neutral in the case of a majority of food and cereal crops which the poor tend to grow.

Horticulture, floriculture and vegetable cultivation on small plots of land, including homestead lands, have proved beneficial for the poor. Agricultural labourers, therefore, need to be provided access to land to improve their economic and social well-being. The scope for lowering land ceilings, which were fixed in 1972, and redistribution of surplus land is limited. The total area declared ceiling surplus after 1972 was less than 2 per cent of the net sown area. National Sample Survey Organisation (NSSO) data for 1992 shows that 72 per cent of rural households had less than one hectare of land.

Therefore, further reduction in land ceilings and acquisition of land for distribution to the poor is not a credible policy option any more. However, this is not to underplay the need to acquire the land declared ceiling surplus. The record of most states in implementing the existing laws is dismal.

Concealment of land is widespread. Land acquisitions have been disputed, with cases piled up in courts for years without resolution. During the Tenth Plan period, states have to concentrate on the detection of concealed land and strive for the speedy disposal of cases so that the land acquired under ceiling laws becomes available for distribution to the poor.

The reform of tenancy in the post- Independence period was taken up as a part of the land reforms agenda. Its basic thrust was to stop eviction of tenants and fixation of rent. Conferment of ownership rights to the tenants was the ultimate goal of tenancy laws. The policy attempted to reconcile twin objectives of protection to existing tenants and resumption of land for personal cultivation by the medium, small and marginal farmers. However, the prohibition of tenancy has not really ended the practice.

On the other hand, it has resulted in agricultural practices that are not conducive to increased production. This, in turn, also depresses employment opportunities for the landless agricultural labourers. Mechanisation of agriculture has enabled families to keep land under personal cultivation even in the absence of ablebodied persons to take care of agricultural operations. The fear of tenant eventually taking possession of the land in these areas has resulted in agricultural practices which are not conducive to increased agricultural production. This, in turn depresses employment opportunities for the landless agricultural labourers.

The changes in the agrarian economy over the past three decades warrant a fresh look at tenancy laws. States are at different stages of agricultural transformation. Patterns of semi-feudal agriculture in some states co-exist with corporate and commercial farming practices in others. Where agriculture has reached the commercial farming stage, middle and large farmers lease land from small and marginal farmers. NSSO surveys show that area owned by the marginal and small farmers is greater than the area they cultivate. These developments indicate the need to revisit the tenancy laws.

One option could be to completely free tenancy laws of all restrictive conditions. Farmers owning land below the ceiling limit may be provided a guarantee that their land would not be taken away. The fixation of rent could be left to the market forces. Given the extent of concealed tenancy in states that have banned tenancy, it is not likely to increase area under tenancy dramatically in the short run. However, in the medium to long run, more land would be expected to come on the land lease market which can be accessed by the rural poor.

Civil society organisations have attempted innovative experiments to rectify inequities of land ownership in the rural areas. Access to land for the landless has been built into their programmes. The Pani Panchayat in Ralegaon Siddhi in Maharashtra is a case in point. Every member of the village has a proprietary right over the harvested water. Every member, irrespective of the size of his land holding, has a share in the harvested water for irrigation. As the water available to each member is limited, members with large land holdings have been persuaded to lease their land to small and marginal farmers and agricultural labourers who have water rights but no land.

The arrangement has allowed landless access to land. The large landholders have also benefited as they receive rent for land which would otherwise have remained fallow for lack of irrigation. Another variant of this approach has been adopted in a few watersheds. While the landholders get water for irrigation, the non-land owning families get a larger share of output from the Common Property Resources (CPRs) which get rejuvenated after the successful completion of the project. This has enabled many families to take up animal husbandry as an occupation and meet their fodder and fuel requirements from the CPRs.

Fishing rights on ponds constructed as part of the watershed project are only given to self-help groups of the landless. These arrangements effectively increase the access of the poor to the land and other sources of livelihood and improve their standard of living. Successful projects change the nature of agricultural land from un-irrigated to irrigated. In such cases, the ceiling laws of the state could come into force and the ceiling surplus land could be distributed to the landless poor.

Alternatively, the guidelines for watershed development projects could be modified to give priority to those watershed projects where the village community, through a resolution, agrees to provide land access to the landless labourers on a continuing basis. In addition, outright purchase of land from farmers willing to sell their holdings also needs to be explored. In many parts of the country, families have migrated to urban areas but continue to hold on to their land holdings in the absence of an efficient land market due to restrictions on the lease, sale and mortgage of agricultural land.

The Government could create an enabling environment for the emergence of land markets or itself enter the land market as a major player. The National Scheduled Castes and Scheduled Tribes Finance and Development Corporation (NSFDC) has a scheme for providing assistance to SC/ST families to purchase land. The scheme received and enthusiastic response in Tamil Nadu, Andhra Pradesh and Karnataka.

While the provision for purchase of land in the erstwhile IRDP continues in the revamped SGSY, the main focus of the scheme is on the creation of self-help groups and setting up of micro enterprises. Land could be purchased and distributed to landless under SGSY and they could be organised under a cooperative society to provide other support services for agricultural operations.

There has been an increasing feminisation of the agricultural labour force in the country. NSSO (50th round) estimates for 1993-94 show that 75.3 per cent of women workers were engaged in agriculture compared to only 58 per cent of male workers. In the rural labour force, 84.7 per cent of women were engaged in agriculture as compared to 73.8 per cent male workers. Data on incremental additions to the rural labour force show that the rural male worker has a greater chance of getting absorbed into non-agriculture pursuits than the rural female worker.

Besides, migration of able-bodied men to urban areas in search of employment, breakup of the joint family system and other social factors such as death of husbands and desertion by husbands have resulted in an increase in the number of female-headed households. However, in the case of land holding families headed by women, if male descendants are present, the ownership right does not devolve on the women. Protecting social cohesion and prevention of fragmentation of land holdings are some of the major arguments advanced against allowing women to inherit land. These gender-biased land laws put women-headed households at a disadvantage.

Without proper title to land, they are denied access to credit and other facilities available to farming communities. This not only affects the income generating capacity of the households but also impacts adversely on agricultural production. Therefore, both on grounds of equity and efficiency, land Inheritance laws need to be gender neutral.

### *Alienation of Tribal Lands*

The influx of non-tribals into tribal areas as a result of various developmental projects, exploitation of natural resources and industrial activities has led to the alienation of tribal land. It is extremely paradoxical that while outsiders/nontribals have come into the Scheduled areas in the name of development, the local tribal population gets displaced and migrate to urban areas in search of employment. This has given rise to severe discontent in the tribal areas.

The process of alienation has taken place because of lack of legal awareness about land rights among both tribals and government officials and ineffective administrative structures. Inherent deficiencies in legal provisions such as the absence of any machinery to initiate suo motu action, general period of limitation for adverse possession, lack of provision against trespass and against fraudulent and collusive transfer of land to non-tribals continue to exist.

Alienation has also been facilitated by improper land records. An in-depth scrutiny of the methods for preparation of land records, and the maintenance and updating of such records must, therefore, be carried out at the earliest. Computerisation of land records in tribal areas should also be accorded the highest priority. The Panchayats (Extension of Scheduled Areas) Act (PESA), 1996 extended the provisions of 73rd Constitutional Amendment Act, 1992, to the Scheduled Areas in the states of Andhra Pradesh, Chattisgarh, Gujarat, Himachal Pradesh, Jharkhand, Madhya Pradesh, Maharashtra, Orissa and Rajasthan.

The PESA enables tribals to assume control over their own destiny and to preserve and conserve their traditional rights over natural resources, including land. However, the stringent provisions of this law have remained only on paper and have not been operationalised by state governments. PESA would be effectively implemented during the Tenth Plan period to resolve the issues of tribal exploitation and alienation.

One of the main reasons for the concealment of land, which has hampered the land reforms programme, has been the lack of a comprehensive land rights database. The CLR and SRA&ULR schemes have placed emphasis on modernisation of cadastral survey procedures and strengthening of training facilities for revenue, survey and settlement staff. Provision of computers and other infrastructure has been made under these schemes.

This process will be carried forward more vigorously in the Tenth Plan not only to detect concealment of land but also to reduce scope for litigation in rural areas.

### *Delivery Mechanism*

Poverty alleviation programmes have been designed to address different facets of rural poverty. Micro credit-linked programmes provide a package of services including credit and subsidy to set up micro enterprises. Wage employment programmes address the issue of transient poverty. Besides, schemes for infrastructure development and provision of basic services contribute to the wellbeing of the rural people.

Successful implementation of these programmes requires an appropriate policy framework, adequate funds, and an effective delivery mechanism. Past experience shows that the mere availability of funds is not likely to eradicate rural poverty. Nor is the design of the rural development programmes, no matter how refined, a sufficient condition.

The success of these programmes ultimately depends on the capability of the delivery system to absorb and utilise the funds in a cost-effective manner. An effective and responsive district-level field machinery with a high degree of commitment, motivation, professional competence and, above all, integrity has been recognised as one of the prerequisites for successful implementation of anti- poverty programmes.

An effective delivery system has to ensure people's participation at various stages of the formulation and implementation of the programmes, transparency in the operation of the schemes and adequate monitoring. International experience shows that greater functional and financial devolution to local governments results in higher allocation of resources for social sectors and more efficient use of resources. Such trends in social spending have been witnessed in many Indian states as well.

The increasing integration of India in the global economy, the budget constraints faced by both central and state governments and inefficiencies in the administrative structure led to the development of a consensus to devolve powers to local institutions to enable people's participation in administration. The 73rd and 74th Constitutional Amendments that conferred statutory status on PRIs and urban local bodies did not have only democratic decentralisation as their objective.

These institutions were also seen as a process for harnessing and channelising the people's innate abilities to bring about rural transformation in a way that every individual acquired his/her rightful place in the social, economic and political arena. The Ninth Plan had called for the devolution of functional responsibilities, administrative control on government functionaries dealing with subjects listed in the Eleventh Schedule of the Constitution and financial resources for taking up developmental programmes to the PRIs.

There has been mixed progress on this front. Political devolution has taken place. Elections have been held and women, SC/STs and other marginalised groups have got political representation in the rural areas. Problems encountered in the process of evolution of panchayats has been taken care of with the intervention of courts, civil society organisations and increased public awareness. The strengthening of forces that facilitate political empowerment of rural communities would be an important area of action in the Tenth Plan period.

Issues of transparency, accountability and development would require greater attention. States which have lagged behind in devolving functions and finances to panchayats would have to be encouraged to empower the panchayats. The gram sabhas in most states have been entrusted with only ceremonial functions. The power and functions of gram sabhas need to be enlarged by giving them effective powers of implementation and monitoring of developmental plans.

Social audit of all development programmes by the gram sabha would be made mandatory. The committee system adopted in many states to facilitate a more participative decision-making process in the panchayats should be incorporated in the State Panchayat Acts. The powers entrusted to a gram sabha in a Scheduled V area could be extended to gram sabhas in non-scheduled areas as well.

Administrative and financial devolution by the states to the PRIs remains an area of major concern. The Constitution has placed onerous responsibilities on PRIs. They require financial resources to discharge the tasks assigned to them and emerge as viable institutions of selfgovernment. Financial devolution is also desirable as the control of investment decisions by local communities leads to better utilisation of scarce resources.

Panchayats would need greater powers of taxation and avenues for non-tax revenue. States could provide matching grants to panchayats to take up specific projects. Apart from the funds that flow to panchayats for centrally sponsored and state sector schemes, untied grants could also be provided to the PRIs. The PRIs need to raise resources from the local community and end their dependence on government funds.

The functional domain of the PRIs can be enlarged only if they pay adequate attention to their resource base. The onus for devolving functions, functionaries and financial resources to the PRIs rests with the state governments. Though the states have, slowly, transferred functions and finances to the PRIs, these institutions are hampered by lack of administrative support. PRIs have to be adequately staffed and the functionaries must be trained in planning, budgeting and accounting tasks. An elaborate system for auditing of panchayat finances has to be put in place.

At present, adequate safeguards against the misuse of resources by elected functionaries do not exist in many states. These issues need to be tackled on a priority basis. The 74th Constitutional Amendment Act provided for the constitution of District Planning Committees (DPCs). However, the Constitutional provision on DPCs is rather weak as it provides for the preparation of only draft Plans by the DPCs.

State governments have not given adequate attention to the DPCs and the Government of India's guidelines on district planning have not been fully operationalised. DPCs should be set up and its functionaries must be trained in the basics of planning. The gram sabha/panchayat should be associated with the preparation of village development Plans based on the felt needs of the people.

These Plans should be integrated with the panchayat samiti and district-level plans to make the grassroot planning process a reality in the Tenth Plan period. The voluntary sector has witnessed a phenomenal growth in the country in the last 20 years. These institutions have played an important role in community mobilisation, providing technical support to the community for developmental projects, especially in the areas of health and education.

It has been clearly established that where panchayats, community organisations and user groups have worked in close cooperation, people have benefited immensely from developmental projects initiated either by the government or the communities themselves. People's organisations, whether in the form of an NGO or a group of experts, provide expertise and competence to the panchayats that they otherwise may not possess.

However, in many places, the emergence of Constitutionally-mandated PRIs has led to a conflict of interest as both voluntary organisations and these institutions occupy the same space. The voluntary agencies have to recognise that PRIs are institutions of governance and must work in close cooperation with them. The PRIs, for their part, have to recognise the critical role that voluntary organisations can play in enhancing their capabilities.

The delivery of programmes would improve only if the PRIs emerge as strong players in the social and economic life of the country. NGOs and other civil society organisations can facilitate the evolution of PRIs as institutions geared to promote the well-being of the rural poor. The preceding paragraphs have described the content and direction of anti-poverty programmes in the Tenth Plan period.

The financial allocations for the Tenth Plan period for these programmes have been stepped up considerably. As against a total expenditure of Rs. 35,866 crore in the Ninth Plan, the allocation for the Tenth Plan period has been increased to Rs. 56,748 crore. Under Pradhan Mantri Gram Sadak Yojana (PMGSY) have been substantially enhanced. These are expected to provide assured wage-employment, enhance incomes and ensure nutritional security. The allocations for direct anti-poverty alleviation programmes would be complemented by investments in other sectors which have a strong bearing on the incidence of poverty.

2

# Structure of Rural Industries

The rural manufacturing activities are largely dominating among various non-farm activities in terms of its size, providing employment to rural labourforce and the generation of income in the nonfarm households in different geographical locations. The expansion of the avenues of industrial employment within rural areas has generally been recognised one of the major ways for diversifying the rural economy and to promote the absorption of surplus agricultural labour.

Moreover, in regions like Uttaranchal where the possibility of developing farming economy are rather limited and the agricultural activities are not in a position to generate additional employment opportunities for increasing rural labourforce, the expansion of rural industrial activities becomes rather crucial and important to address the problem of increasing incidence of unemployment and poverty in these areas.

An attempt has been made separately, to examine the structure, trends in growth, level of investment, absorption pattern of labourforce and issues related to the overall emerging situation and problems existing in the properly functioning and the possibilities for expansion of different product groups of rural manufacturing activities in different geographical locations. The existing manufacturing activities which are forming a largest part of rural non-farm sector, constituting both traditional and non-traditional categories of units.

The black smithy, basket making, matting, rope making, woollen based enterprises, comprises of traditional form of activities, while, tailoring, comb making, iron and steel work, flour mill, repairing and servicing constitute the kinds of non-traditional manufacturing activities. The households belonging to certain social groups as part of village economic and social structure undertake all these traditional rural industries from generation to generation.

The carpentry and Blacksmithy households are engaged in the manufacture and repair of the tools and equipments for traditional agricultural activities while the Basketary and rope making enterprises are purely based on raw materials available in local forests, are manufacturing a variety of baskets, mats and ropes respectively, for the purpose of the collection of forest products. The rural households for storing foodgrains also use the baskets and various other domestic items and the mats are used for performing agricultural activities.

The production of various woollen based commodities is basically based on locally available raw wool from the local sheep and goat rears and a part of shortcoming is also met from outside the state and abroad. The woolen activities are known to be the traditional occupations of the scheduled caste households who have been engaged on them along with the rearing of goats and sheep for the past several generations.

However, during the recent past various other castes of households have also adopted the spinning and weaving of woolen yarn and also in the production of various woolen commodities. Remaining rural industrial enterprises are non-traditional in nature and are involved in manufacturing different commodities according to the local requirements.

The traditional form of rural industrial activities such as Carpentry, Blacksmithy, Basketry and Woolen based enterprise are the dominant product groups of units in each of the geographical locations of the sample areas. These all units together constitutes over three fourth of the representation among the various rural industrial sector. Though the concentration of rural industries is fairly largely confined in high hill areas (41 per cent) followed by low hills (32 per cent) while a lowest proportion of them (27 per cent) are located in middle hill areas.

The traditional categories of household based rural industries, excepting the case of carpentry, have been declining while those are in the production of nontraditional product groups have been fairly well increasing in each of the geographical locations, but largely in middle altitude hill areas followed by high and low hill areas of the state over the years.

Of the 490 rural industrial units as covered in our study, a highest proportion of them (45 per cent) are traditional form of household enterprises those were established before 1980, and another little over of one fourth units came into existence during the next five year period but the pattern of expansion of rural industrial activities slashed largely during 1985 to 1990, though it picked up sharply after 1990-95 but at much lower extent as compared to pre 1985 periods.

The households those were traditionally engaged in rural manufacturing activities for the past several generations have been discontinuing to remain engaged on them further due to one or other reasons but the process of adopting rural manufacturing activities as the source of household income is seen still continuing through starting and joining of the other rural households, though at a smaller extent.

However, over the years the proportions of households opting for the expansion of traditional form of industries in general and those are basically based on locally available raw materials in particular are noted to be relatively at lower level than the case of households initiating for the expansion of modern type of units such as tailoring, flour mills and repairing and servicing units.

**Origin of Industries**

Since a fairly high proportions of rural industrial units are traditional and were established during past several generations ago. Even, among the non-traditional units a majority of them were established during last several years ago. It is, therefore, a fairly high numbers of the rural industries (49 per cent) are inherited by the present owners from their fathers.

However, significantly a highest proportions of the units were established by the present entrepreneurs (41 per cent) followed by 30 per cent were established more than three generations ago and remaining 29 per cent were started by the fathers of the present entrepreneurs.

Among the industrial units those were quite old and were established three generations ago, a fairly large proportion of them are confined in the product line of woolen (51 per cent) and activities such as Blacksmithy (37 per cent) rope making (36 per cent) and basketry and matting (33 per cent) while the first generation entrepreneurs are largely initiating for the expansion of repairing and servicing activities, flour mills and tailoring activities.

This indicates that despite a significant decline in the proportions of traditional household based rural industries and those were confined on the manufacturing of locally available raw material based products, a sizeable numbers of them are still operating in the sample areas. In fact, the rural households are still confronting towards the expansion of certain product groups of rural industries such as carpentry rope making and Basketry, which production system is basically based on locally available raw materials, and activities such as black smithy in spite of the increasing concentration of new entrepreneurs in the expansion of modern type of industrial activities.

This implies the fact that inherited traditional household rural industries may be continued even without a good level of earnings due to lack of better opportunities of employment and the avenues of earnings in fact a overwhelming majority of the entrepreneurs continuing the inherited activity.

These views are further well supported by the evidence that a overwhelming proportion of the present entrepreneurs (62 per cent) were not associated with any economic activity, in fact over 41 per cent of them were unemployed and 16 per cent were students, before joining the rural industrial activities.

Further it revealed that a significantly a highest proportion of already employed population had opted to establish or to join the Blacksmithy (58 per cent) followed by basketry and mat making (54 per cent) and tailoring (45 per cent) while the attraction of the students had been towards the establishment of mainly modern rural industrial activities such as flour mills, repairing and servicing establishments.

Even among the rural population those were employed with other economic activities before starting the present units a fairly larger proportions of (65 per cent) them had entered in modern activities such as flour mills, though 52 per cent had started the carpentry work followed by 41 per cent had established repairing and servicing units.

*Table 1. Origin of Rural Industries*

| SL.NO. | PRODUCT | INDIVIDUAL | | | | |
|---|---|---|---|---|---|---|
| | | Self | Father | Grand Father | Friend/ Relative | TOTAL |
| 1. | Carpentry | 40 (47.62) | 26 (30.95) | 18 (21.43)* | - | 84 (100.0) |
| 2. | Blacksmithy | 21 (20.59) | 43 (42.1 6) | 37 (36.78) | 1 (0.98) | 102 (100.0) |
| 3. | Basketry & Matting | 31 (46.27) | 14 (20.90) | 22 (32.83) | - | 67 (100.0) |
| 4. | Rope making | 22 (36.07) | 17 (27.87) | 22 (36.06) | - | 61 (100.0) |
| 5. | Flour Mills | 25 (62.50) | 7 (17.50) | 8 (20.00) | - - | 40 (100.0) |
| 6. | Woolen Textile | 9 (18.37) | 15 (30.61) | 25 (51.02) | - | 49 (100.0) |
| 7. | Tailoring | 33 (60.00) | 15 (27.27) | 7 (12.73) | - | 55 (100.00) |
| 8. | Others | 22 (68.75) | 3 (9.38) | 7 (21.87) | - | 32 (100.0) |
| | TOTAL | 203 (41.43) | 140 (28.57) | 146 (29.80) | 1 (0.20) | 490 (100.0) |

Thus it may be strongly put forward the arguments that the people those are suffering from the various evils of un-employment are no way hesitating even to join the low earning\based rural traditional household industrial activities. However the relatively young generations are largely initiating to opt for the establishment of better earning profiles of modern rural industrial activities after completing their formal education.

It has also been noted that a very small proportions of women entrepreneurs (4 per cent) had also left working as housewives so as to establish rural industrial activities, though a majority of them were entered into the expansion of their traditional household based enterprises such as woolen activities (33 per cent) and a very low proportion them joined the carpentry and tailoring activities.

In this sense the rural households, either headed by men or the women segments have been quite significantly moving among different occupations and in the expansion of one to another type of rural industrial groups due to the well prevalent reasons of a very low level of income generation capacity of different rural industrial enterprises.

However, there are reasons such as scarcity in the availability of required quantity and quality of raw materials, irregularly of employment and earnings and the problems associated to the marketing of their produced those are equally influencing to the pattern of the movements of entrepreneurs towards the expansion and establishing of various categories and product groups of rural industrial activities.

A highest proportions of all of the 39 per cent of the heads of households, those were employed earlier, had reported that inadequate amount of income available from the past activity had compelled them to start the present rural industrial activity. Another, a second majority of 26 per cent entrepreneurs had changed the product-line of their manufacturing activities due to non-availability of required raw materials for producing goods in the last product group of industry followed by irregularity of work and insecurity to sustain the last industry (25 per cent) while remaining 7 per cent had closed down the last activity due to certain marketing problems in selling of the products and a lowest proportion of 3 per cent had established the present industries after getting retirement from the last employment.

**Motivation for Industry**

Accessibility to various raw material in adequate quantity and the availability of family skill have been visualised as the important influencing factors determining the expansion pattern of different rural industrial activities. Besides, a significant proportions of around over one fourth of the present entrepreneurs were forced to join their family enterprises due to lacking alternative sources of employment and income opportunities in rural areas, followed by 4 per cent of them were motivated by the different government departments for establishing the present industry through providing financial assistance to meet out the cost of starting the concern activity.

Availability of adequate quantity of required raw materials has attracted a highest proportion of the entrepreneurs for establishing mat making and basketry activities (42 per cent) followed by rope making (42 per cent) and carpentry (37 per cent) while the availability of traditionally developed family skill to be used in the production processes of rural industrial activities, has largely influenced the expansion pattern of carpentry, black smithy rope making and woolen activities.

Lacking employment opportunities in other economic activities in rural areas has mainly attracted to the local people either to adopt their traditional household based rural industries such as woolen and Blacksmithy activities or to go for favour of the establishment of relatively better earning modern type of rural industrial enterprises such as flour mills, tailoring and repairing and servicing units.

The initiatives of the Government's rural development programmes those emphasised toward the promotion of rural industrial activities have mainly gone in favour of the expansion of modern product groups of industries and least in the expansion of traditional and locally available raw material based units. Since among the 21 units established under different rural development programmes, a highest proportion of them are tailoring (33 per cent) followed by 19 per cent each in the group of repairing and servicing and woolen activities and flour mills (10 per cent).

### *Capital Intensity*

An important factor, which would determine the potential of employment generation, is the capital requirement for setting up of the enterprise. Setting up of a rural non-farm enterprise require a very low amount of capital investment. Indeed it was very low for the establishment of manufacturing activities as compared to trading, servicing, and transportation activities. Rural industries in most cases do not use separate structure to house their equipment and tools to perform the production of goods.

A part of the normal residence of the proprietor is normally used for this purpose. Even when a separate structure is used it is usually built with mud and stones using family labour and at some extent to the hired labourers from the local areas. The estimated capital requirement for setting up of a household based rural industry accounted for about Rs.5 thousand which seems relatively at higher side because of the amounts of investment required for establishing modern type of industrial units such as flour mills and tailoring activities is reported to be fairly high as Rs.28 thousand and Rs.4 thousand respectively.

Otherwise the amount of fixed investment undertaken for establishing other than tailoring and flour mills is estimated to be rather low at Rs.1155 for rope making units to highest at Rs.3297 for repairing and servicing activities. The amount of financial requirement for meeting the cost of the construction of separate building/shed and acquiring various basic machinery tools and implements at the time of the establishment of rural industrial enterprise is estimated to be almost the same at Rs.2.27 thousand and Rs.2.29 thousand respectively. However, it accounted relatively higher for meeting the cost of land and building as compared to acquiring machinery, tools and equipment in establishing of the units such as black smithy, rope making and tailoring.

Generally, the rural industrial units produce various goods and articles in small quantity at the initial period of its starting and the size and volume of production picks up according to the increasing trend of its demand. It is therefore, initially a very small amount of finances are required for establishing of the different industrial units while the industrial units have to make additional financial investments for acquiring additional machines , tools and equipment with the increase of the size of production to meet the increasing local demands of the various products.

And thus, the trends in further investment in fixed capital of rural industrial enterprises largely depends on the level of increasing trend in the overall size of production and the level of additions to the net income of the entrepreneurs from the concerned activity. Comparing the level of financial investment as undertaken during the period of starting and at present of various rural industrial units, it seems that the volume of production in each of the category of industrial units has been significantly increasing over the years.

As the consequences the level of the present value of financial investment of different rural industrial together has increased nearly two folds as compared to the value of initial investment. A highest level of addition in acquiring machinery tools and other equipment has been visualised in the cases of tailoring (four folds) followed by basketry and mat making (188 per cent) black smithy (156 per cent), woolen activities (144 per cent) carpentry (123 per cent) and lowest at 37 per cent for flour mills followed by 51 per cent for repairing and servicing activities.

It indicates that over the years the volume of production of traditional household based industrial activities has been increasing significantly at much higher level than the case of modern type of industrial activities; though during the recent past, the value of production as well as net earning from modern industrial units have been increasing more sharply than the case of traditional household based rural industries.

### *Raw Materials*

Access to and the availability pattern of different required raw material are among the most important factors which determine and influence the level of productivity and income and thus the overall development prospects of the manufacturing activities.

It has generally been accepted that there has been a substantial decrease in the numbers of rural industrial units which were engaged in the manufacture of different type of rural raw material based products, even after the announcement and introduction of several protective measures to accelerate the development of rural manufacturing activities under the various planned development strategies in the past.

But decrease in the availability and inadequately supply of the required raw materials are universally acknowledged as the major factors responsible for the closer of a majority of these rural industries. Most of the rural industrial units in the state are more or less dependent on the local supply of raw materials. The carpentry, basketry, mat making, rope making and woolen activities are the major rural industrial units which prospects of development are basically based on the availability of raw material in nearby forests and in other local areas.

The woolen activities are using only raw wool in the production of different woolen products. The goat and sheep rearers locally meet the demand of raw wool. In fact, a majority of the households those are engaged in woolen activities are also traditionally involved in the rearing of goats and sheep in the high hill areas of the state. However, during the recent past, the shortage of local wool is also being met through importing from Nepal, Newziland and Australia.

The ringal is the only raw material used in the production of various sizes of mats, candies and several other goods by the mating and basketry rural industries. Ringal is available locally in the forests, even most entrepreneurs are growing it on their waste and fallow land areas. Similarly, the carpentry units are using only different varieties of woods which is largely available in nearby forests. Also, the raw material for the production of different sizes of ropes is available in the forests at adequate quantity.

The black smiths are mainly using iron and wooden products for the production of utencils, agricultural machinery and other daily use items. A overwhelming majority of the rural industries are obtaining various required raw materials from within the villages (83 per cent). Such units are concentrated in the manufacturing activities such as carpentry, black smithy, basketry and mat making.

*Table 2. Value of Raw material procurred from different sources*

| SL. NO. | PRODUCT | Own Sources | Locally | | Outside Region | Per Unit of Raw Materials |
|---|---|---|---|---|---|---|
| | | | Non-Purch-ased | Purch-ased | | |
| 1. | Carpentry | 3.31 | 31.94 | 64.75 | - | 9759 |
| 2. | Black Smithy | 11.17 | 77.01 | 11.82 | - | 4148 |
| 3. | Basketry & Mat Making | 21.90 | 78.10 | - | - | 344 |
| 4. | Rope Making | 25.11 | 74.89 | - | - | 3216 |
| 5. | Flour Mills | - | - | 75.59 | 24.41 | 9771 |
| 6. | Woolen Textiles | 19.53 | - | 71.43 | 9.34 | 6686 |
| 7. | Tailoring | - | - | 84.02 | 15.98 | 4744 |
| 8. | Others | - | - | 35.65 | 64.35 | 1644 |
| | TOTAL | 7.73 | 30.17 | 54.06 | 8.04 | 4590 |

The traditional household industrial activities in general and those are concentrated in activities such as black smithy and woolen textiles are depending on the supply of raw material from own household sources together with it is available within their villages, though the carpentry, basketry, mat making and rope making are obtaining a major supply of required raw material from the local areas alone.

However, the flour mills, woolen and repairing and servicing units are largely depending on the supply of raw material from outside rural areas, even from outside state, besides from local areas (Table 2). On an average the rural industries are spending Rs.4590 in the purchase and procurement of raw material, which constitutes fairly highest for flour mills (Rs.9771) closely followed by carpentry (Rs.9759) and at lowest level for basketry (Rs.344) followed by repairing and servicing units (Rs.1644).

The rural industrial units those are engaged in the production of ringal based products and in rope making are obtaining its required raw material without making any payments on its cost because the entire quantity of concerned martial is largely available in the nearby forests and it could be collected as per their requirement through involving family labourforce without bearing any cost of its collection.

The raw wooden products are also available in nearby forests but the rural industrial units those are engaged in the production of wooden based goods are spending a sizeable amount on the procurement of raw woods. The households of Blacksmithy industrial are mainly engaged in carrying out job work for the farming households. Hence they are spending very little amounts on the procurement of raw material. However, the procurement of raw material as required in the production process of flourmills, tailoring and repairing and servicing units necessarily require a larger investment, either it is purchased from local areas or outside of the state.

**Mode and Size of Production**

The size and volume of production of various goods and articles that is undertaken by rural industrial enterprises is largely governed by the level and extent of the demands, requirements and the purchasing power of the local people. To a certain extent it also depends on the level of the necessity and essentiality for satisfying their basic needs.

Also, the adoption of the primitive and obsolete technology in the production process further limits the volume of production of these traditional household basis enterprises. Because the goods and articles produced by rural industrial enterprises hardly find any markets outside rural areas. It has to be indicated here that the carpentry households are engaged in the production of various wood based furniture and goods required for the construction of houses. These activities are performed by both upper caste and scheduled castes/scheduled tribe groups of households.

The Blacksmithy scheduled castes of households are engaged in the manufacturing and repairing of various agricultural machineries and tools and certain other equipment which are used for cutting grasses and leaves of trees for feeding animals and procurement of forest products for their own use and according to the demands of certain upper castes households which are known their Zajamans. Moreover, in remaining activities both upper and lower caste groups of households are equally participating for last several generations.

The basketry and mating households are engaged in the production of different sizes and categories of mats, baskets, candies and various other articles as per the requirement of local people. The raw materials for the manufacturing of ropes, mats and baskets are locally available. The scheduled tribes social groups of households are mainly engaged in the woolen activities for the last several centuries.

The main articles which are being produced by them are different size of shawls, Pankhi, Chutkas, Thulmas, sweaters and various handicraft products which size and quantum of production is based on the demands of both local people as well as outside rural areas. The size of production of different rural industrial units has been estimated only the tune of Rs.14.7 thousand.

In fact it is much lower level for traditional type of household enterprises, particularly of basketry (Rs.6831), rope making (Rs.9274) and black smithy (Rs.11291), though it is highest for modern type of enterprises related to servicing and repairing units (Rs.25 thousand) and flour mills (Rs.23.5 thousand).

(I) Value added = Value of output - operating cast excluding wages of hired labour - Depreciation (10 per cent of Value of machinery and equipments).

(II) Net Income = Value added - wage paid to hired labour.

(III) Earnings per family worker = Net income per unit/family worker.

*Productivity and Profitability*

The productivity of rural industrial activities is of the interest for various reasons. First, from the micro-economic point of view, it is important to know whether household based industry represents an efficient use of resources as compared to large scale and more mechanised modes of production since this is an important factor effecting the expansion of the rural industrial enterprises.

Secondly, it is important to know, from the point of view of policy making, whether different rural industrial activities represent in principle viable production opportunities, or whether they are merely a sign of distress adaptation, representing basically very low income generating activities to which household only resort when no other profitable employment opportunities are available to them.

The most important question related to this is whether and to what extent the expansion of various rural industrial activities could be a viable option as a strategy for the alleviation of rural poverty. The labour productivity, more or less, follows the order of output per enterprise but the differences in employment size are not large for different rural industrial activities.

The per worker productivity for all rural household industries together is accounted for Rs.11.5 thousand and it ranged lowest at Rs.5.5 thousand for basketry and mating to highest at Rs.22.9 thousand for repairing and servicing activities. A significant level of differences are also well existing in the pattern of income generation of different rural industries, though a marginal extent of variations are prevailing between the level of per unit amount of income and value added being generated from different industries, because most rural industries are no way hiring any paid worker and are running with employing their family workforce only.

Similarly, with a very high raw material content, which is basically obtained from local forests without any cost in the cases of most rural industries, the per unit value added to output ratio is turn out at much higher rate of over 68 per cent. In fact the corresponding ratio is resulted to be as higher as 96 per cent for basketry and mating units closely followed by repairing and servicing activities (95 per cent) though it stands lowest for woolen activities (44 per cent) followed by carpentry (59 per cent).

Due to differences in employment size, the ratio of value added per worker to output for carpentry has reduced significantly at much higher level than the remaining rural industries, and it followed fairly larger for repairing and servicing activities (Rs.21801) followed by flour mills (Rs.12620) and carpentry (Rs.10590) and lowest for woolen activities (Rs.2876). Further it has been recognised that due to lower level of absorption of hired labours in rural industrial activities the differences between value added and income turn out to be at very lower extent as compared to the differences in the ratio of value added to output.

The ratio of per unit value added to net income for different industries together is accounted for 96 per cent, though the corresponding ratio ranged between 90 per cent to 100 per cent, respectively for flour mills and rope making units. Further, the earning per household worker is estimated to be around Rs.8 thousand and the household workers those are engaged in modern type of industrial units such as flour mills and repairing and servicing are generating fairly much larger amount of earnings as compared to those are engaged in traditional form of household based rural industries.

Given the fact that most industrial units in rural areas are carried out as household enterprises with a main objective of earnings a livelihood, and that, a majority of household workers are working on full time basis making them as the principle occupation and source of household income. The rural industrial activities are largely contributing in the incomes of different rural households those are engaged on them along with the amount of income generated from farm activities so as to cross the absolute poverty line.

In this sense initiating for diversification of rural industrial activities through introducing market oriented goods and articles in production system and bring improvement in the quality of the product would be a most important instrumental measure for increasing the income of rural households.

**Productivity and Income Generation**

The changes in the efficiency and importance of different industrial activities for rural households, in terms of providing income. The analysis revealed that over and above, each of the categories of rural industrial activities have been efficiently functioning in rural areas. It is well reflected by the fact that the level of productivity of different rural industries and the pattern of income generation from them has shown a considerable increasing trend of over 37 per cent and 27 per cent respectively.

However, in real terms the income of households those are engaged in modern categories units, mainly in servicing and repairing and flour mills is increasing more sharply than the case of households engaged in traditional household industries such as Blacksmithy and rope making.

The larger increase in the productivity and income as being derived from former categories of units is mainly due the fact that a majority of them are of the recent origin which has consequently increased the total volume of production for current year only while the growth of latter categories of units has shown a margin increase during the same periods since a majority of them were traditional and were established three to four generations ago.

Besides, lacking improvements in the quality of products, use of traditionally developed indigenous mode of production technologies, poor marketing network for selling the produced and the low level of investment capacity of rural households are the important factors of low value added in the traditional household based rural industries.

However, it has to be considered that the development potentials of traditional household based industries in general and those are basically based on locally available raw materials are regarded significantly more brighter than the case of modern categories of repairing activities, flour mills and tailoring.

*Table 3. Workers in Rural Industries*

| SL. NO. | ACTIVITY | TOTAL NUMBERS | | | PER UNIT | | |
|---|---|---|---|---|---|---|---|
| | | Family workers | Hired workers | TOTAL | Family Workers | Hired Worker | TOTAL |
| 1. | Carpentry | 86 (86.00) | 14 (14.00) | 100 (100.0) | 1.02 | 0.17 | 1.19 |
| 2. | Blacksmithy | 125 (99.21) | 1 (0.89) | 126 (100.0) | 1.23 | 0.01 | 1.24 |
| 3. | Basketry and mating | 82 (98.80) | 1 (1.20) | 83 (100.0) | 1.22 | 0.01 | 1.24 |
| 4. | Rope make | 71 (100.0) | - | 71 (100.0) | 1.16 | - | 1.16 |
| 5. | Flour Mills | 42 (87.50) | 6 (12.50) | 4 (100.0) | 1.04 | 0.15 | 1.20 |
| 6. | Woolen Textiles | 84 (97.67) | 2 (2.37) | 86 (100.0) | 1.71 | 0.04 | 1.76 |
| 7. | Tailoring | 68 (91.89) | 6 (8.11) | 74 (100.0) | 1.24 | 0.11 | 1.35 |
| 8. | Others | 34 (80.95) | 8 (19.05) | 42 (100.0) | 1.06 | 0.25 | 1.31 |
| | TOTAL | 592 (93.97) | 38 (6.03) | 630 (100.0) | 1.21 | 0.08 | 1.29 |

Largely, because the wide ranging various goods and articles produced in former categories of units are more market oriented possessing greater demands both inside and outside rural areas and thus are possessing greater advantages of their diversification than the case of latter categories of units.

### *Size of Employment*

Further considering into account the structure of employment in different categories of rural industries it depicts that in spite of higher labour absorption in relation to income derived, the rural industrial units, in fact, have relatively small number of workers per unit. In the sample units as a whole, the average number of workers employed is 1.29, consisting of 1.21 family unpaid workers and 0.08 hired wage paid workers.

Inability of rural industrial activities to provide adequate income in term of sustaining minimum level of household living, the workforce from these households is seen do participate in other non-farm activities both within the rural areas itself or in nearby urban areas so as to supplement the income for their households livelihood.

In fact, in a majority of the rural industrial units, only the heads of households are engaged in different stages of the operation of their units such as collection and obtaining of raw materials, production process and the marketing of goods and articles. Even, over one third of the total rural industrial activities are alone handled by the retired personnel from their last occupation in Government sector and those belonging to the age groups of above 60 years.

Over and above, the rural industrial units are mainly run by the head of households and to a certain extent through engaging their available family workforce while only few units are seen employing hired labour on wages for only specific kinds of work which cannot be performed alone by the heads of the households of the concerned industries.

The proportion of hired worker employed in rural industrial activities accounted for only 6.03 per cent and its proportion ranged highest at 19.05 per cent in repairs and servicing activities to lowest at 0.89 per cent in Blacksmithy with no hired labour is employed by rope making units. It has been well visualised that a very low level of earnings available from the rural industrial activities is restricting the scope for employing of both family and outside family workforce in different rural enterprises. Since these views are well supported by the evidence that the size of workforce employed in different units is significantly well related according to the size of income generated by them.

## Structure of Manufacturing Various Goods

The size and structure of manufacturing various goods and articles in rural industrial enterprises is largely governed by the demand generated by local villages and the requirement of own households for different goods produced by them. Only few enterprises such as tailoring, black smithy, rope making and woolen are involved in the production of various goods for meeting the local demands as well as for selling outside their villages.

However, the size of production of various goods is undertaken according to the demands of local household, therefore, the question of keeping unsold goods and articles as a stock is hardly arisen. The entire quantity of production of various commodities of the rural industries is either sold or it is used by its households, though a major proportion of production (99.25 per cent) is sold to the consumers and a very small part of it is reported to be used by the concerned households itself.

### *Pattern of Sale*

The nature of production of various goods in rural industries is mainly to satisfy the local requirements. These view are further strengthened by the fact that a fairly high proportion of around 63 per cent of the total sale of goods is carried out directly to the local people from the site of the workplace of the industrial units. In all, the local villages, nearby villages and nearby towns are noted to be most preferred destinations for the sale of the goods and articles manufactured in rural industrial enterprises.

*Table 4. Value of Production, Sale and Self consumption*

| Sl. No. | ACTIVITY | Total Production | Total Sale | Total Self Consumption |
|---|---|---|---|---|
| 1. | Carpentry | 1806924<br>(100.0) | 1788924<br>(99.56) | 8000<br>(0.44) |
| 2. | Blacksmithy | 1151682<br>(100.0) | 1146082<br>(99.51) | 5600<br>(0.49) |
| 3. | Basketry | 457677<br>(100.0) | 452627<br>(98.90) | 5050<br>(1.10) |
| 4. | Rope Making | 584014<br>(100.0) | 577764<br>(98.94) | 6250<br>(1.06) |
| 5. | Flour Mills | 439080<br>(100.0) | 936680<br>(99.74) | 2400<br>(0.26) |
| 6. | Woolen Textiles | 558894<br>(100.0) | 534454<br>(96.24) | 24440<br>(3.76) |
| 7. | Tailoring | 899085<br>(100.0) | 891335<br>(99.14) | 7750<br>(0.86) |
| 8. | Others | 801234<br>(100.0) | 795234<br>(99.25) | 6000<br>(0.75) |
| | TOTAL | 7198590<br>(100.0) | 7133100<br>(99.25) | 65490<br>(0.75) |

However, the products of black smithy, tailoring rope making and flourmills are largely being sold in the local villages itself. In fact, the nature of performing repairing and servicing activities, of modern rural industrial units is also basically based on the local demands though a significant level of repairing and servicing work is also being done by them for the individuals of neighbouring villages.

The flourmills are found involved in the processing of various foodgrains for only local villagers while the tailors are engaged mainly to perform work for local villagers and only to a limited extent.for nearby villagers. The carpentry households are seen manufacturing various wooden based furnitures and several other wooden goods for its supply to different nearby villages and towns and even to sale outside the district.

However, the indications are that the traditional household based rural industries such as basketry, woolen and rope making units have started to sale their products through different channels, both within and outside villages, nearby towns and even in the exhibitions those are organised outside Uttaranchal, during the recent past, though a major proportion of the sale of goods is performed at the village level by each of the industrial units.

Thus, it is well evident that the products manufactured in traditional household industrial units are not only meeting the demands of local households but the demands of these products have been considerably increasing in neighbouring villages, nearby towns and even outside Uttaranchal. While the production basis of modern industrial units is limited largely upto the supply of local requirements and only a little proportion of access production is procured outside villages and in nearby towns.

Moreover, it is well depicted that rural industrial units require very low level capital investment, though it was reported to be considerably higher for modern categories of units than the case of traditional household units. Basically using traditionally developed indigenous mode of technological system in the production of goods and articles in rural industries has resulted the very low level of productivity, value added and earnings, as it is measured either in terms of per worker or per household.

Also, in spite of higher labour absorption in relation to income derived, the rural industrial units, in fact, have a relatively small number of workers per unit. On the whole, the structure of production, the productive efficiency of all the industries is still on the increase and the sources of marketing of disposal of different goods and articles manufactured by rural industries has been significantly widening.

# 3

# Contribution in the Rural Economy

The contribution of non-farm sector has been consistently increasing in the creation of additional employment and the generation of income in different geographical locations over the years due to decreasing manland ratio and an overall decline in the net cultivated land area, beside a considerable decline in per capita net domestic production being originated from agriculture and related activities.

The consequences of these all-adverse performances of farming economies have universally been well recognised in terms of a significant decline in the concentration of workforce in agriculture and allied activities and its subsequent shift in non-farm sector during the recent past.

However, the contribution of various components of non-farm sector in general and its manufacturing segment in particular in the process of overall development, especially in terms of creating employment and the generation of income, has been realised at much below the level of its actual expectations in different areas.

This largely due to inadequate initiatives undertaken for the exploitation of various advantages and niche based opportunities that are available in favour of developing variety of non-farm activities in different locations of the state under the pastdevelopment plans.

Besides, several fundamental problems as experienced in terms of lacking improvements in the production technologies, accessibility to the facilities of road transports and required infrastructures, continuing concentration towards the production of limited numbers of commodities based on fulfilling only the local demands for last several centuries, lacking development in the quality and designs of products and related features were also been equally responsible factors behind the slow growth of a numbers of non-farm activities and its lesser extent of contribution in the rural economy of the state.

It can be obviously seen that almost the rural households, especially in hilly and mountainous areas of the state, are obtaining a sizeable amount of income from other than agricultural activities, either through engaging its family workforce in different non-farm occupations within rural areas itself or motivating them, to migrate outside rural areas in near by towns so as to supplement in the incomes of the households through sending remittances.

The real situation which presently emerging is that although almost the households are engaged in the agricultural activities therefore the farming is emphasized as the prime occupation of the workforce of almost the households in rural areas of the state. But the non-agricultural activities are seen providing significantly much higher amount of income as compared to income originated from agricultural activities in the total incomes of the households.

## Income Distribution

A review of the pattern of income distribution among the

households representing different geographical locations. There are significant differences in both per household and per capita income distribution between the farm and non-farm households and also, between the rural households of different locations. The per household income is estimated to be Rs. 18482, and it varied highest from Rs.19.91 thousand to lowest at Rs.17.30 thousand between the households located in middle and low hill areas respectively.

The PCI accounted for Rs.3519, which again stands relatively higher in middle hill areas as compared to high and low hill areas. Also, the per household as well as per capita income of non-farm households is estimated to be significantly much higher than the case of farm households in each of geographical locations. This mainly due to the obvious fact that, first, the farming households are deriving income from only two sources namely; farm sector and as remittances from the migrants family workforce while the non-farming households are noted deriving a sizeable amount of earnings from the various categories of non-farm activities, besides from agricultural activities and through remittances from the migrant family members.

Also, the proportion of workforce engaged in performing different economic activities in rural areas was revealed rather higher among the non-farm households as compared to farm households, though a marginal differences in favour of latter groups of households was revealed in the proportion of migrants to total workforce. Distribution of households according to different income groups revealed that a highest proportions of the households of over 73 per cent, comprising 76 per cent among the farm households and 64 per cent among the non-farm households are confined in lowest income group range of below Rs.2000.

And only little over than 7 per cent of the households are in the highest income group of above Rs.4, 000 though, the proportion of households in respective income range are relatively higher in middle hill areas and in particular among the non-farm households. Moreover, it appears that the inequality in the pattern of income distribution among the households is largely prevailing between different locations and also between the households those are engaged in farm and non-farm activities.

But the non-farm households are better placed as compared to farm households in terms of their economic situation is concerned and the extent of inequalities emerging in the pattern of income distribution among the households in different locations.

### *Source of Household Income*

The households average net amount of income as derived by them from different farm and non-farm activities and from other sources, such as remittances from the migrants family members and the income received in the form of pension by the retired family members during the reference period. The farm households are seen deriving certain amount of income from only the limited sources such as farming activities, pension and remittances from migrant family members.

However, the sources of income of non-farm households are significantly much higher than the farm households. The working family members of non-farm households do engage in numbers of non-farm activities in the capacity of selfemployed as well as wage paid casual workers, besides working in farming activities while the working family members of farm households only concentrate in the activities of own farms rather than to join in non-farm activities even during the off season of the agricultural operations.

In fact, they prefer to migrate outside for seeking employment rather than to participate in locally available wage-paid employment, even the earning and the status of occupations available in rural areas are comparatively better than as are available at the places of migration, partly because of a largely developed inferiority complexes among themselves against the joining of certain categories of wage-paid employment in rural areas and partly due to the fact that most of the rural non-farm activities have been traditionally performed by only a particular social groups of households for the past several generations.

The income of a household consisted of the earnings summed over the diverse sources of employment plus rent payment received, if any, for leasing out land and other assets plus all transfer payments (e.g. pensions, gifts and remittances received). The amount of income derived by the households as remittances from migrant workforce and as pension by the retired family members in favour of services they rendered in the past could be included as a part of non-farm income.

Since, each of the migrant workforce those are contributing to the household incomes through remittances are employed in urban areas, largely in defence and Government services, and the retired personal those are receiving pension were earlier mostly migrants and were working with the defense and Government Services. Practically the amount of pension, which they are currently deriving, is the outcome of services they rendered for non-farm sector. In this manner the income earned through pension and remittances is the income derived from urban non-farm sector and thus, this income could also be treated as a part of non-farm income.

The per household annual average amount of income in the sample areas accounted for Rs.18.48

thousand. And the economic condition of households located in middle hill areas seems relatively more sound as compared to those located in high and low hill areas. The actual amount of income being generated from agricultural and its associated activities is appeared relatively much less as compared to non-farm sector in each of the geographical locations. Per household income from farm sector is estimated to be Rs.6016 as against Rs.12376 from non-farm sector and it varied largely among the rural areas of different geographical locations.

Since every household is possessing at least some cultivated land. As a result, each of the households in Uttaranchal is engaged in different agricultural operations and is generating at least some amounts of income from it. Hence, the income estimated for farm sector is the combined income of both farm and non-farm households. In sample areas, the contribution of income originated from non-farm sector in the total income derived from different sources accounted for around 76 per cent though it varied largely among different locations.

Since in the proceeding analysis the nonfarm activities were found highly concentrated in rural areas of high hills followed by low hills and at lowest level in middle hills. The contribution of income generated from the non-farm sector is more or less originated at a similar pattern as revealed in terms of the concentration of non-farm activities among different geographical locations. The proportion of income derived from farm sector is, however, significantly at highest level in rural areas of low hill areas as compared to middle and high hill areas, though its share follows at much lower level than the case of non-farm sector in each of the geographical locations.

The share of earnings that the household deriving in the form of pension of their family members and as remittances from the migrant workforce has also been noted very high in different geographical locations. However, the combined contribution of pension and remittances in the total income generated in rural areas of middle hill areas is found fairly higher (42 per cent) as compared to high (36 per cent) and low (22 per cent) hill areas.

*Table 1. Percentage share of Farm and Non-Farm Sectors*

| SL. No. | Source of Income | High Hills | Middle Hills | Low Hills | All Areas |
|---|---|---|---|---|---|
| A. | Farm Sector | 23.01 | 29.86 | 45.53 | 33.04 |
| 1. | Shops | 5.09 | 2.77 | 3.10 | 3.53 |
| 2. | Construction Labour | 7.06 | 4.16 | 3.47 | 4.75 |
| 3. | Manufacturing | 14.18 | 8.67 | 13.66 | 11.84 |
| 4. | Transport | 3.79 | 4.87 | 2.24 | 3.71 |
| 5. | Services | 10.38 | 6.90 | 10.22 | 8.98 |
| 6.(a) | Others Pension | 24.35 | 27.33 | 16.35 | 22.91 |
| (b) | Remittances | 12.09 | 15.45 | 5.42 | 11.24 |
| B. | Non-farm Sector | 76.99 | 70.14 | 54.46 | 66.96 |
| | Per thousand Income (Rs.) | 18095 (100.00) | 19912 (100.00) | 17302 (100.00) | 18482 (100.00) |

The manufacturing activities are noted as the most importanss of nonfarm sector in terms of the generation of the size of income and its share in the total income originated from different sources in each of the sample areas. The share of income generated from manufacturing activities is estimated to be around 12 percent, though it varied marginally among different locations. The service sector employment is seen contributing about 9 per cent income in the total income of the sample areas.

The combined contribution of different rural non-farm activities in the overall income of sample areas consisted at 33 per cent which is almost similar to that of farm sector, and the income derived as pension and remittances from the migrants. Considering into account the fact that the amount of income received by the rural households as remittances from migrant workforce and as pension in favour of the services rendered by the rural workforce in urban areas, is the form of income generated by rural workforce from urban areas, the amount of income originated from these two sources should undoubtedly be considered as the transfer of non farm income from urban to rural areas.

In this sense, it could be attributed that the contribution of income generated from rural non-farm sectors and urban modern economies (non-farm sector) in the total rural income, is more or less, at similar proportions but it varied among different geographical locations. The contribution of urban earnings to rural income is visualized highest in the rural areas of middle hills as compared to remaining two areas. Irrespective of the number of rural workforce participating in different non-farm activities in urban areas and the proportions of them remitting a part of their earning to their households in rural areas, the rural workforce employed either in rural or urban non-farm sector is seen contributing almost equal proportion of income in the rural areas.

To sum up, although, the domination of farm sector in the rural economy can be well visualized in the sense that each of the rural households are engaged in agricultural operations and this sector is contributing at least some amount of incomes to all of them. However, the contribution of non-farm sector can also be not oversided in the process of rural development. Since various non-farm activities are employing a very high proportion of rural workforce, even more than the cases of farm-sector in some of the locations, and are contributing significantly much higher percentage of income as compared to farm sector in the rural areas of different geographical locations of the state.

*Farm and Non-farm Income on Household Economy*

It seems that the income derived through pension and as remittances from migrantfamily members together is the major source of income of the farming households in all the sample areas in general and especially in the households located in high and middle hill areas. Since in the farm households, the contribution of income generated through pensions and remittances together is estimated to be significantly much higher than the farm sector; it is reported as higher as 69 per cent and 63 per cent for the farming households which are situated in high and middle hill areas respectively.

However the contribution of income generated from farm sector is noted to be significant much higher than the case of income received as remittances and pension in the farming households particularly of those are located in low hill areas. Over and above, the farming households are highly depending upon the income derived as pension and remittances. It is also clear that the farming households are more likely preferring to motivate its workforce for migration outside villages in search of remunerative employment opportunities rather than to motivate them to engage in rural non-farm activities during the period of off season of agricultural operations.

*Table 2. Percentage share of Farm and Non-Farm households*

| SL. | Sectors/ | Farm Households | | | | Non-farm Households | | | |
|---|---|---|---|---|---|---|---|---|---|
| | Source of Income | High | Middle | Low | Total | High | Middle | Low | Total |
| 1. | Farm Sector | 30.76 | 37.10 | 73.53 | 46.59 | 16.64 | 18.46 | 18.79 | 17.99 |

| | | | | | | | | | |
|---|---|---|---|---|---|---|---|---|---|
| 2. | Rural Nonfarm Sector | - | - | - | - | 73.87 | 73.28 | 64.91 | 69.24 |
| 3. | Others, Total | 69.23 | 62.90 | 26.17 | 53.41 | 9.49 | 11.26 | 17.30 | 12.77 |
| | Pension | 47.00 | 39.98 | 17.44 | 34.95 | 5.74 | 7.44 | 15.02 | 9.55 |
| | Remittances | 22.23 | 22.92 | 8.73 | 18.46 | 3.75 | 3.72 | 2.28 | 3.22 |
| | Total (per household income in Rs.) | 16800 | 18122 | 13165 | 15903 | 19800 | 23569 | 24726 | 22542 |

The rural non-farm activities are noted playing a very important role in terms of the contribution of income in a large number of households in almost the rural areas of different locations. Since, the share of non-farm income in the total income of households generated from different sources is accounted for 69.24 per cent, though the level and extent of its contribution is found varied among different geographical locations.

The share of non-farm in the income of households those are located in high altitude areas is as higher as 73.87 per cent but it narrowed at 70.28 per cent for middle hill areas and reaches at the lowest level at 64.91 per cent for low hill areas. The contribution of farm-sector in the income of non-farm households is estimated to be only around 18 per cent and it is more or less at similar proportion for the households of different geographical locations.

The amount of income generated through remittances and in the form of pension together is contributing only 12.77 per cent, in the income of non-farm households, though it varied largely for the households of different geographical locations, being highest in low hill areas (17 per cent) followed by 11 per cent in middle and 9 per cent in high hill areas.

Largely existing inequalities in the pattern of the distribution of cultivated land among the households seems to be highly reducing the share of farm sectors in the total income of households among those are located in different geographical locations even among those of the same location. But the availability of limited available land for cultivation among the households is compelling to its workforce to participate in different non-farm employment and generate income to contribute for maintaining the livings of its households.

However, the households owing relatively larger size of holdings, are even not in a position to meet their minimum food and other household requirements, from the farms. Therefore they are forcing to its surplus workforce to migrate outside rural areas for seeking employment in urban areas rather than to engage in rural non-farm economies (Table 2).

*Contribution of Non-farm Income*

Further an attempt has been carried out to examine the pattern of contribution of different non-farm activities in the overall income as being generated from rural non-farm sector in different geographically locations. Annually, on an average a non-farm household is generating around Rs.15.6 thousand from engaging its family workforce in performing different non-farm activities within the rural areas, though it is marginally varying from lowest at Rs.14.53 thousand to highest at Rs.16.59 thousand for the households located in high and middle hill areas respectively.

The manufacturing activities are indicated to the most dominating components of non-farm sector in each of the geographical locations in term of its percentage share in the overall income of the households, which they are generating from different non-farm employment. Since the manufacturing activities are contributing around 36 per cent of income in the overall non-farm income of the households; though its share is follows at highest level in the rural areas of low hills (41.80 per cent) followed by high hills (35.20 per cent) and lowest at 31.68 per cent in middle hill areas.

Different services related activities are noted as the second most components of non-farm sector in view of their contribution in the income of non-farm households in different locations. The contribution of services in the non-farm sector's income of households is estimated to be little over than 27 per cent, comprising 31 per cent in low hills, 26 per cent in high hills and 25 per cent in middle hills.

The remaining three components of non-farm sector, i.e. trading, construction and transport activities, are also seen contributing more or less, at similar pattern in the non-farm income of households of different geographical locations. Although the combined share of these all activities is accounted for around little over than the share of manufacturing activities though their combined contribution is seen at greater level in middle hill areas followed by high hill areas and at lowest level in low hill areas.

Further an assessment regarding the contribution of different rural non-farm activities in the income of non-farm households has been analysed in term of the average amount of income that the non-farm households are deriving from different components of non-farm activities. It has to be noted that many sample households are engaged in more than one non-farm activities.

Therefore, the average per households income contributed by each of the non-farm activities has been calculated by working out the total amount of income generated from respective activity and than it is divided by the actual number of households engaged in it.

*Table 3. Contribution of Different Non-farm activities in the Income of Non-farm households*

| Locations | Activities | | | |
|---|---|---|---|---|
| | High | Middle | Low | All |
| Manufacturing | 35.20 | 31.68 | 41.80 | 36.11 |
| Trading | 12.64 | 10.12 | 9.49 | 10.76 |
| Construction | 17.54 | 15.21 | 10.61 | 14.49 |
| Transport | 9.40 | 17.17 | 6.83 | 11.29 |
| Services | 25.91 | 24.91 | 31.27 | 27.39 |
| All Activities (Per Household Income Rs.) | 14529 (100.00) | 16587 (100.00) | 15802 (100.00) | 15608 (100.00) |

The households which family workforce is engaged in service sector are found acquiring significantly highest amount of incomes than the households those are engaged in other rural non-farm activities. The transportation related activities are seen as the second most important non-farm activities those are contributing around Rs.29 per annum in the non-farm households, though the average amount of income being earned from these activities is ranging lowest at Rs.22.53 thousand in high hill areas to highest at Rs.34.70 thousand in middle hill areas.

Average earnings from farmsector and wage paid employment in construction related activities seem to be very low at Rs.4055 and Rs.7327 respectively. Even than almost the households in former sector and a very high proportion of around 31 per cent households in latter sector are engaged on them for the generation of income. The trading and manufacturing activities are observed providing almost a similar amount of income to the non-farm households in different geographical locations, though marginally higher in middle hill areas than the remaining locations.

On the whole almost the non-farm activities, excepting those are confined in construction sector, located in middle hill areas are appeared more productive as compared to those of high and low hill areas from the view of the generation of income in the nonfarm households. Thus, it highlights the fact that in real terms, the different categories of non-farm activities are observed highly concentra ted in the rural areas of high hills. As the consequences over half of the sample households were confined in a non-farm employment in the concern area.

But, the potential for the generation of income from different non-farm activities are noted fairly larger in middle hill areas as compared other sample areas. The extent and nature of participation of households in different rural non-farm and farm activities. Every nonfarm households are partly engaged in traditional farm sector along with the number of various non-farm activities to supplement income for their households.

On an average, one household is simultaneously engaged in more than two activities in each of the geographical locations. The proportion of households engaged in manufacturing activities is constituted to be around 40 per cent, consisting significantly at highest proportion of 46.26 per cent in low hill areas followed by 42.22 per cent in high hill areas and at lowest proportion at 30.83 per cent in middle hill areas.

Also, a little over 41 per cent households, comprising 52.67 per cent in middle hills, 40 per cent in high hills and 11.54 per cent in low hills are engaged in wage-paid employment, available in construction and its related activities. Around 12 per cent of the households are appeared engaged in each trading and service related activities while a lowest proportion of (6.14 per cent) household are seen participating in transport related activities which are indicated to be rewarding highest amount of income as compared to income being generated from rest of the non-farm activities in rural areas of different geographical locations.

It seems that the factors such as differences in the expansion of infrastructural facilities, accessibility situation of rural households to the facilities of road transports and marketing network for the transactions of goods and articles between rural and urban areas are the most important factors which are directly perpetuating certain level of differences in the pattern of income generations of the households even from engaging in similar non-farm activities among different geographical locations.

Since the households in rural areas of middle and low hill areas are possessing relatively better advantages over the hill areas in term of access to the facilities of road transport, marketing network and linkages with urban areas and even in the development of various social and economic infrastructural facilities. The combined implications of these factors have largely reflected higher amounts of return in favour of the households of farmer geographical locations as compared to latter one even in performing similar category of non-farm and in engaging in same non-farm activity as wage paid casual worker.

Similarly, the households those are engaged in different non-arm activities as the self-employed are generating significantly higher amount of income as compared to those are employed as wage-paid casual workers. And the relatively higher amounts of returns as derived by the households through engaging in certain nonfarm activities such as transport services and trading related activities are the outcome of the relatively higher amount of investment undertaken by them in the expansion of concern non-farm activities.

*Table 4. Particopation of Households in Non-Farm activities*

| Activities | High | Middle | Low | All |
|---|---|---|---|---|
| Farm Sector | 495 (100.00) | 412 (100.00) | 428 (100.00) | 1335 (100.00) |
| Trading | 73 (14.75) | 41 (9.95) | 58 (13.55) | 172 (12.88) |
| Construction | 198 (40.00) | 217 (52.67) | 135 (31.54) | 550 (41.20) |
| Manufacturing | 209 (42.22) | 127 (30.83) | 198 (46.26) | 534 (40.00) |
| Transport | 30 (6.06) | 35 (8.50) | 17 (3.97) | 82 (6.14) |
| Services | 56 (11.31) | 44 (10.68) | 65 (15.18) | 165 (12.36) |
| All Activities | 1061 | 876 | 901 | 2838 |
| Sample household | 495 (100.00) | 412 (100.00) | 428 (100.00) | 1335 (100.00) |
| Per household No. of activities | 2.14 | 2.13 | 2.11 | 2.13 |

Thus, providing increasing investment on the expansion and development of various potential non-farm activities could be a suggestive methodology for increasing the incomes of non-farm household in rural areas. However, the expectation from the part of rural households for creating additional investment on the expansion and development of different area specific po:ential non-farm activities are rather minimal because a majority of them are not in a position to generate sufficient income from different sources even for maintaining their minimum standard of livings.

The Government intervention in this regard, through initiating for development of a comprehensive plan approach toward the expansion of certain non-farm activities, which are possessing area specific advantages in terms of their development, would be a rather more instrumented suggestive measure.

## Providing Employment Opportunities

Over the years, the importance of non-farm employment has been gaining increasing very fastly in the rural areas of almost the developing countries including India. Since the concentration of rural workforce in farm sector economies has been rapidly declining and its direct shift in non-farm employment has empirically been visualized in these countries (Islam 1986) Vaidyanathan (1986) Vyas and Mathai (1978) and Chadda (1993).

Similar situation has also been found emerging in the structure of employment in different districts of Uttaranchal. However, still the workforce in rural areas of different geographical locations in largely confined in agriculture and related activities due to lesser extent of growth in the availability of employment opportunities in other economic activities.

*Table 5. Non-Farm Sector Providing Employment*

| Areas | Total workers | | | Non-farm workers | | |
|---|---|---|---|---|---|---|
| | M | F | T | M | F | T |
| High hills | 1215<br>(100.00) | 1166<br>(100.00) | 23.81<br>(100.00) | 54.90 | 50.77 | 52.88 |
| Middle hills | 1713<br>(100.00) | 1301<br>(100.00) | 3014<br>(100.00) | 35.79 | 39.82 | 37.52 |
| Low hills | 1901<br>(100.00) | 954<br>(100.00) | 2855<br>(100.00) | 29.46 | 61.01 | 40.00 |
| All Areas | 4829<br>(100.00) | 3421<br>(100.00) | 8250<br>(100.00) | 38.10 | 49.46 | 42.81 |

The contribution of non-farm sector in providing employment opportunities in different geographical locations is largely varying in the State because of largely existing inequalities in the availability pattern of employment in different economic sectors, distribution of cultivated land and the variations in the fertility and productivity of land, which interacting to a larger differences in per household and per hectare returns of crop production among different rural areas.

In all, the proportion of workforce engaged in different non-farm activities is estimated to be 42.81 per cent, consisting of 49.46 per cent women as against 38.10 male workforce. Among the workforce of non-farm households, over half of them are again seen working in farm activities as self-employees along with working with non-farm activities.

The corresponding proportion of workforce is, however, as higher as 58.53 per cent in the rural areas of middle hills followed by 54.73 per cent in low hill areas and 46.67 per cent in high hills. The manufacturing activities are the most important components of rural non-farm sector in term of role they are contributing in providing employment opportunities to the rural workforce in each of the geographical locations of the State.

The proportion of workforce employed in manufacturing sector, mainly in a capacity of self employees, accounted for over 19 per cent, and it ranged lowest at 14 per cent in middle hill areas to highest at 23 per cent in high hill areas. Of the 10 per cent of total non-farm workforce engaged in rather low paid construction activities as the casual workers, a highest proportion of them are confined in high hills followed by middle and low hill areas.

The concentration of workforce in each trading and services is estimated to be around 6 per cent and the respective proportions of workforce are by and large same in each of the geographical locations. And a lowest proportion of workforce (2.41 per cent) is engaged in transport related activities in a capacity of self-employed.

*Earnings of workforce*

An examination into the pattern of annual earnings of workforce from different non-farm activities reveals that the different occupations and activities confined in services sectors such as personal services undertaken in the form of self employed and various occupations referred to public sector are providing a fairly high amount of earning to its workforce in rural areas of each geographical locations.

The amount of earnings that the workforce is deriving from transport related activities are also as higher as Rs.34.70 thousands in middle hill areas followed by Rs. 27.20 thousands in low hills and lowest at Rs.23.21 thousand in high hill areas. However, the proportion of workforce engaged in concerned activity is noted at lowest level as compared to remaining non-farm activities because the participation of workforce in transportation require a larger amount of investment so as to engage on it as a self employed.

*Table 6. Earnings of Workforce*

| S.L. | SECTOR/ ACTIVITIES | AREA | | | |
|---|---|---|---|---|---|
| | | HIGH HILLS | MIDDLE HILLS | LOW HILLS | ALL AREAS |
| 1. | FARM SECTOR | 2837 | 2709 | 3182 | 2907 |
| 2. | TRADING | 11088 | 10481 | 11059 | 10885 |
| 3. | CONSTRUCTION | 7556 | 10396 | 8439 | 8576 |
| 4. | MANUFACTURING | 7467 | 10117 | 10282 | 9087 |
| 5. | TRANSPORT | 23206 | 34700 | 27201 | 27679 |
| 6. | SERVICES | 29573 | 31909 | 25788 | 28647 |
| | TOTAL NON FARM | 10587 | 14571 | 13082 | 12478 |

Average amount of earnings from trading activities (Rs.10.88 thousand) is noted to be relatively higher than the case of earnings from manufacturing (Rs.9.09 thousand) and construction activities (Rs.8.58 thousand) while the farm sector is visualized providing very low amount of earnings at Rs.2.09 thousand in the sample areas.

On an average the workforce participating in different rural non-farm activities is in a position to earn around Rs.12.48 th ousands in a position to earn around Rs.12.48 thousand annually which stands highest at Rs.14.57 thousand in rural areas of middle hills followed by Rs. 13.08 thousand in low hills and lowest at Rs.10.59 thousand in high hill areas (Table 6).

### *Status of Employment*

The rural workforce is seen involving themselves in undertaking different non-farm activities in a capacity of either daily wage paid casual workers or as the self employed. The self-employed workforce is running the household based non-farm enterprises through engaging its own family workforce and sometimes through engaging outside family workforce on wages in performing certain works of the concerned activity.

In all, the total size of workforce reported to have engaged in non-farm sector is registered to be 1670, of which relatively a higher proportion of them are working as self employed (51.20 per cent) as compared to daily wage paid casual workers (48.80 per cent). The manufacturing and construction activities are noted as the dominating components of rural non-farm sector in terms of providing employment opportunities to the rural labourforce in each of the geographical locations.

Since, of the total numbers of workforce engaged in different non-farm activities the proportion of them employed in these two sectors alone is accounted for around 71 per cent; comprising 41 per cent in manufacturing and remaining 30 per cent in construction activities. However, the construction activities are seen only providing wage employment to its entire workforce but a very high proportion of workforce engaged in manufacturing sector is working as selfemployed (86.6 per cent).

Though, the proportion of workforce engaged in manufacturing activities as self-employed is significantly varying among different geographical locations, as being highest at 95 per cent in middle hill areas to lowest at 84 per cent in each low and high hill areas. The proportion of workforce engaged as self-employed is accounted marginally larger in trading and commercial activi ties as compared to manufacturing activities, particularly in middle and low hill areas.

In remaining two sectors, transportation and services, the proportion of work force employed as wage paid employees is relatively higher than the case of selfemployed. Infact, in services, the proportion of workforce employed as wage-paid employed is as higher as 78.39 per cent, though it is registered fairly larger in high hills (87.30 per cent) followed by middle (83.33 per cent) and low hill (68.29 per cent) areas.

# 4

# Growth of Non-farm Sector

The scope for large scale diversification of economic activities is severely limited in the purely hilly and mountainous areas of the state, because of a number of factors such as the limited and environmentally sensitive resource base, their spread of useable resources across different and inaccessible terrain, inaccessibility to markets and modern inputs and technology, deficient infrastructure and insufficient energy and high transport costs leading to non-competitiveness of products.

Despite the fact that the diversification of economic structure through initiating industrialisation and large-scale production system would adversely effect the ecological system of Uttaranchal, since the most part of it dominated by hilly and mountainous areas. However, initiating development for carrying out small scale production at household level through harnessing certain environmental resources based on traditionally developed indigenous mode of technologies by the local people have been proved no way effect the local ecological system.

Since, almost the districts of Uttaranchal possess several locations specific opportunities and comparative advantages for the establishment and expansion of locally available resources based various categories of non-farm economic activities.

In fact, activities such as carpentry, rope making, ringal work, spinning and weaving of woolen yarn and a few related manufacturing enterprises have been in operation in only few selected hilly areas of the state for the past several generations. These activities are functioning at household level through using family labourforce and are basically based on locally available raw materials from the forests.

Accordingly, a major part of industrial activities in rural areas of almost the districts are mainly as a part of the tradition and they do not form any kind of linkages and integration with the local resources and changing demand pattern. In stead the scheduled caste communities who manufacture and repair various categories of goods sand articles for the domestic use and agricultural purposes of the upper caste households own these units.

Increasing accessibility to the facilities of road transport has also provided some extent of opportunities to the local people for establishing commercial activities in the form of retail shops, eating and refreshment units, repairing activities etc. along the roadside during the recent past.

**Establishing Non-Farm Activities**

The total numbers of existing non-farm activities in Uttaranchal accounted for 2.05 lakhs, comprising 1.43 lakhs own account non-farm enterprises and 0.62 lakh nonfarm institutions in 1998. Considering into account the structure and establishment pattern of different non-farm activities across the district levels, it revealed that these both the categories of activities are largely concentrated in three agriculturally and industrially highly developed districts; Nainital, Haridwar and Dehradun. Since a sizeable area of these districts is in the plains, land is very fertile showing fairly high productivity of the major foodgrains, agriculture is more or less diversified, and over 91 per cent of the total registered industrial units are found alone located here. It may, therefore, be pointed out that persisting significant level of agricultural and industrial development in these districts have directly or indirectly influenced to and the opportunity of establishing different non-farm activities to a certain extent. As around 58 per cent of the total non-farm activities are alone located in these industrially and agriculturally developed districts.

However, the concentration of these activities is more largely observed in urban areas (78 per cent) than in rural areas (48 per cent). In addition, the non-farm institutions which are indicated to have been employing a larger volume of labourforce as compared to own account enterprises, are again found highly concentrated in these three districts though largely in urban areas than in rural areas.

In urban areas, the proportion of non-farm institutions in these districts together accounted for over 88 per cent, constituting as larger as 31.23 per cent in Dehradun followed by 28.21 per cent in Nainital and 20.55 per cent in Haridwar. However, in rural areas the differences in the proportion of non-farm institutions located among different districts are not varying to the extent as is revealed in the cases of urban areas, it varied lowest at 6.47 per cent in Uttarkashi to a highest level at 17.86 per cent in Nainital.

As far as the expansion pattern of own account enterprises is concerned, over half of the total units are confined in these agro-industriallydeveloped districts. In fact the concentration of concerned units in urban areas of these districts reaches as larger as 77.74 per cent as against 38.24 per cent in rural areas. In purely hilly and mountainous districts, the expansion of own account units is visualised at highest level in district Almora while a lowest proportion of them are located in Uttarkashi (3.36 per cent).

The analysis revealed that the expansion of various categories of non-farm activities has taken place at greater extent in the districts of Kumaun division as compared to the districts comprising of Garhwal division. Despite the fact that the availability of various natural and forest resources and thus the opportunities of developing different categories of non-farm activities based on using available resources is larger in high mountainous areas than in the middle and low areas. But, in real terms, the situation in the expansion pattern of various non-farm activities is emerging into a different direction.

As the expansion of both own account enterprises and non-farm institutions has largely occurred in low hill areas, in fact in plain part of the district Nainital, Dehradun and Haridwar followed by district like Almora, Pithoragarh and Chamoli while least expansion is visualised in high hilly districts such as Uttarkashi.

Thus, over and above accessibility to road transport facilities, the development of market links, level of agricultural and industrial development and the pace of urbanisation are seems to be mainly determining the development and expansion pattern of various non-farm activities though largely for non-manufacturing components of non-farm sector in the State.

## Concentration

Further considering into account the pattern of changes that has been occurred in the concentration of non-farm activities in the state between the period 1990 and 1998, the analysis revealed that over the years, the concentration of own account enterprises and non-farm institutions together is declining marginally in four districts out of nine districts representing the state, but at large level in agriculturally and industrially developed districts such as Nainital and Dehradun than in the purely hilly districts.

Among the developed districts, the concentration of non-farm activities, in both rural and urban areas of districts Nainital and Dehradun has been declining while it has been increasing in the case of Haridwar. On the other, in purely hilly and mountainous districts, the expansion of both the categories of units together is consistently increasing in urban areas of all the six districts with a marginal decline in the rural areas of districts Chamoli, Pauri and Pithoragarh, which mainly due to decrease in substantial numbers of own accounts enterprises in Pithoragarh and both the categories of activities in district Pauri and Chamoli.

Further dealing into the establishment pattern of non-farm activities between rural and urban areas the analysis revealed that the proportion of units located in rural areas are significantly at higher level than in urban areas 46.86 per cent. This kind of situation is found highly emerging in each of the hilly and mountainous districts but there is a reversal situation in the cases of districts Dehradun, Haridwar and Nainital in this regard. The concentration of non-farm activities in rural areas is revealed as higher as 82.40 per cent in district Tehri Garhwal followed by 81.38 per cent in Almora and at lowest level in Pauri (63.17 per cent).

However, in non-hilly districts, the proportion of concerned activities confined in rural areas are as low as 27.41 per cent in Dehradun to highest at 43.84 per cent in Haridwar. It is also recognised that in rural areas, the concentration of own account enterprises is relatively at larger level as compared to non-farm institutions in both hilly and nonhilly districts of the state, but it is at fairly higher level in former category of districts than the latter one.

It is obviously the fact that non-farm institutions constitute relatively larger category of units than the own account enterprises, in terms of the size of production, employment, investment level etc. and thus the properly functioning and growth of these units require a greater level of certain infrastructural facilities and easy access to and linkages with various components which may be associated to their promotion and development.

In this context the entrepreneurs prefer to locate non-farm activities mostly in urban areas than in rural areas because the urban areas possess greater advantages in terms of market linkages in favour of the supply of raw materials and disposal of final products, availability of infrastructural facilities and certain opportunities for developing their activities.

Across the districts of the state, the concentration of own account enterprises revealed at highest level in rural areas of Tehri Garhwal (83.85 per cent) closely followed by 82.88 per cent and 82.47 per cent in Almora and Uttarkashi respectively. However, over the years, the concentration of own-account enterprises has been narrowing down considerably in the rural areas. In contrast of it, they are expanding in urban areas of almost the districts, excepting the case of high hill areas such as district Uttarkashi.

This gives an impression that increasing pattern of urbanisation and a significant level of improvements in the accessibility situation to information system and the road transport facilities in Uttaranchal which have experienced during the recent past have not only increased the frequency of visits of local people to the nearby markets to purchase their basic requirement at lower prices than they were getting from the local shops but also the pattern of shifting the rural non-farm enterprises into nearly market towns have also seen equally influenced to a greater extent.

Also, the increasing competitions prevailing in marketing of goods and articles manufactured by own accounts enterprises from the increasing flow of similar types of goods and articles from urban segments has been adversely effecting the growth potential of their activities in rural areas.

**Sectoral Distribution**

The classification of different non-farm activities according to various product groups, indicates that the non-farm sector in the state is dominated by the activities such as retail trading, personnel and community services and to a little extent by manufacturing, refreshment and eating establishments. Though, by and large, different product groups of non-farm activities are evenly distributed in almost the districts of the state.

In the existing numbers of various non-farms activities, the activities engaged in retail trade and commerce constitute at highest proportion of 45.33 per cent as against 28 per cent personnel and community services followed by around 14 per cent manufacturing activities and a lowest proportion of 0.03 per cent activities associated to mining and quarrying sector.

The domination of trading and commercial activities has been visualised at much larger level in all the districts, though these categories of activities are forming a major share in the total non-farm activities of the three most developed districts, Dehradun (52 per cent), Haridwar (49 per cent) and Nainital (48 per cent).

Though, in purely hilly districts the share of trading and commercial activities in the total non-farm activities is as higher as 48.58 per cent in Pauri to lowest at 32.56 per cent in Uttarkashi. On the other hand, the expansion of activities, which are involved in providing personnel and community services, has taken place relatively at greater extent in the districts of purely hilly areas as compared to districts with plain areas.

Similar, situation is found emerging in the cases of the development of manufacturing activities among these two groups of districts. As the share of manufacturing activities among the total non-farm activities is found at lowest level in Dehradun (10 per cent) and it constitute 12 per cent and 14 per cent in Nainital and Haridwar respectively.

But in purely hilly districts the corresponding figure ranges lowest from 10 per cent for Pauri to highest at 20 per cent for district Almora. Considering into account the expansion pattern and contribution of three major categories of non-farm activities, i.e. manufacturing, trading and commerce and services, separately and, examining the relationship between the share of trading and commercial activities on one hand and together of services and manufacturing activities on the other in the total numbers of existing non-farm activities across the districts of the state.

It appears that the development of agriculture and industrial sector are positively influencing the expansion pattern of trading and commercial activities but their little linkages are establishing in promoting the expansion of manufacturing and service related activities. Since, in agriculturally and industrially developed districts the trading and commercial activities are forming significantly larger share than together of the manufacturing and service related activities among the various existing non-farm activities. However, in agriculturally and industrially backward hilly districts the share of latter categories of activities together is seen comparatively at larger level than the cases of former categories of activities in the total non-farm activities.

### *District Level Concentration*

Despite of the fact that the trading and commercial activities constituted at highest proportion among the various non-farm activities and the domination of these activities is more or less pronounced in three developed districts of the State. Over 50 per cent of the non-farm activities are alone located in these developed districts. The proportion of units located in hilly districts varied lowest from 3.59 per cent in Uttarkashi to highest at 11.12 per cent in Almora.

It is further pointed out that the different product groups of non-farm activities are, more or less, evenly distributed among the districts of purely and mountainous areas. Only the exception is the case of mining activities those are not existing in Chamoli and Pauri Garhwal and are mainly concentrated in district Almora. The manufacturing and service related activities, those were found dominating among the existing various product groups of activities in the purely hilly districts in the analysis undertaken earlier, are found concentrated relatively at higher level in Almora and Pithoragarh and at lowest proportion in Uttarkashi.

However the construction-related activities are more particularly dominated in Tehri Garhwal due to the obvious reason that a large Dam is under construction in this district. The concentration of trading and commercial activities ranges lowest from 2.58 per cent in Uttarkashi to highest at 9.37 per cent in Almora. Expansion of eating and refreshment activities in Almora has undertaken significantly to a higher level than in Dehradun and Haridwar and almost at similar extent to that of district Nainital.

**Trends in Growth**

In real terms, the total numbers of non-farm activities are largely declining in the state over the years. During the periods, 1980 and 1998, the numbers of all nonfarm activities has reduced from 2.11 lack to 2.05, showing an absolute decline of 3.03 per cent points. The decrease in overall numbers of non-farm activities has been reported due to the declining trend in the growth of non-farm enterprises to the tune of 9.34 per cent while the own account enterprises have shown a positive growth rate of 0.15 per cent point during the same period of reference.

The own account enterprises and non-farm institution together has shown a declining trends in six out of nine districts with a highest level of decrease in Pauri (24.23 per cent) followed by Chamoli (12.88 per cent) and Dehradun (11.36 per cent). Appreciable growth of these activities is noticed in the district of Haridwar (23.12 per cent) with a marginal increase in Uttarkashi and Pithoragarh.

As far as the growth of own account enterprises is concerned, a very high level of growth is again revealed in Haridwar while in remaining two developed districts these activities have been gradually moving out, though relatively at unprecedented level in Dehradun (21.78 per cent) as compared to Nainital (0.66 per cent). In hilly districts, a high rate of negative growth is estimated for Pauri (18 per cent) and Chamoli (16.78 per cent), otherwise in remaining districts these traditional kind of household enterprises have been increasing at least at some extent.

Though a highest growth of this categories of units is found in Pithoragarh (10.04 per cent) followed by Uttarkashi (8.49 per cent) and it is around 2 per cent in each Almora and Tehri. This seems that in high hill areas of districts Uttarkashi and Pithoragarh where woolen activities have been traditional household activities of local people for the past several generations are still finding an appreciable opportunities in their development.

As the consequences of these phenomena increase of traditional household enterprises in these two districts the overall growth rate of own-account enterprises has shown a positive growth trends in the State during the reference periods. Further, it is observed that in spite of the positive growth rate that has witnessed of own account enterprises, the non-farm institutions have been largely washing away from most of the districts excepting the case of Dehradun and Haridwar. The highest level of negative growth of these activities is revealed in district Nainital (18.89 per cent) followed by Tehri Garhwal (15.13 per cent).

**Growth Performance: Rural and Urban Areas**

It is striking to note that non-farm activities has been loosing its relative importance in rural areas while a very little growth of 2.52 per cent has been observed in favour of urban area of the state during last one decade. Surprisingly, the expansion of various non-farm activities in urban areas of all the districts, those are in hilly areas has been consistently increasing while they are washing away from the urban areas of two agro-industrially developed districts Nainital and Dehradun.

Again, the growth of non-farm sector has been declining in most of the districts, excepting Haridwar and Uttarkashi. This indicates the fact that their does not establish any strong relationship between the level of agro-industrial development and the expansion pattern of various non-farm activities at least in Uttaranchal. Exception is the case of district Haridwar, non-farm activities of both, own account enterprises and non-farm institutions are quite significantly increasing in its rural as well as urban areas.

In rural areas, the decline in the numbers of non-farm enterprises is revealed at highest level in Pauri 34.29 per cent followed by Chamoli 17.21 per cent and at lowest level of 0.27 per cent in Uttarkashi with a positive growth rate of 39.42 per cent in rural Haridwar. In urban area, the non-farm activities have been growing at the rate of 2.52 per cent as against the declining trend of over 7 per cent in rural areas.

The surprising perceptions regarding the emerging pattern of growth of different categories of non-farm activities among rural and urban areas is that the small scale own account enterprises have been increasing in urban areas instead of rural areas which base of establishment has generally been well recognised in rural areas because they form a part of a traditional household activities.

On the other, the nonfarm institutions those constitute relatively larger as compare to own-account enterprises in term of both size of production and employment are moving out from rural as well as urban areas, though they should have remained functioning, successfully in urban areas because they posses favourable forward and backward development linkages and locational advantages in urban areas.

The analysis on the structure of growth of own account enterprises across the district level reveals that these units are heavily decreasing in rural areas as compared to urban areas of different districts except in

Haridwar they are expanding in both urban and rural areas. In rural areas a highest level of declining trend of these activities is revealed in Pauri (32.27 per cent) followed by Dehradun (23.55 per cent) and lowest in Almora (0.42 per cent) while a positive growth rate of 10 per cent is the exception in the case of concerned activities in Uttarkashi.

The most striking feature to be noted here is that these categories of units have been significantly increasing in urban areas in stead of rural areas of almost the districts excepting Dehradun while the origin of establishment of these categories of activities has generally been well recognised in rural areas.

On the other, the non-farm institutions are moving out from rural as well as urban areas while they should be remain, in functioning, in fact the hypothesis was that these categories of unit should have been grown positively in urban areas because they posses the opportunity to maintain linkages with different sectors of economies in the perspective of their favourable development in urban areas as compared to rural areas.

Even in the urban areas of industrially and agriculturally developed districts the numbers of non-farm institutions have been decreasing at least for last one decade. However, the concern activities have been well growing in most of the districts falling in purely hilly areas. This attributes the fact that the development and expansion of non-farm sector is, more or less, influenced by the accessibility situation to road and basic infrastructural facilities while a little impact and linkages of agricultural and industrial development in this regard are found establishing at least in the case of Uttaranchal.

The expansion of roads in rural areas has only been influencing the local people forwards the establishment of various non-farm activities, mainly retail trading shops, repairing and servicing activities and tea and refreshment shops along the roadside and in the villages nearly roads.

### Different Categories of Non-farm Activities

There exits extremely a larger level of variations in the opportunities for expansion and establishing different categories of non-farm activities among different locations of the state. Even, the contribution that non-farm sector performs in providing employment to the labourforce and in originating income in the households of different socio-economic groups varied from one to another locations even within a district of purely hilly areas of the state.

It is, therefore, attempts have been made to examine the mode of establishing and pattern of different product groups of non-farm activities in different geographical locations. The concerned analysis is based on primary data collected among a sample of 32 villages comprises of three selected catchment areas of both the districts. The information regarding the expansion pattern of various non-farm activities in the sample villages was collected for the period of 1990 and 2000, through making door to door visits while undertaking the listing of existing households on census basis in the sample areas of the study.

In view of examining the structure of existing different non-farm activities in sample areas we have distributed them into four major economic sectors such as manufacturing, trade and commerce, personnel services and transportation. Of the 723 different categories of total non-farm activities currently existing in different locations of the sample areas a fairly large proportion of them (68 per cent) comprises manufacturing activities and a second majority of them (24 per cent) are engaged in the retail trades and commercial activities followed by 4 per cent each in services sector and transport sector.

The non-farm activities are visualised evenly distributed in different geographical locations of the sample area rather than their concentration is specific locations, though significant level of differences are noted existing in the establishment pattern of manufacturing activities among different locations. Since the proportion of nonfarm activities established in different areas varied lowest from 29 per cent in middle hill areas to highest at 39 per cent in high hill areas and 32 per cent in low hill areas.

The domination of manufacturing activities among the various existing non-farm activities is well realised in all the geographical locations though they are concentrated at a larger level in high altitude areas (70.77 per cent) as compared to low (69.30 per cent) and middle altitude areas (62.09 per cent). On the hand, the trading and commercial activities are noticed confined to a relatively larger extent in middle hill areas (29 per cent) followed by 23 per cent in low hill areas and 21 per cent in high hill areas.

However, the concentration of service related activities is almost at similar level in high and middle hill areas, though their concentration is relatively at higher level in low hills. The concentration of transport related activities seems at fairly larger level in middle hill areas (46 per cent) followed by high hill areas (36 per cent) and lowest at 18 per cent in low hill areas. The manufacturing activities which are forming a largest part of rural non-farm sector; are both traditional and non-traditional categories of units and are functioning at household level through employing mainly family labourforce and locally developed indigenous mode of production technology for the manufacture of goods and articles.

Among them the traditional types of manufacturing activities are generally largely developed in each of the locations, though largely in high and middle hill areas as compared to low hill areas. The black smithy, basket and mat making, rope making, woolen-based activities are the important traditional activities of a majority of the households, particularly of scheduled castes households.

In rural areas the scheduled castes households have been engaged in the production of various goods and articles as required by the households of upper castes for performing agricultural activities, collection of forest products and certain other purposes for the past several generations. This kind of production linkages and the nature of performing work by scheduled castes for upper caste is locally known as Zajmani system of work relationship.

However, the Zajmani system of work relationship has been gradually reducing in most part of the hill areas, particularly in low hill areas. Since, the proportion of traditional manufacturing activities located in low hill areas are only 36 per cent as against 75 per cent in high hill areas and 59 per cent in middle hill areas. In stead the expansion of non-traditional, modern manufacturing activities have been greatly visualised in low hill areas as compared to remaining geographical locations.

The carpentry, black smithy, basketry, rope making and tailoring are the dominant manufacturing activities, in terms of its numbers and from the point of providing employment to the family members of the rural households. These all units together constitute over 75 per cent of the total manufacturing activities existing in the sample areas. Also, most of these units, excepting tailoring, are basically using locally available row materials in their production process.

However, the carpentry, basketry, rope making, woolen-based activities, comb making and pottery have been the prominent rural household manufacturing activities in the sample areas for last several centuries though these units have reduced in numbers over the years. Over and above it appears that the different categories of manufacturing activities are well spread over in all the geographical locations.

The structure, however, differs somewhat with altitude. While some product groups of units, mainly identified dominant activities are evenly functioning in all areas, these are certain product groups of units such as comb making, pottery, Iron work etc. which are confined to certain locations. Similarly, the trading and commercial activities, eating and refreshment units, construction and transportation related activities are also evenly established in almost the areas of the state but are largely concentrated in low hill areas.

Among the various non-farm activities a major increase in the structure of establishment has further been experienced in favour of trading and commercial activities in the state, particularly in middle and low hill areas. Since the per cent share of trading and commercial activities in the total numbers of non-farm activities in middle hills areas has increased from 7.08 per cent in 1990 to 29.38 per cent in 2000 and in low hill areas it increased from 9 per cent to 23 per cent during the same period.

The proportion of service related activities has gone down from 4.65 per cent to 3.60 per cent while the share of transport activities has increased from 1.28 per cent to 4.70 per cent while it has narrowed from 85.60 per cent to 67.77 per cent for manufacturing activities during the last decade. A major downfall in the concentration of manufacturing activities is seen in the middle and low hill areas and in particular of manufacturing activities those were in the product line of rope making, black smithy, basketry and tailoring.

However, the carpentry is observed gaining its ground quite satisfactory in the middle and low hill areas while a marginal decline is reported in the high altitude areas. But in absolute terms, the share of non-traditional manufacturing activities such as tailoring, iron work, repairing and services related activities has considerably been increased in the sample areas as against a major decline in the concentration of almost the traditional manufacturing activities in the low altitude areas of the state.

The absolute numbers of non-farm activities in all the three segments of Uttaranchal have been consistently declining over the years at the rate of 12.76 per cent, comprising at highest level in high hill areas (20.43 per cent) followed by middle (8.99 per cent) and low hill areas (5.57 per cent). However, the non-traditional activities such as trading, eating and refreshment, photography and transportation are still on the way of expansion in almost the part of the state.

Among them the trading and transport related activities have shown a remarkable growth in all the geographical locations, particularly in middle hill areas. The expansion of road transport facilities and increasing accessibility of rural areas to the nearby towns is perhaps the most important factor for providing an increasing opportunities and advantages to the local people to go for the expansion of these two groups of nonfarm activities.

The trading activities are involved in the procurement of certain consumption goods and articles from nearby towns and its supply to the rural people through establishing small retail shops in rural areas. It is expected that the concerned activities will continue to rise in different rural areas but their scope and level of further expansion would mainly be determined by the level of general increase in the income level of rural people and its distribution pattern among them. A greater set back in the expansion pattern is revealed in the case of different manufacturing activities in general and those of the traditional household activities in particular in all the geographical locations of the state during the last decade.

The actual number of manufacturing activities has declined from 737 in 1990 to 490 in 2000, showing an overall negative growth of 33.51 percent. It is noted that non-traditional modern industrial activities which production system is not based on the locally available raw materials are expanding to a certain extent in different locations, though at larger level in low hill areas.

But, the major industrial activities, those were mainly traditional and were basically using the locally available row materials are largely declining in almost the geographical locations but at a surprising rate in low and middle altitude areas. The carpentry, black smithy, basketary, woolen and rope making activities, those together accounting for over three fourth strength among the total existing non-farm activities have been greatly getting close down in high and middle hill areas.

Inadequacy in the supply of basic raw materials from the nearby forests and the lacking interest of new generations to engage in these low earning traditional manufacturing activities are postulated to be the most important factors behind increasingly decreasing trends of the major industrial activities in the rural areas of different geographical locations.

Besides, the commodities, which are manufactured through indigenous mode of production technologies and using family unskilled labourforce by the households of basketry, carpentry and woolen activities are facing larger competitions with the similar goods and articles of better quality arriving in the nearby markets from many other villages.

### Expansion of Non-farm Activities

The trends in the growth of establishment, type of entrepreneurship and several issues related to the elements which have influenced the expansion pattern of different categories of non-farm enterprises during the past in the sample areas. The analysis revealed that around one-third of the non-farm activities, largely those confined in manufacturing and service sectors, were established before 1980 and are mainly traditional household level activities.

Another second majority of (23 per cent) them were established during 1980-85. But the trend, of establishing rural non-farm activities declined to 11.34 per cent during next five years period, though it picked up further during the period 1990 to 1995 and again after 1995. It has further been pointed out that a majority of manufacturing (45 per cent) and service related professional services (50 per cent) activities were established before 1980 and are still expanding but the trend of expanding of manufacturing activities has been consistently declined untill 1995 with a marginal increase after 1995.

While the establishment of service related professional activities has picked up considerably after 1995. However, the existing trading and transport related activities are mainly established after 1980 and the trends of expansion of both the categories of activities has been consistently increasing over the years. In fact, of the total existing activities, a majority of both transport (62 per cent) and trading (34 per cent) activities were recently established in the sample areas.

It indicates the fact that the rural non-farm activities which are involved in selling urban originated commodities in rural areas, transactions of goods and services from urban to rural areas and the certain activities confined in rural professional lines are finding favourable opportunities for their expansion while the household based traditional manufacturing activities are seen to have little chances of expansion in rural areas.

*Entrepreneurship*

The non-farm activities in rural areas function at household level through engaging its family members in running of the concerned activities. In general sense, all the members of non-farm households which are attached with their family enterprises in any form, may be regarded as the entrepreneurs of the concerned activity. Because, all of them participate at one stage or other in the various activities of the non-farm activity.

However the head of household holds a key position that handles, controls and manage all kinds of work involved in the operation of concerned household based non-farm activities. The head of non- farm household has been regarded as an entrepreneur of the concerned non-farm activity. It has generally been believed that beside various fundamental factors and locational aspects, the basic socio-economic and personnel characteristics of entrepreneurs of different enterprises are equally important determining factors to the growth pattern and expansion of non-farm enterprises.

In this background the age and educational characteristics and the sex composition of the entrepreneurs are focussed among the various other most crucial personnel characteristics which directly influence the functioning and operational aspects of any enterprise. Male entrepreneurs, except in the cases of certain tradition form of manufacturing activities such as spinning and wearing of woolen yarn, dominate the rural non-farm sector. Women entrepreneurs heading to around 34 per cent of the woolen activities only.

### *Age*

The households established a substantial numbers of non-farm activities during the past several generations ago. In agreement to this findings the analysis to the age composition of the entrepreneurs revealed that a large majority of around 44 per cent of them constituted quite old of above 45 years, in fact 10 per cent entrepreneurs accounted for over 60 years of age and only 27 percent entrepreneurs followed to young age groups of below 35 years.

The young generation entering into the expansion of non-farm activities is noted relatively at higher level in low hill areas than in high and middle hills. This is indicated by the fact that the proportion of present entrepreneurs with young age group of below 35 years constituted 34 percent in low hills as against 28 percent in high hills and lowest at 18 per cent in middle hill areas.

The young age groups of entrepreneurs are notably engaged at larger level in activities confined as non-traditional trading and commercial activities and relatively higher rewarding activities such as transportation. The average age of non-farm entrepreneurs ranged between 42 years to 45 years following highest for those of middle hills and lowest for low hills.

### *Educational Level*

The rural non-farm activities involve every categories of skilled, un-skilled, literate and illiterate workforce in its different stages of operations. Like-wise, these activities can be headed equally by different age groups of individuals with differential level of educational standards and even by illiterates and highly educated personnel of the rural households.

Around 12 percent of the entrepreneurs of sample non-farm enterprises, comprising 14 percent in high hills followed by 10 percent in middle hills and 9 per cent in low hill areas are illiterate and another 17 per cent are possessing only functional literacy while around 4 per cent entrepreneurs have attended graduation level of education and a major chunk of 37 per cent of them have the secondary level of educational attainment.

It further revealed that the entrepreneurs heading transportation, trading and commercial and service related activities are relatively better educated than those are heading manufacturing activities. In fact, any illiterate personnel is found heading the transport related activities while a little over 16 per cent of the entrepreneurs are operating various manufacturing activities.

Of the 26 personnel with above graduation level of education around 63 per cent of them are alone heading the trading and commercial activities and over half of the entrepreneurs of trading and commerce, services and transport activities are possessing above secondary level of education while over 66 percent of the entrepreneurs of manufacturing activities constitute only below primary level of functional literacy or no educational attainment.

Thus, it indicates that the individuals with their young working age groups and possessing relatively better level of educational attainments are mainly initiating towards the establishment of such non-farm activities only, which provide higher incomes while the illiterates and individuals with functional literacy are noted mainly dominating in the expansion of low paid manufacturing activities.

## Origin of the Enterprises

A sizeable proportions of the non-farm activities are quite old, and were established before 1980. It further revealed that around 22 per cent of them were established during last two generations ago of the present owners of these activities and almost similar proportions of units are originated by the father's of the present entrepreneurs. However, a majority of around 56 per cent non-farm activities are the origin of the first and present generation.

Among the first generation of non-farm activities the trading and commercial activities are in majority (92.49 percent) followed by transportation (88.24 per cent) and the respective proportions of units among manufacturing and service related activities accounted for 44 percent and 35 percent respectively. The second generation non-farm activities are, however, confined largely among in the manufacturing sector (29 percent) followed by service sector 12 percent, though over half of the service related and 30 percent manufacturing activities were established three generations ago by the grand-fathers of the present entrepreneurs.

### *Preferential non-farm Activity*

The locational decision of the entrepreneurs of opting the preferential non-farm activity for establishment is governed by several factors like the availability pattern of required raw material, man power with required skill for performing concerned activity, the available marketing facilities for selling the products, finance, linkages of location with basic communication and information sources, and urban areas and the availability of required infrastructural facilities for properly functioning of the respective venture.

But the lacking opportunities of employment in rural areas, the availability of local raw material and the skills among the family members for performing various work related to concern activity are noted to be the major factors, which initiated the head of the family toopt for establishing non-farm activities at the present location.

The contribution of Government in promoting non-farm activities is seen in terms of providing financial and technical assistance to 4.98 per cent households for favour of the establishment of non-farm activities. The proportions of entrepreneur who opted for starting the non-farm activities due to the availability of lower level of earnings in locally available wage-paid employment were noted to be 5.12 percent.

Lacking employment opportunities in local areas is seen forcing the educated and young rural workforce to establish mainly modern non-farm activities such as trading and commercial and transportation units instead of manufacturing and servicing and repairing activities. However, the availability of required raw material in local areas have attracted to a highest proportion of entrepreneurs to opt for the establishment of various manufacturing activities and the availability of skills among the family members of the current entrepreneurs for establishing over a half of the service related activities.

**Motivation of Entrepreneurs**

In regard to examining the motivation of the entrepreneurs over deciding for the adoption of respective activity as a households' occupation it is observed that although a fairly larger proportion of nearly one-third of the non-farm activities were traditional by nature and were established over three generations ago, even then, the establishment of around

42 per cent of them, consisting a highest proportions among the transport activities (56 percent) followed by trading and commercial activities (54 percent), manufacturing activities (38 percent) and lowest among service related activities (10 percent) took place through the motivation of the family members of the non-farm households.

And around 23 percent of the entrepreneurs were motivated by their friends and relatives and remaining only 3.04 percent of the entrepreneurs had decided to establish concerned non-farm activities after motivating them by the Government. Since, a quite large numbers of the non-farm activities in sample rural areas, either forming the traditional household activities or the non-traditional activities were reported to be quite old.

In fact, the proportions of entrepreneurs who have been engaged in manufacturing activities and service related activities before 1985 are as higher as 60 per cent and 50 per cent respectively. However, a very large proportion of entrepreneurs among those are involved in transportation (56 per cent) and trade and commercial activities (34 percent) had joined their concerned non-farm activities very recently after 1995.

The traditional households based low paid non-farm activities such as manufacturing and professional services are the origin of past several generations while the most modern form of relatively better earning non-farm activities such as trading and commercial and transportation are of the recent origin in rural areas of the Uttaranchal.

### Joining Non-Farm Activity

A very large proportion of the present entrepreneurs had opted to join different non-farm activities due to non-availability of employment opportunities in rural areas.

Further, enquiring about the activity status of the entrepreneurs before joining or starting of the present non-farm activities. Highest proportion of them (42 per cent) moved from other occupations to join the present non-farm activity. While a second majority of the entrepreneurs were lacking employment opportunities.

Increasing incidence of unemployment among rural population is appeared largely forcing them to start even low earning profile of non-farm activities, while the already employed rural workforce is seen mainly initiating for the expansion of relatively better paid modern non-farm activities in the rural areas.

Since, a majority of the present entrepreneurs who joined or started high earning activities such as transportation and trading and commercial activities were reported to have moved from other occupations. While a very high proportions of them who joined manufacturing and services were unemployed.

### *Occupational Mobility*

The rural workforce have been leaving different occupations so as to move into the employment available in different rural non-farm activities. They were neither been employed in any economic sector before joining the present activity nor they did change any occupation. Significantly highest proportions of them (19.23 per cent) were earlier employed as daily wage labourers before starting the present non-farm activity.

And a second majority of around 12 per cent of the respondents had moved from one non-farm activity to the other, while remaining 9.27 per cent of them were moved from farm to non-farm sector in the sample areas. Among the presently employed heads of households in manufacturing sector, a highest proportion of them were moved from undertaking wage-paid-labourers work (20 per cent) followed by from farm sector (9 per cent) and only one per cent from the shop and commercial activities.

*Table 1. Occupational Mobility of the Entrepreneurs*

| | | Activity | | | | |
|---|---|---|---|---|---|---|
| Sl. No. | Past Occupation | Trade and Commerce | Manufat-uring | Transport | Service | Total |
| 1. | None | 87 (50.29) | 299 (61.02) | 16 (47.06) | 17 (65.38) | 419 (59.95) |
| 2. | Agriculture | 18 (10.40) | 45 (9.18) | 4 (11.76) | - | 67 (9.27) |
| 3. | Shop/Trad-ing | 1 (0.58) | 5 (1.02) | - | - | 6 (0.83) |
| 4. | Manufac-turing | 9 (5.20) | 22 (4.49) | 5 (14.71) | 2 (7.69) | 38 (5.26) |
| 5. | Service (Govt.) | 22 (12.72) | 23 (4.69) | 4 (11.76) | 5 (19.23) | 54 (7.47) |
| 6. | Labour | 36 (20.81) | 96 (19.59) | 5 (14.71) | 2 (7.69) | 139 (19.23) |
| | TOTAL | 173 (100.00) | 490 (100.00) | 34 (100.00) | 26 (100.00) | 723 (100.00) |

However, a highest level of movements of rural workforce is seen among labourers to trading and commercial activities (21 per cent) followed by labourers to manufacturing (20 per cent), and Government service to transport sector (12 per cent) and a lowest level of below 1 per cent of workforce had moved from one category of trading to another one activity and also no workforce had moved from trading and commercial activities to the transport and service related activities and from farm sector activities to the services.

*Changing Occupations*

Availability of lower level of earnings and the irregularity of work are visualized as the most determining factors behind the moving of rural workforce from one occupation to another. Inadequacy in the availability of required raw materials and the problems occurring in the marketing of the produced have been reported to be the major factors that the rural households have been moving from undertaking work in manufacturing activities to the another rural non-farm activities.

However, only 3.29 percent of the heads of rural households had joined the non-farm activities after retirement from the Government employment. It is, further, pointed out that due to non-availability of raw material in required quality to run their manufacturing activities a highest proportions of sample heads of rural households had changed the product line of the manufacturing activities (75 per cent) followed by (22.67 per cent) had joined the trading and commercial activities and a lowest proportions of (3 per cent) them had joined to the service related activities.

The problems related to irregularity in the availability of work and inadequate amount of earnings in wage-paid occupations available in rural areas has forced a highest proportions of individuals to establish manufacturing and trading activities, while the problem of marketing for the commodities produced in manufacturing sectors is compelling its entrepreneurs to change product groups of the concerned activity.

*Capital Investment*

The level of investment undertaken by different non-farm activities at the initial period of the establishment and the present value of capital available in the concerned activity . The value of initial investment is inflated at current prices. The value of productive capital includes the value of land and buildings, machinery and equipments and working capital being used in carrying out present business.

It has to be mentioned before looking at the pattern of investment in different non-farm activities that the household based tiny manufacturing activities do not require any additional investment on land and building because these activities are generally function at the same houses in which the family members live. Though, these units are investing on the procurement of raw materials and towards meeting the cost of paid workforce.

Accordingly, each of the sample households those are engaged transport sector are the owners of taxi, auto-rickshaw and other means of transportation. Therefore, they have made a sizeable amount of investment only on acquiring the means of transport. The rural households who are engaged in trading and commercial activities are only seen making additional investments on land and building for undertaking concerned activity.

In all, the establishment of rural non-farm activities do not require any large scale of capital investment, excepting the case of transport activities, for which the rural households have to spend a large amount on the purchase of mechanized means of transport. Initially the rural households make only a little amount of investment in the establishment of rural non-farm activities through acquiring necessary machinery, equipment and other basic capitals as required for starting the concerned activity.

But they continued to make investment on their non-farm activity through adding additional machinery and equipments on different non-farm activities after its establishment. However, the level of capital investment on different nonfarm activities during its post-establishment period is largely determined by the pattern of income generation from the respective activities and its extent and level of contribution in the total income of rural non-farm households.

Though, the pattern of investment during pre and post establishment periods has increased at fairly larger level for trading and commercial activities (128 per cent) followed by manufacturing (97 per cent), services (76 per cent) and lowest for transportation (18 per cent).

## Turn Over Nonfarm Activities and Sale

Average annual amount of turnover of all nonfarm activities together is estimated to be around Rs.30 thousand with a significant degree of differences in different geographical locations, as varied lowest at Rs.28.4 thousand in high hill areas to highest at Rs.31.6 thousand in middle hill areas.

The households engaged in transportation are reported to be generating significantly a much higher amount of output as compared to remaining non-farm activities, is the result of relatively much larger amount of investment undertaken by them as compared to others. The turnover of transport activities constituted as higher as Rs.109.3 thousand as against Rs.58.5 thousand for trading followed by Rs.14.7 thousand for manufacturing and Rs.10.9 thousand for services.

Almost a similar level of variations are found reflecting in the pattern of sale/turnover being generated from various non-farm activities among different geographical locations. It is further recognized that more or less, the different non-farm activities have been successfully functioning in the sample areas. This is in the sense that the turnover of non-farm enterprises together has been increasing at the rate of 8 per cent.

In fact it is fairly higher for service related activities (9 per cent) followed by manufacturing (8 per cent), transportation (4 per cent) and lowest for trading activities (3 per cent). However, fairly a large differences in the growth of annual turnover of similar type of activities is seen prevailing among different geographical locations and even among different categories of non-farm activities those are located within a same locational settlement.

Since the turnover of non-farm activities located in middle hill areas has been increasing at much higher rate of 10 per cent as against of units located in high hills (6 per cent) and low hill areas (4 per cent). Also, the turnover of services and trading activities in middle hill areas continued to be much higher than the case of high and low hill areas. In fact, the growth in the gross turn over of each of the non-farm activities in middle hill areas is significantly much higher as compared in remaining geographical locations.

Even the turnover of trade and commercial activities and transportation is noted to be declining in low hill areas. This indicates the fact that the possibilities of expansion of different non-farm activities with sustainable sales and providing gainful employment to the rural households seems to be fairly more favourable in middle hill areas and to a certain extent in high hill areas while the low hill areas have the advantages of developing only manufacturing and service related activit ies.

*Net Earnings*

The net earnings are estimated at prices received by non-farm households for their products and prices paid by them for meeting out the cost of production and sale. Thus, the level of productivity and profitability depend not only on the amount of physical output produced or the total turnover of the non-farm activities but also on prices received and paid by the proprietors. The rural non-farm activities in sample areas are seen generating a very low amounts of earnings through mainly employing its family workforce.

However, undertaking non-farm activities in rural areas of Uttaranchal is noted to be a very profitable occupation. Since the margin of profit of all non-farm activities together is estimated to be around 42 per cent, consisting fairly higher for services (83 per cent) followed by manufacturing (65 per cent), transportation (51 per cent) and lowest for trading and commercial activities (21 per cent).

It may also be pointed out that the input cost of traditional manufacturing activities and certain occupations in services is very minimal because these activities mainly use locally available inputs with minimal or no cost involved in its utilization, is providing significantly higher returns than the non-traditional trading and commercial activities and transport related activities.

However, the amount of earnings as being derived from non-traditional activities, i.e. transportation and trading and commercial activities, constituted to be fairly higher than the case of traditional services and manufacturing activities. The rural non-farm households those are engaged in trading and service related activities are noted earning significantly higher amount of incomes in high hill areas as compared to their counterpart in middle and low hill areas.

The manufacturing activities are seen providing fairly higher earning to its households in low hill areas as compared to remaining two locations while the amount of income available from transportation seems to be relatively much higher than the case of other non-farm activities in each of the geographical locations.

Similarly, the income of non-farm households those are engaged in transportation is appeared increasing at much faster rate (78.59 per cent) as compared to services (48 per cent), manufacturing (27 per cent) and trading and commercial activities (22.33 per cent). Thus, over and above, it seems that the expansion of transport related activities is taking place at greater extent in almost of the geographical locations.

Also the household engaged in different modes of transportation are possibly earning fairly higher amount of income than those are engaged in other rural non-farm activities. But, over a period of time the value of gross turn over as well as the amount of income of non-farm households those are engaged in transportation have been narrowing down, in fact, it is declining to a certain extent in low hill areas, in stead of its significant increase in the household of comprising in middle and high hill areas.

This is happening partly due to increased expansion of various means of transportation and partly as a result of the increase of a significant number of rural households into transport related activities in low hill areas than in remaining locations during the recent past.

**Rural Development Programmes**

In the past, fairly a large numbers of employment oriented programmes and schemes have been launched in the state. Initially Integrated Rural Development Programme was the only scheme introduced for providing self employment opportunities to the rural people during the fourth plan period and the employment oriented schemes such as TRYSEM, IREP, ISB, RCGP, etc. were the main components included with the IRDP. Latter, a number of allied programmes have been added to create the self-employment and casual employment opportu nities for the rural poor.

Prominent among them were DWCRA, Supply of Improved Toolkits to Rural Artisans, Jawahar Rojgar Yojana, JGSY, Employment Assurance Scheme etc. The multiplicity of programmes has resulted in a lack of proper social intermediation, absence of desired linkages among programmes inter se and the implementation being more concerned with achieving individual programme targets rather than focussing on the substantive issue of sustainable employment creation and income generation.

It is, therefore, the Government has decided to restructure the employment oriented progrmames and a new programme known as Swarn Jayanti Gram Swarojgar Yojana (SGSY) was launched in April 1999. The concerned progrmme, covering the all aspects of self-employment such as organizing rural poor to form self help groups and providing the facilities of training, credit, infrastructure, technology know-how, and marketing is the centrally sponsored scheme.

The SGSY programme is being funded by both the Central and State Government in the ratio of 75 and 25 respectively. The objective of initiating SGSY scheme has been to facilitate the rural poor households through providing self employment opportunities and various required assistants, in terms of know-how technology and financial assistance, so as to bring them above the poverty line within three years of the implementation of concern programme.

The identified beneficiaries to be covered under the SYSY are facilitated by providing income generating assets through a mix of bank credit and Government subsidy cum loan facilities. It is emphasized that before the implementation of the SGSY programme a detailed survey would be undertaken to identify the potential economic activities which possessing various development linkages in different rural areas. Thereafter it has been proposed to prepare a comprehensive project report in specific to each of the identified economic activity.

Besides, the review of existing infrastructural facilities and its additional requirement in project areas would be assessed for developing cluster of identified economic activities in rural areas of each of the districts. Involvement of banks and financial institutions for financing groups of beneficiaries and project areas has also been highly appreciated. The SGSY also focuses on providing importance on group approaches with maximizing the participation of rural women on priority basis.

The SGSY programme provides 30 per cent amount of the project cost as subsidy with a maximum limit of Rs.7500. However, the limit of subsidy amount exceeds to 50 per cent of the project cost with a maximum amount of Rs.10,000 for the households belonging scheduled castes and scheduled tribes. Since the Swarn Jayanti Swarozgar Yojana lays emphasis on group activities the proportion of 50 per cent subsidy on the total cost of the project has been made for each of groups of swarozgaries and the maximum ceiling of subsidy is limited to Rs.1.25 lack for each group.

However, no limit in providing financial subsidy has been fixed in the cases of large irrigation projects though the whole amount of subsidy as provided at the time of the implementation of the project will be back ended in such cases. It has also been emphasised that the SGSY programme will be implemented by the District Rural Development Agency (DRDA) through the Panchayati Raj Institutions. It seems that the State Government has been providing a significant amount of budget for implementing various rural employment oriented programmes over the years. Alone for the SGSY scheme, the actual amount of expenditure was initially Rs.103.49 crores during 1997-98, it increased to Rs.138.12 crores during 1999-2000, though it has relatively much higher at Rs.311.19 crores for the year 1998-99.

But the striking feature is that both the budgetary provisions as well as actual amount of expenditures on the implementation of SGSY has been showing a declining trend over the years. In addition, a significant level of inequalities is found persisting in the allocation of funds for implementing SGSY schemes among the districts of the state. It revealed that a major share of SGSY funds has mainly gone in favour of the districts Tehri Garhwal, Haridwar and Nainital beginning from the initiation of concerned programme in the State.

*Table 2. Physcial Progress of S.G.S.Y*

| SL. NO. | DISTRICT | No. of SHGs | Coverage Members | Total No. of Swaroj-garies |
|---|---|---|---|---|
| 1. | Tehri | 332 | 4000 | 2272 |
| 2. | Almora | 547 | 7176 | 1190 |
| 3. | Bageshwar | 150 | 1725 | 1190 |
| 4. | Chamoli | 309 | 3587 | 947 |
| 5. | Haridwar | 168 | 1862 | 848 |
| 6. | Rudrapraya g | 91 | 1022 | 897 |
| 7. | Pauri | 643 | 7067 | 619 |
| 8. | Uttarkashi | 144 | 1728 | 330 |
| 9. | Udham Singh Nagar | 176 | 1810 | 516 |
| 10. | Pithoragarh | 83 | 996 | 385 |
| 11. | Dehradun | 434 | 5082 | 910 |

| | | | | |
|---|---|---|---|---|
| 12. | Champawat | 77 | 864 | 287 |
| 13. | Nainital | 136 | 1360 | 500 |
| | TOTAL | 3290 | 38279 | 10127 |

During 1999-2000, around 99 per cent of the total funds released under the SYSY have alone been distributed among these three districts and a lowest amount of fund was allocated to district Bageshwar followed by Uttarakashi and Dehradun. Initially, the SGSY progrmame was not launched in district Bageshwar. Uttarkashi, Udham Singh Nagar, Almora and Dehradun during first two years of its announcement i.e., 1997-98 and 1998-99.

# 5

# Khadi and Village Industries

A large portion of India's population lives in the villages where illiteracy still prevails and large industry is not in a position to absorb the work force from rural areas. In view of this, it is necessary to create more employment opportunities in villages by utilising local resources and skills so that rural people can get work in the villages itself.

This would also reduce the migration of unemployed rural youths to urban areas in search of jobs. Only a few of them get absorbed in urban areas and this constant flow of people to urban areas has put the existing civic infrastructure under severe pressure. As a result, the number of jhuggi-jhonpari clusters and slum dwellers in urban areas is steadily increasing.

The khadi and village industry sector has got the potential to create new jobs in rural areas. During the Ninth Plan period, new policy measures were provided to the sector for enhancing production and employment. A committee on strengthening of the khadi and village industries sector was set up under the chairmanship of Shri K.C. Pant, Deputy Chairman, Planning Commission.

The report of the Pant Committee, submitted in November 2001, recommended a special package for the development of the sector. The Ministry of Agro and

Rural Industries, which is the nodal ministry for the khadi and village industry sector, is implementing this package. The package includes:

— providing the option of market development assistance (MDA) or rebate for khadi cloth;

— continuity of rebate/MDA for five years;

— creation of a database for the sector; and

— intensive marketing support so that the sector may fulfil the objectives of generating rural employment and improving the quality of life of the rural people.

In the areas of research and development (R&D), various sponsored projects were taken up and funded by the Khadi and Village Industries Commission (KVIC) from the science and technology grant from the Department of Science and Technology. The Jamnalal Bajaj Central Research Institute (JBCRI), Wardha, one of the prominent R&D institutes under the KVIC, is in the process of being revamped. It is proposed to upgrade JBCRI to the National Institute of Rural Industrialisation (NIRI), involving an estimated expenditure of Rs. 8 crore.

Some of the technologies developed by the R&D institutions under the KVIC are:

— High productive 6, 8 and 12 spindle all steel new model charkha (NMC).

— Development of semi-automatic and Nepali looms for weaving.

— Development of nine spindle charkhas for muslin khadi.

— Production system for 500 and 600 counts muslin khadi.

— New shades of herbal dyes.

— Suitable and modern Jacquard looms for weaving.

— Improvement in loom for northeastern states. I Production of portable Ghani for vegetable oil extraction.
— Isolation and naturalising of bitter aspect from neem.
— Isolation of various components from sunflower cake.
— Development of LYMPO bricks from ash of rice husk and broken brick lumps.
— Formulation of new herbal formulations and herbal soaps.
— Development of bio-manure, bio pesticides and bio insecticides.
— Use of non-edible oils in soap formulations.
— Use of cashew nut liquid in rubber manufacturing.
— Use of different fibres in hand made paper.
— Decorticators for oil seeds and pulses.
— Development of paddy de-huskers and rice polishers
— Improvement of the potter wheel.
— New technology for tile making.
— Neera preservation.
— Value added products of honey, bakery and fruit products.
— Curing of bee diseases and artificial insemination of bees.

Over the years, the production of khadi cloth has been on the decline. Hence employment in this area is also falling. However, production and employment in village industries have grown from Rs. 3,895 crore in 1997-98 to Rs. 6,607 crore in 2001-02 (anticipated) and new job creation has been reported.

The main reasons for the poor performance in khadi production were (a) uncertainty over the continuation of the rebate policy for khadi, which upset the production schedule and output of khadi producers; (b) high stock of unsold khadi and mismatch in khadi production; (c) the project finance approach adopted in place of existing pattern approach for village industries units took the rural entrepreneurs some time to get used to; and (d) there was a shortfall in availing funds from banks and budgetary resources.

In a major initiative during the Ninth Plan, the marketing of a select range of village industry products was launched under the brand name 'Sarvodaya', with a focus on quality. The National Institute of Design (NID), Ahmedabad, has been entrusted with a project to introduce new and trendy designs in khadi. New designs developed by the National Institute of Fashion Technology (NIFT), New Delhi, would be taken up for production by khadi industries. These initiatives are expected to improve the demand for khadi and to boost production and employment.

Apart from announcing the khadi package in line with the recommendations of the Pant Committee, the Government would emphasise on the concept of 'No Loss' against the earlier concept of 'No Profit' in order to strengthen the khadi and village industries and to make the sector viable and vibrant. In 1994, the High Powered Committee to examine and suggest appropriate policy support to strengthen the khadi and village industry sector under the then Prime Minister had envisaged the creation of two million jobs in the khadi and village industries sector during the Eighth Plan.

This was to be done by the Rural Employment Generation Programme (REGP) and the KVIC was to be the implementing agency. Taking into account the progress of job creation, the target for REGP has been revised and a total of 1.5 million jobs was envisaged to be created by the end of the Ninth Plan. Till 31 March 2001, one million jobs had been created in the sector under REGP. During the Tenth Plan period, two million new jobs would be created in the khadi and village industries sector.

Since 1995-96, under the REGP, 25 per cent of the project cost is provided as margin money for projects that cost upto Rs. 10 lakh. For projects costing between Rs. 10 and 25 lakh, an additional 10 per cent of the remaining cost of the projects is also provided as margin money. For the northeastern region, Sikkim, Andaman & Nicobar Islands, Lakshadweep, hill areas, border areas, tribal areas and for weaker sections (scheduled castes, scheduled tribes, other backward classes, women/ physically handicapped/ex-servicemen and minority community beneficiary/institution), margin money is provided at 30 per cent of the project cost.

In order to extend the quality control network of the sector, 17 national level laboratories have been identified. These laboratories have been accorded accreditation for testing and standardisation of khadi and village industries products and will cater to the needs of local artisans as well as institutions. Marketing is the key to the success of any product. KVIC is providing the necessary marketing inputs to the khadi and village industries sector for both domestic as well as export marketing.

Its main focus, however, is on domestic marketing. Financial assistance is provided to directly aided institutions, State/Union Territory KVI Boards and their aided organisations for setting up sales outlets, renovation or expansion of existing sales outlets, purchase of mobile vans and organising exhibitions to create awareness about khadi and village industries products. KVIC has been participating in international exhibitions being organised by the India Trade Promotion Organisation (ITPO).

Representatives of non-government organisations (NGOs) and KVI Boards are provided financial assistance for ITPO exhibitions. Khadi Gramodyog Bhawans are proposed to be opened in countries like the United States, the United Kingdom, Germany, South Africa, etc. for export promotion. Accordingly Export Promotion Council (EPC) status for khadi and village industry product exports is being envisaged.

An 8 per cent per annum growth in khadi cloth production has been envisaged during the Tenth Plan period. Employment in khadi industries is expected to increase at 3 per cent per annum and major efforts would be made up to improve the quality and value of khadi production by focusing upon design inputs and improving the quality of khadi cloth. Anti-crease treatment for khadi cloth would be achieved by technology tie-up with renowned laboratories and research institutions. Khadi institutions would be strengthened to become economically viable by developing backward and forward linkages.

In order to increase the earnings of khadi artisans attention would need to be given on ensuring higher productivity by introducing improved tools and equipments. Programmes to upgrade skills through training for khadi artisans would be taken up. Use of improved tools and techniques would encourage artisans to produce value-added khadi cloth items, decoratives, etc. With an eye on developing a niche market for khadi, it is proposed to restructure and strengthen the marketing strategy.

For village industries efforts would be made to provide adequate finance, tax exemptions, particularly in sales tax, octroi, purchase tax, etc. Awareness would be generated in village industries about the Margin Money

Scheme of the KVIC and to prepare economically viable and bankable projects by village industries entrepreneurs. Efforts would be made to increase full time employment in village industries and enable the artisans to produce items round the year.

Special quality assurance and product development programmes would need to be taken up for village industries to increase their marketability. Cluster development of village industries need to be undertaken in a way that makes all inputs available at one place and provides marketing inputs to increase sales of village industries units. Technology interfaces are proposed to be established in the Tenth Plan to disseminate information as well as function as technology adoption centres.

One-time financial assistance would be provided to such technology interfaces. The technologists/scientists and experts attached to these interfaces will interact with the local institutions, individuals and artisans for on-the-spot assessment of their technology-related or technical problems. NIRI would act as the coordinating agency for all such technology interfaces.

In the Tenth Plan, it is proposed to set up rural industrial estates and artisan clusters to provide necessary infrastructure and support services to the village industries. Developed land, power, water, common facility centres, training and skill upgradation centres, design and quality inputs and common packaging facilities would be provided at such clusters. The Common Facility Centres would be managed by the implementing agency for the industrial estate.

Financial assistance would be provided to Common Facility Centres by KVIC or by agencies like the National Bank for Agriculture and Rural Development (NABARD), Small Industries Development Bank of India (SIDBI), Council for the Advancement of People's Action and Rural Technology (CAPART), etc.

## National Programme for Rural Industrialisation

Under the National Programme for Rural Industrialisation (NPRI), 50 clusters have been identified by the KVIC for cluster development. Twelve clusters were taken up in 1999-2000, out of which five have commenced production. Further work on the promotion of clusters for increasing rural employment and establishment of backward and forward linkages, setting up of Common Facility Centres, common service network support for satellite cluster units, etc, have been taken up by the KVIC.

# 6

# Review of Progress - Kisan Card Scheme

Kisan Card Scheme was introduced in the year 1998-99, subsequent to the announcement of introduction of this scheme in the union budget for the year 1998-99. Based on the announcement, a model kisan card scheme was formulated by NABARD and was circulated among the banks in August 1998.

Since then the scheme has made rapid strides and upto 31 December 2000 (latest available position) all the banks taken together had issued 104.97 lakh kisan cards in the various states throughout the country. Period wise breakup of the total cards issued since the inception of schemes and upto 31.12.2000 (Table 1).

It may be observed from table-1 that the scheme picked up momentum in the year 1999-2000 and as a result as many as 51.3 lakh cards, forming about 49% of the total cards issued upto 31.12.2000, were issued to farmers by the banks during the said year. The momentum gained by banks was continued during the next year i.e. 2000-2001 also and within 9 months as many as 47.5 lakhs Kisan Credit Cards (45% of total) were issued by banks. These achievement against the target fixed. During 1998-99 as it was the year of inception, no target was fixed.

*Table 1. Kisan cards issued - Year-wise*

| Year | Target | No. of cards issued | % to total cards issued |
|---|---|---|---|
| 1998-99 (w.e.f. August 1998) | N.A. | 607225 | 6% |
| 1999-2000 | 2000000 | 5134081 (256%) | 49% |
| 2000-01 (upto 31.12.2000) | 8708525 | 4756346 (55%) | 45% |
| Total | | 10497652 | 100% |

However, during the year 1999-2000, a target of covering 20 lakh farmers under kisan card was announced by the Finance Minister in his budget speech. Towards this end, NABARD advised various Cooperative Banks and RRBs, through its regional offices in various states to fix their own target with a view to covering at least about 10 per cent of the crop loan beneficiaries during the year 1999-2000.

The response of the banks, against the target of 20 lakh, was overwhelming. Banks issued cards totaling almost two and half times (256% achievement) of the target. Encouraged by the response from banking system, Finance Minister in his budget for 2000-01fixed the target, for the year 2000-01, at 75.0 lakh cards, which later on was further raised to 87.0 lakh based on the targets indicated by various banks particularly cooperative banks. The progress in achieving this target upto 31.12.2000 was 55%.

## Agencywise Progress

Commercial banks, Regional Rural Banks (RRBs) and Co-operative banks are the agencies to implement the kisan card scheme. It has been reported that all 27 public sector commercial banks had implemented the schemes.

Similarly, all RRBs had also issued circulars to implement the scheme.

However, there had been certain delay in implementing the schemes by Co-operative banks in states like Haryana and Punjab due to certain apprehensions. Later on, after issue of necessary clarifications and meeting with officials of State Cooperative banks and Department of Cooperation of these states, both the states have commenced implementation of the kisan card scheme. All the three agencies, upto 31 December 2000, had issued 104.97 lakh of cards. Agency-wise and period-wise break up of the cards issued.

*Table 2. Agencywise Kisan Cards issued*

| Agency | 1998-99 | 1999-2000 | 2000-01 (31.12.2000) | Total |
|---|---|---|---|---|
| Commercial Banks | 445451 | 1365911 | 1153574 | 2964936 (28%) |
| RRBs | 6421 | 173301 | 405969 | 585691 (6%) |
| Cooperative Banks | 155353 | 3594869 | 3196803 | 6947025 (66%) |
| Total | 607225 | 5134081 | 4756346 | 10497652 |

As may be observed from the table above, Cooperative Banks had major share of the cards issued. This was natural as Cooperative Banks (SCBs and CCBs) are the major agencies for purveying short term credit for raising crops in India. Cooperative Banks had 66% share of total cards issued upto 31.12.2000.

This was followed by Commercial banks with 29.6 lakh card forming about 28% of the total card issued. Though the RRBs have good number of branches in rural area, their share in crop loan had been only modest (8%). RRBs had issued 4.06 lakh cards which was about 6% of the total.

As has been mentioned already, no targets were fixed for the year 1998-99, hence comparison of target with the achievement was not possible. Further, during 1999-2000 an overall target for coverage of 20.0 lakh farmers was fixed by Government of India, but, agencywise break-up was not available. Target for the year 2000-01 has been fixed at 87.0 lakh. Agencywise break-up of this alongwith achievement upto 31.12.2000 (latest available information) has been shown in the table 3:

*Table 3. Progress in issue of kisan cards by various agencies during 2000-01 against target*

| Agency | Target | Cards issued | % Achievement |
|---|---|---|---|
| Cooperative Banks | 5708500 | 3196803 | 56.0% |
| RRBs | 500025 | 405969 | 81.2% |
| Commercial Banks | 2500000 | 1153574 | 46.1% |
| Total | 8708525 | 4756346 | 54.6% |

As may be seen from the table given above the overall achievement of the target upto 31.12.2000 had been 54.6%. RRBs had done well. As against a target of 5.0 lakh, RRBs had issued 4.05 lakh cards, thus achieving 81.2% of the annual target within first 9 months of the year. At this rate, it is expected that RRBs would fully achieve their target fixed for the year.

On a review of statewise position given in annexure-3.1 it was revealed that the performance of RRBs in majority of the states was excellent. In as many as 12 states, performance of the RRBs had been excellent (80% or above). In two states, it was moderate whereas in 6 states, it was poor. Noticeable feature of RRBs performance is that in some states, like Arunachal Pradesh, Tripura, Assam, where performance of Co-operative banks was poor, in contrast RRBs had done exceedingly well.

*Table 4. State-wise Performance of RRBs in issuing kisan Cards*

| Performance | % of achievement of target (31.12.2000) | Name of states |
|---|---|---|
| Excellent | 80% and above | Arunachal Pradesh, Bihar, Gujarat, Himachal Pradesh, Jammu & Kashmir, MadhyaPradesh, Karnataka, Maharashtra, Orissa, Tripura, Rajasthan, Uttar Pradesh(12 States) |
| Moderate | 50% - 80% | Haryana, Assam (2 states) |
| Poor Below | 50% | Kerala, Meghalaya, Punjab, Tamil Nadu, West Bengal, Andhra Pradesh (6 states) |

There is need to pay more attention in certain states where performance of co-operative banks as well as RRBs had been poor. These states are Kerala, Punjab, Tamilnadu and West Bengal. Performance of Co-operative banks was at 56% which cannot be considered satisfactory. As can be seen from the table given above, among the major states, having significant share of target, the performance of Bihar, Karnataka, Maharashtra and Uttar Pradesh had been excellent at 80% and above, whereas in states like Andhra Pradesh and Gujarat, the performance had been moderate between 50 to 80 per cent.

Among the major states, where performance had been poor (below 50%), include Himachal Pradesh, Kerala, Madhya Pradesh, Orissa, Punjab, Rajasthan, Tamil Nadu and West Bengal (8 states). Performance of states in North East, though their targets were small, was very poor. Special attention is required in North-East to motivate the bankers, State government as well as farmers to implement the scheme.

This position was obtained from Reserve Bank of India and it relates to cards issued up to 31 December 2000. This was due to non-availability of state-wise break up of card issued by some of the banks. Since there was no allocation of targets for issue of kisan cards among various commercial banks, it may not be possible to compare their achievement against target as has been done in case of RRBs and Cooperative Banks.

*Table 5: Kisan card issued by Commercial Banks*

| Number of cards | No. of banks | Name of Banks |
|---|---|---|
| Above 5.0 lakh | 2 | Canara Bank, State Bank of India |
| 3.0 - 5.0 lakh | 1 | Syndicate Bank |
| 1.0 - 3.0 lakh | 5 | Andhra Bank, Bank of Baroda, Bank of India, Punjab National Bank, State Bank of Hyderabad |
| Below one lakh | 19 | Allahabad Bank, Bank of Maharashtra, Central Bank Of India, Corporation Bank, Dena Bank, Indian Bank, Indian Overseas Bank, Oriental Bank Of Commerce, Punjab & Sindh Bank, State Bank of Bikaner & Jaipur, State Bank of Indore, State Bank of Mysore, State Bank of Patiala, State Bank of Saurashtra, State Bank of Travancore, UCO Bank, Union Bank of India, United Bank of India and Vijaya Bank |

As can be seen from Table 5, Canara Bank and State Bank of India had recorded a good progress and distributed over 5 lakh cards. Syndicate Bank was the only bank to fall in the second slab of 3.0 to 5.0 lakh cards. 5 Banks were in 1.0 to 3.0 lakh bracket, whereas 19 banks were in the below 1.0 lakh bracket. The progress of Kisan card is reviewed in state level Banker Committee meeting (SLBC) in each state as per guidelines given by RBI. Commercial banks whose performance has been rather poor may be followed up by RBI and respective State Government to cover all eligible farmers in the area of operation falling under their respective branches.

**Statewise Position of Kisan Cards**

A comparison of target versus achievement is not possible, as the targets for the commercial banks are not available statewise. However, on a closer scrutiny of the number of cards issued, it can be inferred that in certain states, the number of cards issued is quite significant (more than 5 lakh). These states are Andhra Pradesh, Maharashtra, Rajasthan, Orissa, Karnataka, Gujarat and Uttar Rradesh.

*Table 6. Kisan Card issued and coverage of Farmers state-wise*

| Percentage of farmers covered | Nature of performance | States |
|---|---|---|
| 50 % and above | Satisfactory | Andhra Pradesh, Gujarat, |
| 25% to 50% | Moderate | Haryana, Maharashtra, Orissa, Punjab and Rajasthan |
| Below 25% | Poor | Bihar, Delhi, Goa, Himachal Pradesh, Jammu & Kashmir, Karnataka, Kerala, Madhya Pradesh, All N.E. States, Tamilnadu, Uttar Pradesh & West Bengal |

In absence of target, another yardstick to compare the performance of banks in issuing kisan cards could be measuring the performance of banks by number of kisan cards issued. This may be done by comparing the number of kisan card issued with the number of farmers borrowing from banks in each state. The number of farmers borrowing from banks has been calculated by assuming that 50% of the operational holding as borrowing farmers.

As can be observed from the table, only Andhra Pradesh has covered more than 50% of its farmers (61.2%). The performance of states like Gujarat, Haryana, Orissa, Maharashtra, Rajasthan and Punjab may be regarded as moderate. In the other remaining states, banks have to cover a lot of farmers under the scheme. They may have to make all out efforts to bring in more number of new farmers hitherto not having access to banks, into the banking fold using kisan card.

## Zonewise Review of Performance

Various states of the country have been clubbed into 5 geographical Zones viz., Western Zone, South Zone, North Zone, North-Eastern Zone and Eastern Zone. The position in respect of kisan card issued in various zones. As could be observed from the table, the progress in South Zone and West Zone had been good as in these two zones 30.7% and 26.7% of the farmers accessing bank credit have been covered under the kisan card scheme. Progress of North Zone is poor as Co-operative Banks' performance has not been upto mark.

Punjab State Co-operative Bank had delayed the implementation of the kisan card owing to certain reservations and apprehensions. It is learnt that the authorities in NABARD, Chandigarh and Punjab State Cooperative Bank, Chandigarh have later on clarified these apprehensions and fears have been cleared and that necessary intimation in this regard have been issued by Registrar, Cooperative Societies, Govt. of Punjab.

It is, therefore, expected that by the end of the year i.e. 31 March 2001, all Cooperative banks in Punjab would achieve their targets of issuing 175000 cards during the year 2000-01. This would push up the performance of north zone. The real cause of worry is the very poor progress in North-Eastern Zone and Eastern Zone.

The matter should be given urgent attention by the concerned state government and also by the apex agencies including Reserve Bank of India and NABARD. The problem, if any, may be discussed in the meeting of State Level Bankers' Committee. It may be mentioned that the progress of Kisan Cards had been good in those states where state governments took interest and following up the scheme with the banks.

**Small & Marginal Farmers under Kisan Card Scheme**

Since most of the banks have not been monitoring the data in respect of cards issued to farmers category-wise (small and marginal farmers), it has not been possible to present a national picture in this regard. However, based on the data compiled by some banks at the request of BIRD in this regard and the information collected during their field visit to banks by consultants, certain inferences and conclusions have been drawn.

Coverage of small and marginal farmers has been satisfactory. The range of coverage is from 33% to cent percent. Thus, if this sample is taken as a representative of national scene, it is quite satisfying to note that small and marginal farmers have been adequately covered under kisan card scheme by banks. The coverage of small and marginal farmers is sizeable in RRBs which may be quite obvious as majority of cards so far had been issued by the banks to their existing clients and most of the clients of RRBs had been in the target group i.e., small and marginal farmers and poorer strata of the society.

RRBs are followed by co-operative banks. Since co-operative banks operate through primary agriculture cooperatives (PACs) where most of the farmers are also small and marginal, it was expected that their coverage of small and marginal farmers would be quite high.

As regards commercial banks, the sample data shows that Commercial banks have also covered many small farmers. In view of instructions from GOI and State Governments and continuous monitoring by RBI, Commercial banks are under compulsion to issue as many kisan cards as possible. It would be difficult for them to achieve their target without covering small and marginal farmers, which are in substantial number in rural areas.

Another way to assess the coverage of small and marginal farmers by various agencies under kisan card scheme, in absence of availability of complete data on coverage of small and marginal farmers, may be to examine the average amount sanctioned per card.

*Table 7. Average Amount Sanctioned per Kisan Credit Card*

| Period | Average amount sanctioned per card (Rs.) | | | |
|---|---|---|---|---|
| | Coop. Banks | CBs | RRBs | Total |
| 1998-99 | 53716 | 27986 | 16633 | 34310 |
| 1999-2000 | 10030 | 27986 | 23393 | 14702 |
| 2000-01 (31.12.2000) | 23690 | 25744 | 23488 | 24171 |
| Overall Average | 17281 | 26151 | 23385 | 20127 |

The trend of average amount sanctioned per kisan card issued by all agencies, it would be interesting to note that in the first year i.e., 1998-99 of introduction of kisan card scheme, the average amount sanctioned per card was Rs. 34310. This would in turn imply that banks were focussing more on big farmers in this year. It is very surprising to note that average amount of loan under Kisan Credit Card scheme of cooperatives was highest followed by commercial banks and thereafter RRBs. In the next year i.e. 1999-2000, when Kisan card scheme gained considerable momentum (50% of the total card issued upto 31.12.2000 were issued during 1999-2000) the amount sanctioned per card came down substantially to Rs.14,702/-, less than half of that of previous year.

This meant that during this year, all agencies would have covered a substantial number of small and marginal farmers, which had brought down the average. Another reason for more coverage of small and marginal farmers by banks could be the removal of minimum ceiling of Rs.5000/- for issue of kisan card. Further, as the staff of banks found the scheme useful, their good experience led to removal of some apprehensions and inhibitions, which were harbouring in their minds earlier. Good demand from farming community for kisan card would have also encouraged the banks to cover more of small and marginal farmers.

## Ground Level Credit Flow

The amount of ground level credit flow in the country during the last 5 years i.e. 1996-97 to 2000-01 have been presented in the table below:

*Table 8. Ground Level Credit Flow for Agriculture Sector*

| Year | Production Credit/ Crop loan | Agriculture Term loan | Total Agriculture |
|---|---|---|---|
| 1996-97 | 17058 | 9353 | 26411 (20%) |

| | | | |
|---|---|---|---|
| 1997-98 | 20640 | 11316 | 31956 |
| | (21%) | (21%) | (21%) |
| 1998-99 | 23903 | 12994 | 36897 |
| | (16%) | (15%) | (15%) |
| 1999-00 | 27239 | 14525 | 41764 |
| | (21%) | (12%) | (13%) |
| 2000-01* | 30983 | 20477 | 51460 |
| | (14%) | (41%) | (23%) |

Total credit to agriculture sector during the year 2000-01 has been estimated to touch Rs.51460 crores, recording an annual growth rate of 23 per cent over the previous year. Production credit/crop loan has been estimated at Rs.30983 crores with a growth rate of 14 per cent over 1999-2000. The estimated growth rate in flow of production credit in 2000-01 at 14 per cent is much less than that was achieved during 1999-2000 (21%).

In contrast, the growth rate in flow of term loan to agriculture is expected to touch 41 percent i.e. about 3.5 times higher than that of 1999-2000 (12%). The picture was almost reverse during 1999-2000 where growth rate in production credit/crop loan recorded a significant rise but growth in term credit to agriculture came down by 3%. It may be mentioned here that 1999-2000 was the year in which sizeable number of kisan cards were issued.

However, the positive correlation between kisan card and flow of production credit may be difficult to establish as during the very next year i.e. 2000-01, the growth rate fell down significantly. Further, to explore any correlation between kisan card and flow of production credit at ground level using statistical methods, the number of records available is only 3, which is too small to derive any meaningful conclusion or correlation.

The flow of ground level credit particularly crop loan is dependent on many factors and weather is one of the very important variable affecting crops and thereby demand for production credit. The significant rise in the flow of production credit in 1999-00 could be partially due to the good monsoon during the year 1999. During 1999, out of 35 meteorological subdivisions, in as many as 28 sub-divisions, rainfall was excess to normal.

Similarly, 81 per cent of the gross cropped area in the country received normal to excess rainfall during the year 1999. On the whole, country received 96 per cent of the normal rainfall (852mm) during south-west monsoon period during the year 1999.

Even though at present, while kisan card scheme is in full swing, the data may not be sufficient to arrive at the relationship between number of kisan card and ground level flow of production credit, yet the comparative analysis of total amount sanctioned under kisan card in the country with that of actual ground level flow of production credit gives a fair amount of indication that this scheme would play a significant role in flow of credit to agriculture sector in the coming years.

*Table 9. Comparative Analysis of kisan card and Ground level Production Credit*

| Year | Nos. of Kisan card* | Total Amount sanctioned under kisan card* | Production Credit (Actual) | Col. 3 as % of Col.4. |
|---|---|---|---|---|
| (1) | (2) | (3) | (4) | (5) |
| 1998-99 | 607225 | 2083 | 23903 | 8.7 |
| 1999-00 | 5741306 | 9631 | 27239 | 35.3 |
| 2000-01 | 10497652 | 21128 | 30983 | 68.2 |

During 2000-01, two third of the ground level production credit would be through KCC which is quite significant.

However, at this stage, it may be premature to conclude that kisan cards would lead to increased ground flow of production credit in India but this would certainly facilitate stabilisation of flow of production credit.

The position agencywise. Historically, Cooperative Banks (short-term structure) had been the major outlets for channelising production credit in India. During 1999-00, Cooperative banks had a share of 56% of total production credit disbursed at the ground level followed by commercial banks and RRBs.

Thus, cooperative banks have tremendous influence on flow of production credit. In total, by 31 December 2000, cooperative banks had issued 6947045 kisan cards forming 66% of the total cards issued by all agencies. The amount of limit sanctioned through these cards was Rs.12,005 crores.

*Table 10. Comparative Analysis of kisan card issued and Ground level disbursements*

| Year | Nos. of Kisan card* | Amount sanctioned under kisan cards | Production Credit disbursed | Amount sanctioned under kisan card as % of production credit disbursed |
|---|---|---|---|---|
| 1997-98 | - | - | 10895 | - |
| 1998-99 | 155353 | 826 | 12489 (19%) | 6.6 |
| 1999-00 | 3750242 | 4432 | 15224 (18%) | 29.1 |
| 2000-01 | 6947045 | 12005 | 17598 (16%) | 65.7 |

As can be observed from table given above, the growth rate in production credit disbursed by Cooperative bank was more or less same since 1998-99, the issue of kisan card does not appear to have led to increase in ground level credit flow for crop production. There is nothing surprising about it.

If the circulars regarding kisan card scheme launched by cooperative banks are perused carefully, it would be seen that most of the SCBs/DCCBs had not provided anything extra in the kisan card limit as compared to the credit which a farmer or a member of PACS was availing of in the past.

Though, a few banks have indicated that a farmer may be provided Rs.10000 extra in addition to crop limit to meet his other short term agriculture and non farm sector requirements, in practice, very few banks have allowed drawals against this limit. Thus practically the farmer is getting more or less same amount of credit as he was getting earlier under usual system of cooperative banks.

The advantages which farmer got through kisan card is more flexibility and a simple sanction for a period of three years, thus avoiding year to year hassles of procuring revenue records and other documents for availing bank loan. Further, since cooperative banks had been calculating credit requirement of a farmer using the scales of finance as approved by Technical Committee of the district, even prior to the kisan card scheme, the limit under kisan card was no different to the earlier limit.

Flow of credit would increase only when -

— Scales of finance are revised upwards or

— More land is covered under crops by farmer or

— More members are enrolled or

— Cropping pattern is changed or

— Individual Maximum Borrowing Power (IMBP) is periodically reviewed and increased.

Therefore, one should not expect any significant increase in production credit at ground level as long as cooperative banks do not plan to either enroll new members or restrict crop loans to IMBP without taking into consideration the actual requirement. . However, the figures of kisan card issued by the cooperative banks show rapid strides. Within a span of two years of launching of scheme, as much as 65.7% of the total ground level flow of credit in 2000-01 would be through kisan cards. By any standard, this is a remarkable achievement.

The share of RRBs in total production credit disbursed during 2000-01 is about 8%. Although in comparison to Cooperative and Commercial banks, it is quite small, yet in view of their extensive branch network in rural areas and their clientele being small borrowers, RRBs have played a vital role in covering small and marginal farmers under the scheme which hitherto did not have good access to bank credit.

*Issued and Amount Sanctioned by RRBs*

The sanctioned amount under cards during 2000-01 formed about56.8% of the total ground level disbursement during 2000-01, which can be considered moderately satisfactory. As regards impact of kisan card on ground level flow of production credit, the situation in RRBs is akin to that at national level. There was a significant upsurge during the year 1999-00 (32% growth rate) which came down sharply in 2000-01.

So, it would be difficult to draw any definite conclusion whether kisan card had led to increase in ground level flow of production credit in RRBs based on this limited data. Commercial banks had issued 2964916 kisan cards by end of December 2000. Against these cards, total limit of Rs.7753 crore had been sanctioned. The trend in ground level disbursement of production credit in commercial banks was in contrast to that obtaining in RRBs and cooperatives.

During 1999-00 when cooperatives and RRBs recorded good growth rate in ground level disbursement due to favourable monsoon, Commercial banks could hardly record a rise of 1% in this year. However, they were able to restore their normal growth trend in 2000-01; but the trend in flow of credit at ground level did not appear to exhibit any marked correlation with the number of kisan card issued.

The performance of commercial banks in coverage of farmers under kisan card was quite good as can be judged from the fact that by the end of December 2000, the amount sanctioned under kisan card (Rs.7753 crores) formed 71% of the total ground level disbursement of production credit by commercial banks.

# 7

# Non-Farm Employment and Women

There are certain limitations in using the employment data from different census documents. Since it is widely known that many definitional and conceptual modifications were effected in one census after the other so that one is bound to discover diverse conceptual absurdities if the population data were to be used without making qualified adjustments in some cases,

Broadly speaking the employment data for the years 1981 and 1991 is more or less comparable in the sense that in both the census as the concept and definition used for the classification of workers is almost similar. The size and structure of rural non-farm sector can be measured in terms of

— number and size of establishments

— income and earnings and

— employment

In both the census the work force has been divided into two groups one, main workers and two, marginal workers. And the sectoral distribution of workforce has been carried out in the case of main workers only. However, in the 1991, the definition and methodology used for inclusion of women in the categories or work force in rural areas is somewhat different than it was used during the other census periods.

**Farm and Non-farm Employment**

The agricultural and its related activities are forming the economic base of the State. Hence, these activities are the main sources of providing employment opportunities to the workforce and the avenues of income to the households in different districts of the State. Still, over three fourth of the work force is engaged in performing different agricultural work in the state.

However, over the year, the concentration of workforce on agricultural activity has been consistently declining in the state. And the shift of workforce from agricultural to non-agricultural has been quite significant in each of the districts of the state. In other words, the concentration of workforce in productive economic sectors, confined in primary and secondary sectors has been narrowing down and its shift has subsequently been visualized in tertiary sector of economies, particularly in informal sector economies in different districts.

Distribution of workers into farm and non-farm sectors revealed that the concentration of workforce in farm sector stands at a highest level in Tehri, closely followed by Chamoli and Uttarkashi while the non-farm employment is noticed confined largely in Dehradun and Nainital in all the last three Cencus years. But, over the years, the non-farm employment has been increasing at a faster rate in former group of districts as compared to latter one.

It indicates the fact that the shift of workforce from farm to non-farm sector is greatly taking place in areas where the workforce was largely confined in farm sector as compared to those areas where the workforce was already largely concentrated in non-farm sector. A shift in the structure of employment in favour of non-farm sector is considered to be an index of economic development.

In this sense, given the increasingly fragmentation of land holdings decreasing trends in the availability of arable land and the degradation in the quality of land leading to the stagnation in the productivity of major crops over the years, a structural shift in the concentration of workforce in favour of non-farm activities becomes all the more imperative for reduction in emerging situation of poverty and un-employment in the state.

*Non-farm Employment in Rural and Urban Areas*

The comparison of farm and non-farm employment between rural and urban areas is reflecting a universalised fact that the workforce in urban areas is largely confined in non-farm sector while the rural workforce is mainly engaged in farm sector. However, the proportion of workforce engaged in non-farm sector in urban areas is relatively at lower extent than that of workforce engaged in farm sector in rural areas.

Also, the absorption of workforce in rural non-farm sector is revealed at higher level as compared to urban farm sector. A significant point which emerging with this analysis is that the employment in different component of non-farm sector in urban areas is consistently declining while in rural segments it has shown a remarkable increase over the years.

The concentration of workforce in rural nonfarm sector has increased from 16.12 per cent in 1971 to 19.39 per cent in 1981 and 23.8 per cent in 1991 while in urban counterpart the respective proportions have declined from 93.70 per cent to 91.36 per cent during 1971 to 1991. Similarly across the district level, the absorption of workforce in non-farm sector is recorded fairly well increasing in each of the districts, but relatively at highest level in Chamoli and Dehradun.

However, in urban areas it has been increasing only in Almora, Pithoragarh and Chamoli and marginally in Pithoragarh. Thus, in rural areas the non-farm employment is on the increase at the cost decrease in the absorption capacity of farm sector to employ additionally increasing level of workforce in rural areas, while the employment in urban non-farm sector has been narrowing down largely due to negative performance in the growth of various non-farm activities in general and in particular of those possessing greater employment absorption potentials.

The farm sector is limiting the chances of labourforce to engage into different farm activities, more particularly in agricultural operations, due to the already over pressure of workforce on it. It is, therefore, the shift of increasing volume of labourforce into nonfarm activities has depicted a very high growth of employment in non-farm sector relative to farm sector during the recent past.

Across the districts level, the trends in the growth performance of employment in farm sector has been declining in absolute terms in districts Tehri and Pauri while it has been proportionately narrowed in Dehradun, Nainital and Pithoragarh with a sharp increase in district Uttarkashi, Chamoli and Almora during the year 1981 to 1991 as compared to 1971 and 1981.

On the other, the growth pattern of employment in non-farm sector has been consistently increasing in the districts Chamoli, Dehradun and Nainital to a greater extent while in remaining districts, in spite of the positive growth trends in non-farm employment the progress in absorption of workforce in different non-farm activities, has been reduced largely during 1981 to 1991 as compared to 1971 to 1981.

In all, the analysis reflected that a very high pace of industrialisation which has taken place in agro-industrially well developed districts Dehradun and Nainaital of the State, has positively influenced the growth of non-farm sector as a substantial level in both the districts as compared to remaining districts of the State, during the recent past.

Similarly, a decline of a sizeable numbers of traditional manufacturing activities in districts Uttarkashi and Almora, as reflected in earlier analysis have further witnessed a very high incidence of decline in the rate of growth of non-farm employment with a positive growth of farm-employment in both the districts. Though the non-farm employment in the State is still increasing with a varied degree of differentials in its growth pattern across the districts level.

**Structure of Rural Non-farm Employment**

The comparison related to the structure of employment between farm and non-farm sector in the proceeding part of the analysis revealed a significant changes occurring in the shift of workforce from farm sector to non-farm sector and the extent of differences are further prevailing in the concentration of workforces, changes in the structure and growth pattern of both male and female workforce in farm and non-farm sectors between rural and urban areas and among different districts of the state.

The nature and the magnitude of changes existing in the structure of non-farm employment and the concentration of workforce in different components of non-farm sector between rural and urban areas of the state. The analysis on the size structure of rural non-farm employment as presented in members of the households than the women. Since the domination of men workforce is fairly largely visualised in non-farm employment in each of districts of the state in fact, it has consistently been increasing at much larger level further than the case of women workforce in almost the districts.

However, the concentration of both men and women workforce in rural non-farm sector is satisfactorily increasing in each of the districts of the State though more sharply in favour of women workforce as compared to their male counterparts. The share of non-farm employment in total rural labourforce has considerably risen. Also, with a considerable shift of workforce from farm to non-farm sector the employment in latter sector has been increasing to a much larger extent than the case of overall growth of employment in both urban and rural areas.

In so far as the comparison of growth trends in non-farm employment between rural and urban areas suggest that initially during the period 1971 and 1981 the non-farm employment in urban areas increased at much larger level than in rural areas. But since last one decade or so a reversal situation is emerging in the growth of employment in non-farm sector between these two areas.

It suggests that the expansion of different non-farm employment has been greatly taking place in rural areas as compared to urban areas despite the fact that both the categories of activities together has shown a negative growth performance in both the areas over the years. However the expansion of non-farm activities has highly been undertaken in the rural areas of districts Chamoli, Dehradun and Pithoragarh where the employment in non-farm sector has growth quite a large extent, accounting for 76 per cent, 63 per cent and 52 per cent respectively during 1981 and 1991.

While the lowest growth is reported in rural areas of Pauri (17 per cent) followed by Uttarkashi (19 per cent) during the same period. Between 1981 and 1991 the employment in non-farm sector in rural areas has grown at larger scale as compared in urban areas of almost the districts, except in district Tehri, where extremely a larger pace of urbanisation has occurred with the initiation of the construction of a large dam during the recent past, had led to increase the expansion of different categories of non-farm activities to a large extent.

### *Sectoral Concentration*

A major shift of workforce, however was, well recognised from farm to non-farm sector in each of the districts of the State. To find out about what are the main components/ activities confined in non-farm sector those are favourably influencing the concentration and growth pattern of rural workforce over the years, in the context of drawing some concrete policy perspectives for developing different nonfarm activities.

### *Rural-Urban Concentration*

The classification of workforce into different components of non-farm sector postulates that both in urban and rural areas, the workforce is largely concentrated in service sector which include Government sector employment and personnel and community services but it largely constitutes of personal and community services in rural areas. However the proportion of workforce confined in services is reported to be significantly at higher level in rural areas as compared to urban areas and also, it has been increasing more sharply in former areas than in the latter areas over the years.

The manufacturing, trade and commerce and construction activities are the another main components of non-farm sector employment in both rural and urban areas. However, the trading and manufacturing together are forming second most groups of non-farm activities after the services, which are employing little over one fourth of the urban workforce. The share of agriculture based non-farm activities such as livestock, fishing, hunting and forestry in providing employment is noted significantly at higher level in rural areas as compared to urban segments. Also the concentration of workforce in these activities is on the increase in both the segments is significantly increasing over the years.

In rural areas itself, the traditional household manufacturing activities seems to be moving away at a much larger extent than the non-household manufacturing activities as a result the concentration of workforce has declined to a much higher level in the former category of activities with a marginal decline of around one percent point in latter category of activities.

**Role of Women in Non-farm Sector**

The agriculture and its related activities are the main sources for providing employment to a majority of work force in the State. The women participate along with their family members in performing different economic activities as well as in household related activities. In fact, the participation of women in performing household related activities in recognised significantly at a higher level than their male counterpart. The women are provided almost full freedom by the prevailing social system and by their families to participate in their family business and agricultural operations.

The work participation rate of women workers in Uttaranchal is consistently relatively at larger level than the cases of most of the States in India. The census data for the year 1991 revealed that a little over one fourth of women population in the state is engaged in performing different economic activities. In fact, the corresponding figure reaches as higher as 45 per cent for district Uttarakashi followed by 40 per cent for Chamoli. It has been further pointed out that due to unprecedently increasing volume of migration of male workforce out side state for the purpose of seeking employment and earning opportunities the burden of work among the women workforce has been consistently increasing over the years.

Hence, it has resulted to a considerable increase in the work-participation rate among the women, while for men workforce it has been declining in almost the districts excepting the case of district Pithoragarh and Nainital, over the years. Also, the direct implication of increasing incidence of out-migration of male workforce has been seen in terms of a relative decline in the overall work participation rate of worker in a majority of the districts with a marginal increase of less than one per cent point at the state level during 1981 and 1991.

### *Men and women in farm and non-farm*

Distribution of men and women workforce in farm and non-farm sectors revealed that the non-farm sector in different districts of the state is highly dominated by the male workforce while the in farm sector, the concentration of women force is significantly much higher as compared to male workforce. Further, the analysis shows that while farm sector is the dominant source of employment for both men and women in a majority of the districts, except in Dehradun, in the sense that the proportion of both men and women workforce engaged in farm sector in remarkably higher than in non-farm sector is most of the districts.

However, both the sexes have increasingly been influenced to engage themselves in non-farm sectors during the last couple of decades, though in absolute terms the concentration of male workforce in non-farm sector is increasing more sharply than the case of women workforce. The women workforce in rural areas of the state mainly remain confine in performing household related, both economic and non-economic activities while the men workforce do participate partly in household related economic activities during the agricultural operations and partly in wage-paid employment or self-employed activities during rest of the duration from agricultural work.

Expansion of non-farm employment in rural areas of the state has been providing increasing opportunities to the male workforce to concentrate in different non-farm activities. As a result the proportion of male workforce engaged in performing both farm and non-farm activities has been recorded almost at same level in the State. In fact, as per 1991 census report, in the districts Pauri and Dehradun the proportion of male workforce engaged in farm-sector is reported to be significantly much higher than in farm sector.

However, over the years greater performance in the expansion of non-farm employment has been revealed in Chamoli and Tehri and at lowest level in district Uttarkashi and Almora. Also, only exception is the case of district Almora and Nainital, the concentration of women workforce in non-farm sector has declined to a certain extent as a result of a significant increase in their concentration in the farm sector during the last one-decade. Contrary to this, a highest level of increase in the absorption of women workforce has been reported in two industrially districts Dehradun and Nainital of the state beginning from the year 1971 to 1991.

The pattern of growth in the absorption of men and women workforce in farm and non-farm sectors points out that there has been a progressive and substantial increase in the proportion of both men and women workforce in to both non-farm sector as well as in farm sector, but it is at much higher rate in former sector than in the latter one. Also, the growth of women workforce is revealed significantly at much higher level than the men workforce in both the sectors. In fact, during last decade, the combined growth rate of workforce engaged in non-farm and farm sector is reported to be 29.39 percent for women workforce as against 20.06 per cent for men workforce.

Significant levels of differences are also revealed between districts in terms of direction and rate of change in the pattern of the absorption of men and women workforce in farm and non-farm sectors. A negative growth rate in the pattern of absorption of both men and women workforce was revealed farm sector for districts Uttarkashi, Chamoli Pauri and Almora between 1971 to 1981 however, it increased marginally during 1981 and 1991 for both men and women workforce in district Uttarkashi, Chamoli and Almora with a greater jump for both men and women workforce in non-farm sector; but it further, fell down for both the sexes in Pauri with a marginal positive changes in the shift of workforce in non-farm sector.

Between the period 1981 to 1991, the concentration of women workforce in farm sector is found growing very fastly in three districts Nainital (119 per cent). Dehradun (90 per cent) and Almora (88 per cent) with a marginal decline of 2 per cent point in nonfarm sector employment for Almora and the increase of over 90 per cent for each Nainital and Dehradun. It gives an impression that the farm sector still possesses a greater potential for absorbing increasing level of labourforce in Almora, Dehradun and Naintial as compared to remaining districts.

Also, a large scale of concentration of various manufacturing and commercial activities that has achieved in districts Nainital and Dehradun during the past several years ago and are still in the process of expansion are greatly providing an open opportunity to the expansion of different non-farm activities so as to offer increasing level of employment to both the sexes of labourforce. The pattern of concentration of men and women workforce in different sectors of non-farm activities, the analysis revealed that the women workers are more or less equally participating in performing different categories of non-farm activities in rural areas.

In fact, in two main components of non-farm sectors, manufacturing households and services, the concentration of women workforce has been over lapping to that of men workforce since the period of last three decades. However, the concentration of both men and women workforce has shown a declining trend in both household and non-household manufacturing activities but largely in household manufacturing than the non-household manufacturing.

And it is declining more sharply for women workforce as compared to their men counterpart. In fact, a consistent increase in the share of service sector in providing employment opportunities to both the sexes has been reported in rural areas, though, again, the concentration of women on it has increased more sharply than the case of men during 1981-91. However, in livestock, forestry, fishing and hunting, mining and quarrying, non-manufacturing, construction, trade and commerce and transportation, the concentration of men is leading over the women workforce in rural areas.

In fact, it has been consistently declining for women workforce in most of the activities except in transportation and trade and commerce. Further it is observed that in trading and commercial activities, despite the much lower level of concentration of women than their male counterpart, the proportion of women is appeared increasing more sharply than the case of male workforce over the years.

Thus it appears that the women workforce is better moving from relatively low paid occupations available in traditional household manufacturing, construction and occupations confined in primary sector to the better paid occupations in tra ding and commerce, mining and quarrying and service sectors in the rural areas of the State during the recent past.

### *Sectoral Growth*

An inquiry into the trends in the growth of employment in dif ferent components of non-farm sector highlights that initially during 1971 to 1981 the absorption of men workforce in non-farm sector increased at slower level in rural areas as compared to urban areas but it picked up in favour of former areas than the latter areas during 1981 and 1991. On the other, the corresponding growth rate of women in rural areas has been relatively at lower rate than in urban areas during each of the reference periods, but on the whole, it increased in rural areas with a negative growth pattern in urban areas during 1981 to 1991.

The concentration of male workforce in rural areas is growing more sharply than in urban areas in each of the major components of the non-farm sectors, particularly in manufacturing, trading and commerce and service related activities during the recent past. In fact, the concentration of rural women is increasing more sharply than its urban counterparts in almost the activities of non-farm sector, except in the construction. Thus the overall analysis indicates that the non-farm employment in its different sectors is increasing fairly at higher level in rural areas as compared to urban areas, though the concentration of workforce in different non-farm activities is reported to be significantly larger in urban areas than in the rural areas.

The absorption of women workforce in different sectors of non-farm employment is consistently increasing both in urban and rural area but more sharply in latter areas than in the former one. In rural areas itself, initially the concentration of men workforce was increasing more sharply than the case of women workforce in different non-farm activities but latter, during the period 1981 to 1991, the corresponding growth pattern of women workforce turn up significantly at higher rate than the male workforce; 67.23 for women as against 40.85 per cent for men.

In fact, expecting in primary sector related activities, the concentration of women workforce is increasing relatively at much larger level as compared to their male counterpart. Even a negative growth rate for men workforce is revealed in certain activities such as construction, traditional household manufacturing and mining and quarrying during 1981 to 1991. On the other hand, the concentration of women workforce has increased at much faster rate in mining and quarrying followed by trading activities with a marginal decline in fishing, forestry livestock, planting and hunting activities.

In fact the in rural household based manufacturing activities the concentration of women workforce has declined at 12.77 percent during 1971 and 1981 but it has further increased over 42 percent with a decrease of 35 percent for man workforce during 1981 and 1991. It is further revealed that over the years the concentration of both male and female workforce in non-farm activities is declining in urban areas, though more sharply in case of females as compared to male workforce.

Excepting the case of construction in remain and services activities the concentration of women in remaining non-farm activities has been increasing significantly much higher rate in rural areas as compared to urban areas. As far as the pattern of concentration of the workforce in non-farm activities in different geographical locations is concerned the analysis depicted that the proportions of them employed in non-farm sector are relatively much higher than the case of men workforce in low and middle hill areas while a reversal situation is emerging in high hill areas. However, in absolute terms, the men workforce is highly dominated in non-farm employment in each of the geographical locations.

The concentration of women workforce is largely seen in certain numbers of occupations confined in traditional household manufacturing livestock, forestry, plantation and services activities. However, a very small size of women workforce is formal employed in construction activities in low hill areas.

# 8 Public Distribution System

The problem facing the country today is not one of shortage of foodgrains but of managing the surplus. Ironically, even as the godowns of the FCI are overflowing, stray cases of starvation deaths are still being reported. A civilised society in the 21st century cannot allow this to happen.

Therefore, while there is need to produce adequate food grains domestically, supplementing with imports whenever required, it is also necessary to look at the food grain distribution network. The Public Distribution System (PDS) in the country facilitates the supply of food grains to the poor at a subsidised price.

However, doubts have been raised about the efficacy and cost-effectiveness of the PDS, especially in the light of the growing food subsidy and food stocks. The PDS needs to be restructured and there is a need to explore the possibility of introducing innovative ideas such as smart cards, food credit/debit cards, food stamps and decentralized procurement, to eliminate hunger and make food available to the poor wherever they may be in cost-effective manner.

There are two aspects to the paradox of overflowing godowns and vulnerable sections of society not consuming adequate food. One is the issue of having enough purchasing power or income to buy food and the other is the access to food in terms of physical availability of food. Though the overall employment generation is closely connected to efficient economic growth, there are some issues that must be kept in mind. In remote, inaccessible and backward regions both job opportunities and access to food may be constrained. In such situations, food-for-work and related schemes are necessary.

These may need to be supplemented by more innovative schemes like grain banks. Community grain banks can be set up in such areas from where the needy can borrow grain in times of need and repay the grain once the crisis is over. Natural disasters such as earthquakes also create conditions in which the Government must provide emergency assistance and the administration has to be alert to such situations.

Finally, a minimal amount of social security must be provided to those who are old, sick or disabled and cannot take on work even if it is available. Special schemes must ensure that they do not go hungry.

**Food Consumption Patterns**

Dramatic changes in food consumption patterns have taken place in India in the post Green Revolution period. Between 1972-73 and 1993-94, the food basket has become much more diversified, with the share of cereals seeing a dramatic decline of ten percentage points in most regions.

At the all-India level, cereal consumption in the rural areas declined from 15.3 kg per capita per month in 1972-73, to 13.4 kg per capita per month in 1993-94. The corresponding decline in the urban areas was more modest - from 11.3 kg to 10.6 kg over the same period. At the same time, consumption of milk and meat products as well as vegetables and fruits has increased. Such changes are a natural outcome of economic development. This trend towards a more diversified diet is also discernible among the poorest 25 per cent of the population.

Thus although cereals continue to dominate food expenditures, over time their importance has decreased. At the same time, cereals have become cheaper in relation to other food groups. In rural Uttar Pradesh, for example, the per capita monthly consumption of cereals for the lowest quartile income group has declined from 13.6 kg in 1972-73 to 12.3 kg in 1993-94.

During the period, the consumption of coarse cereals declined from 5.0 kg per capita per month in 1972-73 to 0.8 kg per capita per month. This was only partly offset by an increase in the per capita monthly consumption of rice from 2.6 kg to 3.5 kg and that of wheat from 6.1 kg to 8.1 kg.

During the same period, the share of cereals in the total food expenditure among the lowest quartile income group in the state declined from 69 per cent to 49 per cent while that of milk, meat, vegetables and fruits increased from 7 to 12 per cent and that of other food items from 17 to 28 per cent.

Thus the growth of aggregate demand for cereals in the country can be said to have been kept in check due to two factors - slowdown in the pace of population growth and shift in consumer preference towards non-cereals. However, some of the studies on cereal consumption requirements in the country have not taken into consideration the full implications of changing consumer preferences and have led to exaggerated demand projections for cereals.

At the same time, other demand projections which take these changing preferences into account, come out with estimates which match the supply projections, indicating that the requirements of cereals will be adequately met by domestic supplies at least up to 2020. Thus there is no need for undue concern on this front.

### MSP and Food Procurement Policy

The stock of food grains available with the government agencies as on 1 July 2002 was 63.01 million tonnes (mt) - 21.94 mt of rice and 41.07 mt of wheat. This was well above the prescribed buffer stock norms. While the changing demand patterns is one reason for the accumulation of surplus food grains, another factor is the tendency of successive governments to fix minimum support prices (MSP) for paddy and wheat in excess of the levels prescribed by the Commission for Agricultural Costs and Prices (CACP).

While this has given the farmers an incentive to produce more, it has raised the market prices and reduced the demand for cereals. Studies conducted at the National Council of Applied Economic Research, New Delhi, show that fixing of procurement prices at levels higher than the CACP's recommendations has led to the procurement of an additional quantity of 12.8 mt of wheat and 3.4 mt of rice. This points to the need to strictly adhere to the recommendations of the CACP. A realistic MSP will help promote the diversification of cropping patterns.

The system of MSP served the country well in the past three and a half decades but has started encountering certain problems in recent years. This is because the agricultural production scenario has undergone significant changes over the past four years. Many states, including formerly deficit states like Bihar, Assam and Uttar Pradesh, have reported surpluses of several agricultural commodities, especially cereals and this trend is likely to continue in the coming years as well. The average production of food grains, which was 187 mt during the Eighth Plan, is expected to have increased to 205 mt in the Ninth Plan.

Thus, the increase in average total food production is in excess of the total food grains requirements of around 196 mt at the end of the Ninth Plan as worked out on the basis of normative approach. The policy of recommending a relatively higher MSP for wheat and rice as compared to the MSP for other crops served the cause of the country well in the 1980s and 1990s.

It helped exploit the opportunity created by the Green Revolution and led to much higher average productivity of these two crops, compared to the average productivity of pulses or coarse cereals. The higher MSP increased the profitability of these crops and motivated the farmers to divert their areas to these crops from coarse cereals, pulses and even oilseeds, as in the case of Punjab.

This enabled the country to achieve higher output of food grains and achieve surpluses. However, the need to rethink this approach is overdue. There should be a marked incentive for growing pulses and oilseeds by increasing the MSP of these crops. The MSP for oilseeds should not, however, exceed the long-term international price. It should also be noted that attempts to support prices of some oilseeds through public procurement met with limited success despite the huge resources invested in the process.

In this connection, it would be desirable to introduce commodity-specific limits on food procurement operations based on indicators like total production of a commodity during the previous five years. Such limits on total procurement operations during the year should apply to all commodities, including rice and wheat. The

CACP or some other suitable agency could be asked to work out a suitable criterion on which such limits can be based.

### *Food Subsidy and Public Distribution System*

It is now well recognised that the availability of food grains is not a sufficient condition to ensure food security to the poor. It is also necessary that the poor have sufficient means to purchase food. The capacity of the poor to purchase food can be ensured in two ways - by raising the incomes or supplying food grains at subsidised prices.

While employment generation programmes attempt the first solution, the PDS is the mechanism for the second option. With a network of more than 4.62 lakh fair price shops (FPS) distributing commodities worth more than Rs 30,000 crore annually to about 160 million families, the PDS in India is perhaps the largest distribution network of its kind in the world. This huge network can play a more meaningful role only if it ensures the availability of food to the poor households.

*Table 1. Food Subsidy of the Central Government*

| Year | Amount (Rs crore) | % of total Government Expenditure |
|---|---|---|
| 1990-91 | 2450 | 2.33 |
| 1991-92 | 2850 | 2.56 |
| 1992-93 | 2785 | 2.27 |
| 1993-94 | 5537 | 3.9 |
| 1994-95 | 4509 | 2.8 |
| 1995-96 | 4960 | 2.78 |
| 1996-97 | 5166 | 2.46 |
| 1997-98 | 7500 | 3.23 |

| | | |
|---|---|---|
| 1998-99 | 8700 | 3.11 |
| 1999-00 | 9200 | 3.03 |
| 2000-01 | 12125 | 3.61 |
| 2001-02 | 17612 | 4.83 |
| 2002-03 | 21200 | 5.17 |

All is not well with the PDS. The annual food subsidy involved in maintaining the system is huge (Table 1). The food subsidy bill for 2002-3 is budgeted at Rs. 21,200 crore, which works out to 5.2 per cent of total Central Government expenditure. The level of food subsidies as a proportion of total government expenditure has gone up from a level of 2.5 per cent or below in the early 1990s to more than 5 per cent today. The per capita food subsidy expenditure by the government in 2002-3 is estimated at around Rs. 200 or Rs. 17 per head per month.

This, however, does not mean that consumers got Rs. 17 per head per month, for the cost of distributing this subsidy has to be deducted from the subsidy expenditure. The high carrying cost of stocks in excess of the buffer norms pushes up the food subsidy bill and actually amounts to subsidy to the cereals producers/ surplus farmers. The Expenditure Reforms Commission (ERC) has recommended that the cost of holding stocks in excess of the requirement for food security and for PDS could be reflected in the budget as producers' subsidy rather than consumer subsidy.

### *Targeted Public Distribution System*

The PDS in its original form was widely criticised for its failure to serve the below poverty line (BPL) population, its urban bias, negligible coverage in the states with the highest concentration of the rural poor and lack of transparent and accountable arrangements for delivery. Realising this, the government streamlined the system by issuing special cards to BPL families and selling food grains under PDS to them at specially subsidised prices with effect from June 1997.

Under this Targeted Public Distribution System (TPDS), each poor family was entitled to 10 kg of food grains per month at specially subsidised prices. This was expected to benefit about 60 million poor families. The state-wise poverty estimates of the Planning Commission, based on the methodology of the expert group on the estimation of the proportion and number of poor chaired by late Prof. Lakdawala, defined the number of poor in each state. The identification of the poor is done by the states.

The emphasis is on including only the really poor and vulnerable sections of the society such as landless agricultural labourers, marginal farmers, artisans/craftsmen (potters, tappers, weavers, blacksmiths, carpenters etc.) in the rural areas and slum dwellers and daily wagers in the informal sector (porters, rickshaw pullers and hand cart pullers, fruit and flower sellers on the pavements etc.) in the urban areas.

In keeping with the consensus on increasing the allocation of food grains to the BPL category and to better target the food subsidy, the Government increased the allocation to BPL families from 10 kg to 20 kg per month at 50 per cent of economic cost from 1 April 2000. The allocation for above poverty line (APL) families was retained at the same level as June 1997 but the Central Issue Prices (CIP) was fixed at 100 per cent of economic cost from that date so that entire consumer subsidy could be directed towards the BPL population.

The number of BPL families increased with effect from 1 December 2000 because the base was shifted from the population projections of 1995 to the population projections of the Registrar General of India as on 1

March 2000. The change has resulted in increasing the number of BPL families to 65.2 million as against 59.6 million estimated when the TPDS was introduced. The allocation of foodgrains for the BPL category thus increased to 147 lakh tonnes per annum.

In order to reduce the excess foodgrains stocks with the FCI, the Government initiated the following measures under the TPDS from 12 July 2001:

— The BPL allocation of food grains was increased from 20 kg to 25 kg per family per month with effect from July 2001. At Rs. 4.15 per kg for wheat and Rs. 5.65 per kg for rice, the CIP for BPL families is 48 per cent of the economic cost.

— The Government decided to allocate food grains to APL families at the discounted rate of 70 per cent of the economic cost. The CIP of wheat was reduced from Rs. 830 per quintal to Rs. 610 per quintal and the CIP of rice reduced from Rs. 1,130 per quintal to Rs. 830 per quintal.

In addition, 25 kg of food grain was to be provided to the poorest of the poor families under the Antyodaya Anna Yojana at a highly subsidised rate of Rs. 2 per kg for wheat and Rs. 3 per kg for rice. The Public Distribution System (Control) Order 2001 was also promulgated which seeks to plug the loopholes in the PDS and make it more efficient and effective.

On 23 March 2002, the Government reduced the issue price for APL rice and wheat by Rs. 100 per quintal for a period of three months. The scale of issue for APL, BPL and Antyodaya households was also increased to 35 kg per month. Cumulatively, the offtake under TPDS between April 2002 and June 2002 has been 23.54 lakh tonnes for rice and 16.09 lakh tonnes for wheat against 18.46 lakh tonnes and 9.87 lakh tonnes respecitvely for the corresponding period in 2001.

Thus, there is a clear indication that offtake under TPDS has improved at the national level. However, the situation is not uniform across states and there are certain states where conditions need to be improved. For instance, between April 2001 and March 2002, total offtake of rice in Bihar was only 13.8 per cent of total allocation and in the case of wheat this was only 27.9 per cent.

*Restructuring of PDS*

The following points need to be taken into consideration in order to make the implementation of TPDS more effective:

a) Items other than rice and wheat need to be excluded from the purview of TPDS. The main objective of providing food subsidy to the poor is to ensure food security. Since rice and wheat are the basic necessities for the poor, food subsidies must be restricted to these two commodities.

b) Sugar should be kept outside the purview of PDS. It should be decontrolled and the system of levy on sugar discontinued.

c) It is argued that encouraging production of coarse cereals in dry land areas can check environment damage like degradation of soil to some extent. However, there is difficulty in supplying coarse cereals through PDS and bringing them under the cover of food subsidy.

   The average shelf life of coarse grains is limited, making them unsuitable for long-term storage and distribution under PDS. The inclusion of coarse cereals under PDS cannot be taken up as a national level programme since there is no standard variety of coarse grain. However, initiatives on the part of state governments catering to the needs of specific localities are possible.

d) Kerosene oil is also supplied through PDS and is intended for the poor. However, there is large-scale diversion of this commodity and subsidised kerosene is used for adulteration with diesel. The subsidy on kerosene is thus cornered by the non-poor. A study of four states carried out by Indira Gandhi Institute for Development Research (IGIDR), Mumbai shows that there is huge leakage of kerosene meant for PDS.

   It is irrational, therefore, to continue to subsidise kerosene at such high rates and continue its distribution through the PDS. The subsidy on kerosene should be phased out by raising its supply price under PDS while eliminating all domestic central (e.g. Cenvat) and state (e.g. sales tax) taxes on it so as to encourage private supply through petroleum retail outlets and small dealers rather than FPS. Alternately, if kerosene is to be retained under PDS, the extent of subsidy given should be reduced so that there is less incentive for diversion.

e) All further attempts to include more and more commodities under the coverage of food subsidy should be resisted

f) The FPS should be permitted to sell all commodities (other than rice and wheat) at full market prices in order to ensure their economic viability.

g) The coverage of TPDS and food subsidy should be restricted to the BPL population. For the APL population, which has the purchasing power to buy food, the Government needs to only ensure the availability of food grains at a stable price in the market. Stability in food grain prices should be ensured through the maintenance of buffer stock and open market operations of the FCI. Any attempt to revert to the old concept of a universal PDS will be a retrograde step and needs to be resisted. However, in the current situation, where the FCI has huge surplus stocks of foodgrains, it may be necessary to continue supply of cereals under PDS to the APL population at below economic cost as a temporary measure.

h) With the liberalisation of external sector, the operation of the buffer stock can be supplemented by timely exports and imports and this will effectively mean that a smaller buffer stock will be required.

i) Ration cards should not be used by the administration as an identification card for various purposes. That role should be assigned to multi-purpose identity cards.

j) There are several Plan schemes involving distribution of foodgrains which are in the nature of welfare or income transfer schemes. Such schemes could be merged and some sort of convergence achieved.

### *Food Stamps and Food Credit Cards*

In order to contain the level of food subsidy, major reforms are required in the system of marketing of food grains. All restrictions on interstate movement of food grains should be removed once and for all. Second, the system of private trade and marketing of food grains must be strengthened. Third, the idea of having FPS across the length and breadth of the country should be looked into afresh.

It may be more efficient to move towards a new system of providing food subsidy through the normal food supply shops (including the FPS), supplemented by new/additional FPS in remote and inaccessible regions where such shops do not exist. This could be achieved through the introduction of food stamps or the food credit card system. Under the system of food stamps, the State Governments could issue a subsidy entitlement card (SEC) instead of issuing ration cards. The SEC should show, among other things, the number of members in a poor family and their age and indicate their entitlement level for food stamps.

There could, in principle, be different levels of entitlement based on age. All adult members from a poor family, for example, could be entitled to 'a' number of food stamps per month while the entitlement for a child could be 'b' number of food stamps. There could also be a higher subsidy entitlement for old and infirm people. The SEC will indicate the total number of food stamps a family is entitled to every month.

Each family would collect its monthly quota of food stamps from prescribed distribution centres on showing their SEC. They could then use these food stamps at any food supply shop to buy food grains (rice and wheat) at a price (Rs x) below the market price. The retailer will then be reimbursed by the State Government.

There is less scope for corruption under a system of food stamps. Under the existing system, FPS owners declare on paper that they have sold a certain quantity of food to the poor at subsidised prices when, in fact, they have made huge profits by selling the food at market prices. There is less possibility of such diversion of food supplies under the system of food stamps. The retailer can claim food subsidy only if he acquires food stamps by selling food to the poor at subsidised prices. Under this system, it could be made mandatory for retail traders to display the selling price of foodgrains prominently in their shops.

Two potential problems with the system of food stamps need to be kept in mind while designing the system. There is a distinct possibility of food stamps being counterfeited. Secondly, reimbursement of subsidy to the participating retailers can run into logistical problems. These problems are, however, minuscule compared to the problem of physically procuring, storing, transporting and delivering foodgrains to FPS across the country by the FCI and the state food corporations/ agencies.

The food stamp system can be introduced in phases. Initially food stamps can be allowed to be redeemed only at the FPS currently used by the consumer. This will allow food stamps to be printed with the identification number of the FPS so that the totals can be matched and cross-checked later, thus reducing the scope for counterfeiting. This could be followed by the consumer designating any participating retailer and having the identification number of that shop printed on the food stamp.

Normally consumers purchase their daily food provisions from the most convenient shop or, in very rare cases, two shops. As the problem of reimbursing money is a fraction of the problem of delivering food, it should not be too difficult to set up a re-imbursement system, perhaps by sub-contracting the task to a financial service provider. To reduce malpractices, there is an opinion that the food stamps should be issued to female members of the family who can be designated as heads of households for the purpose. The system should be introduced cautiously on an experimental basis in areas where a proper market infrastructure exists. The conventional FPS system may have to be continued in remote and inaccessible areas.

A food coupon system for distribution of rice and kerosene through PDS was introduced in Andhra Pradesh in 1998-99. Informal trading of food stamps can also convert the food subsidy into an income subsidy. The use of smart cards in the form of a food credit/ debit card can remove these problems. The card can have in-built security features that make it difficult, if not impossible, to trade.

A food credit card system could be a superior alternative to the prevalent system of FPS and perhaps even a food stamp system. The customers could use food credit/debit cards to buy subsidised food grains from the market and the retailers can claim the subsidy from the Government. Though the initial cost of issuing a food credit card and setting up a leakage-proof system are likely to be higher than for the existing ration card, the running costs of the system may be lower as the credit/ debit card can be used in existing retail shops that accept such cards.

Besides, the cost would also be compensated by the elimination of leakage at all stages of the current food procurement, storage and distribution system (including the FCI). To minimise the cost, existing credit card companies could be persuaded to set up and run the food credit/debit card system at a cost, in return for advertisement rights to this social service. Specialised credit card companies can also ensure that the food retailers are reimbursed on time, thus giving them an incentive to sell food to the poor.

The food debit/credit card can also have the in-built flexibility of changing over from a food subsidy to an income transfer system if there is a subsequent change in the policy. The card can also be made applicable to all cereals including coarse grains. If desired, a different subsidy rate can be specified for different cereals. As coarse cereals are consumed mainly by the poor, the smart card will allow some self-selecting/self-targeting features to be built into the system.

The food debit/card card could also be integrated with a food-for-work programme without incurring the additional administrative and logistic costs of transporting food to each area where there is need to provide work. Payment for the work would be done by adding the food grain to the food credit of the worker. Once this system is set up, it can also be used to provide social security to the old, infirm, disabled and handicapped citizens. This could be done by programming a higher subsidy proportion for such groups. However, in the rural areas the smart card system may have to be preceded by a food stamp system.

### *Decentralisation of Operations*

One possibility that could be considered is that based on the net consumer subsidy spent on providing food through the PDS, the Central budget should make a provision for a national food subsidy. This subsidy can be distributed among the states according to a prescribed formula based on the latest available data and updated poverty ratios. It would then be left to individual State Governments to determine the quantum of food subsidy based on the contribution they get from the Centre and their own contribution.

The Centre could also agree to enhance the quantum of its contribution to compensate for any increase in prices. The new system will also result in a more equitable distribution of the benefits of food subsidy among different states. However, it needs to be ensured that the food subsidy distributed by the Centre is utilised for the purpose for which it is meant and not diverted for other purposes.

The operation of the PDS should be the responsibility of the State Governments. If a State Government feels that its administrative and managerial resources are inadequate to the task, it can sub-contract this job to other State agencies or the private sector. The role of the Centre should be limited to the allocation of food subsidy to the states and the maintenance of buffer stock through the FCI. Procurement, storage and distribution of food grains should be the joint responsibility of the central and state governments.

The scheme of decentralised procurement, which is in operation, should be promoted and more states should be encouraged to adopt this scheme. The issue of food stamps will be the responsibility of the state governments. The subsidy in each food stamp could be decided by them based on the resources available. The state's own resources could supplement the subsidy provided by the Centre.

As long as the Centre fixes the issue price, changes should be made every time there is a revision in the procurement price of food grains. This will drive home the message to the public that the issue price is being raised because of an increase in the cost of production. There will, then, be less resistance to increase in the issue price. One reason for the burgeoning food subsidy bill is the non-neutralisation of the increase in MSP by a corresponding increase in issue prices.

However, any attempt to increase the issue price following an increase in MSP has the undesirable effect of reducing the offtake, leading to further accumulation of excess stocks. There is a suggestion that the task of fixing the issue price of foodgrains, deciding the quantum of food subsidy per food stamp, amount of food grains to be supplied to beneficiaries etc. may be left to the discretion of state governments, whose decision will be based on their individual capacities. The implications of this suggestion need further examination.

### *Buffer Stocks and FCI*

The high level of market prices of wheat now prevailing in India are primarily due to the rise in procurement prices over the past three years and taxes and charges on cereals imposed by state governments. The difference between the economic cost of FCI and the market price also contributes to the higher price. Notwithstanding the criticisms against FCI, it has to be admitted that it does play an important role in the country's food economy. The contribution of the FCI would be enhanced if there were greater competition in food trade from other public, co-operative and private organisations.

While the provision of food subsidy is an important element of the food security system in India, the food procurement and buffer stock operations play an equally important role. Since agricultural production tends to fluctuate due to climatic factors, it is necessary to maintain an adequate level of buffer stock to ensure stability in food grain prices. Based on a study done by Dr Kirit Parikh of the IGIDR, the ERC has recommended that a food security buffer stock of 10 mt - 4 mt of wheat and 6 mt of rice - would be adequate.

The present levels of buffer stocks in the country are far in excess of requirements and create more economic instability than stability. The FCI can maintain a minimum level of buffer stock and then undertake open market operations within a prescribed price band. It can release stocks in the open market when there are shortages and prices increase. It can also purchase food grains from the open market when there is excess supply and prices are depressed.

However, its objective should not be to procure all that is offered by the farmers but only to maintain an optimum level of buffer stock. Recognising the fact that a high level of buffer stock can itself contribute to inflationary pressures, the FCI can be instructed to limit its role to more manageable and optimum levels in the future. Presently, the level of food credit is more than Rs. 40,000 crore.

Large food credit will have significant macro economic implications since it has a significant impact on money supply. The FCI could also play a role in the international market for food grains by importing when stocks are low and exporting food grains when there are surplus stocks. The private sector and the farmers must also be allowed a role in the export of food grains, by removing all restrictions on the export of wheat and rice. In fact, there should be no restriction on the export of any agricultural commodity.

The lifting of quantitative restrictions on the import of wheat and rice has been accompanied by import duties that are well above the general 'peak' rate of duty of 35 per cent. The relationship between these duties and the 'peak' rate can be defined in the context of the continuing custom duty reform. The FCI will continue to play a vital role in the maintenance of the buffer stock to insulate the food economy from fluctuations in food grains production.

However, its monopoly in food procurement must be ended by allowing State procurement agencies to be set up in all states. Restrictions on private trade must be lifted so that competitive forces can have a free play, thus reducing intermediation costs. Curbs on the entry of modern food procurement, transport, processing and distribution companies must also be removed, so that the agriculture sector can benefit from modern management practices like silo storage, logistics and large-scale processing.

This will benefit both farmers and consumers. It has also to be noted that when procurement prices for food grains are fixed, these should not be pegged at such a high level that it leads to accumulation of surplus stocks in FCI godowns. In this connection, there is a need to strictly adhere to the recommendations of the CACP and not resort to fixation of procurement prices much in excess of the estimated costs of production.

The high market prices of wheat now prevailing in India are due to primarily the rise in the procurement prices over the past three years or so and taxes and charges on cereals imposed by State Governments. The difference between the economic cost of FCI and the market price also contributes to the higher price.

A study by the Indian Statistical Institute researchers using NSS data for 1993-4 along with other data for Andhra Pradesh and Maharashtra estimated both the extent of leakage as well as the economic inefficiency of the public food procurement system relative to the open market. The study shows that only 56 per cent to 58.5 per cent of the total food subsidy (i.e. Centre and State) reaches the PDS consumers.

A major part of the subsidy is lost in the process of administering it. While leakages (grains shown as issued by the PDS system minus grains actually received by households from PDS) can range from 15 per cent to 28 per cent of the subsidy, another 16 per cent to 26.5 per cent of the subsidy is eaten up by the inefficiency of the Government procurement and distribution system (FCI plus State level) relative to the market.

The contribution of FCI would be enhanced if there were greater competition in food trade from other public, co-operative and private organisations. Most of FCI's storage godowns are small-scale, lowquality structures. Sometimes, grains are also stored in the open (known as covered and plinth storage-CAP) leading to heavy storage losses. The quality of the FCI's food stocks is also questionable.

As noted in the approach paper to the Tenth Plan, a June 2000 research report found that half of FCI's grain stocks is at least two years' old, 30 per cent between two and four years old, and some grain as old as 16 years1 Immediate disposal of all the stocks that are more than three years old should be undertaken. A credible physical audit of the FCI stocks is necessary.

The main objective of the food procurement policy should be the stabilisation of food prices rather than subsidising producers. Currently, even though food subsidies are provided to the BPL population, the PDS meets only a limited part of their food requirements. They depend on private traders to meet the rest of their requirements. This makes the objective of stabilisation of foodgrain prices even more important. Such stabilisation has to be achieved by appropriate buffer stock operations and market interventions by the FCI.

### *Private Trade in Foodgrains*

The FCI should gradually hand over its role of MSP-related procurement to private trade. This requires a comprehensive reform of policies, rules and procedures to strengthen the role of the modern private sector in the matter of storage, distribution and processing of foodgrains. Various restrictions that inhibit private initiatives in this regard need to be removed so that the private sector has an incentive to make huge investment in grain handling operations and food processing.

There is urgent need to upgrade market infrastructure, cold storage facilities, mandi facilities and roads, areas in which the private sector should be encouraged to make productive investment. While the National Policy on Handling, Storage and Transportation of Food Grains 2000 is timely, its success is largely dependent upon highly regulated and controlled sectors of the economy.

Under the policy, integrated bulk handling facilities with silos of large capacity for wheat along with testing facilities for quality control would be created for the storage of foodgrains procured by the FCI at about 20 locations in producing and consuming areas as well as a few port towns.

These facilities, including the infrastructure for bulk transportation to these centres, will be created and maintained by the private sector under the overall supervision of the FCI. Private sector participation in this sector will be encouraged through measures such as Build-Own-Operate-Transfer (BOOT), Build-Own-Lease-Transfer (BOLT), Build-Own-Operate (BOO), Lease-Develop-Operate (LDO), joint ventures etc. It is proposed to provide several fiscal incentives to make the scheme a success.

However, the success of the proposed public-private partnerships will be limited unless the existing controls on storage and movement of foodgrains and other essential commodities is suitably relaxed. Many of these controls have outlived their utility since the country has achieved self-sufficiency in food and their continuance hampers the market from performing its productive and commercial role. There is an urgent need to withdraw them, and legislative and administrative measures to ensure this need to be accorded top priority.

The Essential Commodities Act, 1955 is one legislation that is the source of stifling controls. A large number of permits and licences are required to be obtained from the authorities under the Act, periodic returns have to be submitted and regular inspections are carried out, all of which add to transaction costs. Some notifications under the Act restrict the movement of goods from the surplus states to deficit states.

These controls and restrictions, and the constant threat of arrest in case of violations, discourage private companies from producing and distributing essential commodities, thus denying the food sector the benefits of economies of scale and modernisation. In order to facilitate the free trade and movement of foodgrains, the Government issued a Control Order tilted, 'Removal of (Licensing Requirements, Stock Limits and Movement Restrictions) on Specified Foodstuffs Order, 2002' on 15 February 2002.

The Order allows any dealer to freely buy, stock, sell, transport, distribute, dispose, acquire, use or consume any quantity of wheat, paddy/rice, coarse grains, sugar, edible oilseeds and edible oils, without a licence or permit. State governments would require the Centre's prior permission before issuing any order for regulating, by licences or permits, the storage, transport and distribution of the specified commodities.

According to the Expenditure Reforms Commission, the induction of the private sector in procurement operations will indirectly lead to a reduction in the cost of procurement to FCI. The report points out that even though the MSP for wheat in 1999-00 was only Rs. 550 per quintal, the costs by way of statutory and non-statutory charges paid to agencies in Punjab and Haryana totalled up to an additional Rs. 60 per quintal. Of these, mandi charges were Rs. 28.46 per quintal and the purchase tax was Rs. 17.12 per quintal.

Some of these charges are in the nature of economic costs and unavoidable like mandi labour costs, local transport costs, forwarding charges etc. However, the remaining items clearly reflect an attempt by the State Government and various other agencies involved in the process to maximise the returns to themselves on these transactions. The following combination of policy reforms can benefit both farmers and food consumers:

— Single Market

— Amend the Essential Commodities Act to make it0 an emergency provision that will have to be formally invoked by a notification for a limited period.

— Enact a Central Act to ban controls on movement within and between States.

— Abolish octroi and all sorts of taxes/levies on food articles.

— Competitive Grain Procurement

— Phase out all forms of monopoly purchase.

— State Food Corporations should be allowed and encouraged to operate in all States.

— The role of private agencies in food procurement activities should be gradually enhanced.

— De-Licensing

— Remove licensing controls and de-reserve all agro-based and food-processing industries in a time-bound manner.

— Phase out controls on sugar and its byproducts and also remove sugar from the PDS.

— Remove the present restrictions on establishing new milk processing capacity under the Milk and Milk Products Order, (MMPO).

— De-reserve roller flour mills.

— Remove rapeseed and groundnut processing units from the small-scale industries (SSI) list.

— De-reserve all pesticides and fungicides.

— De-license and de-control fertiliser production.

— Export De-control

— Announce a policy renouncing the use of export restrictions on agricultural commodities. Domestic shortages should be met by imports, not by imposing export controls.

— Remove all restrictions (e.g. canalisation) on the export of agro-products.

— Lift the ban on futures trading and stocking of all agricultural commodities, and on institutional credit and finance for such activities.

— Amend the Agricultural Produce Marketing Acts of states to allow direct purchase of grain and other produce from farmers by agro-produce trading, storage and processing companies.

— Support and promote provision of all types of insurance (health and hospitalisation, crop and weather) to farmers and other rural inhabitants.

— Give income tax incentives to insurance companies for a specified promotional period (five years).

— Allow 100 per cent foreign direct investment (FDI) in insurance for agriculture and rural areas.

— Modernise the information and extension system for farmers.

— Overhaul the agricultural research and development system so as to replace the bureaucratic financial/ administrative system with a modern system of professional management and accountability under the Societies Act and provide for academic autonomy and peer review.

— Remove all central and state taxes on production and marketing of cereals and other food products.

— Allow 26 per cent FDI in food retailing. Food retailers would also be free to sell other agrobased and rural industrial products.

These reforms will set the stage for largescale entry of the private sector into agricultural procurement. While these reforms are being introduced in a phased manner, the following steps can be considered to start the process of replacing the FCI operations by private trade:

— Public-private partnerships in setting up modern food procurement, handling, storage and transport systems.

— The Government should operate a market intervention scheme with the support of private trade - purchasing from the farmers when prices are low and offloading in the market when prices are high.

— The number of commodities covered under the procurement scheme should be reduced till finally the scheme is restricted to only rice and wheat. The procurement policy must not be extended to cover more and more commodities.

State governments should be asked to immediately do away with all taxes on foodgrains. This is an unnecessary addition to the price of the essential food items, which, in turn, adds to the burden of subsidy. This should be accompanied by ending the compulsory routing of agro-commodities through regulated grain markets/mandis . Farmers must be allowed to borrow working capital from the banks against hypothecation of their stocks, a step that is long overdue. All banks and financial institutions must be instructed to grant this facility. The same facility must be provided to traders as well.

### *PDS Plan Schemes*

While the provision for food subsidy is made in the non-Plan budget of the Central Government, the Planning Commission provides funds under its Plan programmes for the following schemes to strengthen the operational machinery of the PDS: construction of Godowns; purchase of mobile vans/trucks; and training, research and monitoring. The godowns scheme was intended to assist State Governments and Union Territories in the construction of small godowns of up to 2,000-tonnes capacity.

*Table 2. PDS Plan schemes (Rs crore)*

| Scheme | 1999-00 Actual | 2000-01 Actual | 2001-02 (R.E) |
|---|---|---|---|
| 1. Construction of Godowns | .22.29 | 8 | 11.5 |
| 2. Purchase of Vans/Trucks | 1.06 | 0.23 | 0.3 |
| 3. Training, Research and Monitoring | 0.36 | 0.16 | 0.5 |
| *TOTAL* | *23.71* | *8.39* | *12.3* |

The mobile vans scheme provided financial assistance for the purchase of mobile vans/trucks for distributing essential commodities in rural/hilly/remote and other disadvantaged areas where it is not feasible or viable to set up regular FPS. The training scheme aims at strengthening and upgrading the skills of personnel managing the PDS and to improve the management of supplies.

The efforts of the State Governments/Union Territory administrations and Civil Supplies Corporations etc. are supplemented by providing financial assistance for organising training programmes on PDS. Evaluation studies and research studies on various aspects of PDS are also sponsored under the scheme. The Plan outlay and expenditure under the schemes are shown in Table 2.

According to a report of the Comptroller and Auditor General (CAG) between 1983 and 1999, the Government of India released Rs. 58.73 crore and Rs. 62.96 crore for the construction of godowns and purchase of mobile vans respectively. However, the response of State Governments was lukewarm, at best. A large number of godowns for which the Central Government provided funds were not constructed and many were not put to the intended use.

Many state governments did not purchase mobile vans. A large number of vans were out of order or used for purposes other than the doorstep delivery of foodgrains. A decision has, therefore, been taken to abolish the schemes for construction of godowns and purchase of vans during the Tenth Plan. The funds under the training, research and monitoring scheme need to be diverted towards sponsoring studies on the operation and viability of the food security system.

A pilot project for the introduction of smart cards in the PDS is proposed to be taken up for implementation during the Tenth Plan. The schemewise break up of Tenth Plan outlay of Department of Food and Public Distribution is given in the Appendix.

### *Grain Bank Scheme*

As a part of the Government's efforts to prevent deaths of children in remote and backward tribal areas due to malnutrition, a Village Grain Banks scheme was launched in 1996-97. A onetime grant is provided by the Ministry of Tribal Affairs towards the purchase of grains, at the rate of one quintal per family, storage facilities for the grains and purchase of weights and scales. The funds are provided through TRIFED, which acts as the canalising agency.

The bank is managed by the village committee, which is elected by the beneficiaries themselves who are also members of the bank. They can borrow grains from the grain banks during times of scarcity. A grain bank scheme is also being run under the aegis of the Department of Rural Development in the Jhabua district of Madhya Pradesh. The scheme was launched in 1995 on a pilot basis in 18 villages.

The performance of the scheme in the last two years encouraged DRDA to adopt the strategy in all villages under the Integrated Watershed Development Programme. Presently, there are 184 grain banks functioning in watershed areas and these are managed by the community itself. In the last season, 12,363 families took loans from the grain bank. The Madhya Pradesh government has proposed the evolution of community-based support systems to substitute/supplement PDS operations in areas where PDS does not exist.

Self-help groups of BPL families will be formed and charged a membership fee of Rs. 50. These groups will be eligible to receive supplies of foodgrains and other infrastructure-based assistance from the government. They will organise activities, under the grain bank scheme, to develop degraded lands on the periphery of forests with significant Adivasi population through food for work programmes.

The grain banks will be managed by committees of women beneficiaries to be called anaj samitis. The government will give a one-time supply of 100 kg of wheat or rice to each grain bank. The grain will be stored by the traditional method in earthen kothas constructed with local material and free family labour. Grain banks can be set up in remote and isolated areas beyond the reach of PDS and in regions where there is inadequate employment generation such as in tribal and forest areas.

In order to be successful, the grain bank scheme has to be combined with a food for work programme, so as to ensure generation of income, which is necessary in order to ensure repayment of borrowed grain by the beneficiaries. A grain bank scheme should function with minimum interference on the part of the government. It should be run under the supervision of self-help groups headed by women.

The moment beneficiaries realise that grain under the scheme is being supplied by the government, there will be a tendency not to repay. However, the government may provide the initial supply of grain and the storage capacity may be created under the food for work programmes. The scheme may work well during times of surplus. Besides, a system of food distribution running parallel with the current PDS could result in lack of accountability on the part of both. In the longrun, therefore, there should be only one system.

Despite the huge stock of food grains available in FCI godowns, stray cases of hunger deaths are still being reported. The food distribution system, therefore, needs to be reformed and made more efficient. The present system could be replaced by a system of food stamps and eventually by a food credit card system. The excess stocks of food grains that have accumulated with the Government is partly a result of the high MSP which often exceeded the levels recommended by the CACP. There is, therefore, a need to adhere to the recommendations of the CACP in this regard.

The MSP should encourage diversification of agricultural production. Surveys by the National Sample Survey Organisation (NSSO) show that consumers today prefer to consume less of cereals and more of fruits, vegetables and animal products than before. This changing food consumption pattern may also have contributed to the accumulation of surplus food grain stocks.

Studies show that a buffer stock of 10 mt is adequate to meet food security needs. The FCI could intervene in the market by timely sales and purchases to maintain stability in food grain prices. The buffer stocking agency could also take resort to exports and imports of food grains as per requirements. The scheme for decentralised procurement of food grains should be encouraged and more states could be brought under its fold. Similarly, the operation of the PDS could be decentralised with the states taking their own decisions regarding issue prices, quantum of food grains to be supplied etc.

The national food subsidy could be distributed among the states according to a prescribed formula. The private sector should play an enhanced role in the food distribution system. The Essential Commodities Act should be amended to make it an emergency provision that will have to be formally invoked by notification for a limited period for specific commodities. All restrictions on inter-state movement of food grains should be removed. Octroi and all sorts of taxes/levies on food articles should be eliminated.

The ban on futures trading in all agricultural commodities should be lifted. Twenty-six per cent FDI should be allowed in food retailing along with 100 per cent FDI in insurance for agriculture and rural areas. These and other policy recommendations outlined in the chapter would make the food distribution system in the country more vibrant and efficient and capable of meeting the requirements of a liberalised economy.

# 9

# Tourism

As observed in the Planning Commission Report of the National Committee on Tourism (1988), the public sector made a significant contribution to the growth of tourism in the initial stages of planned development by providing a reasonable infrastructure base. During the Ninth Plan it was recognised that a reappraisal of the role of the State in tourism development and the extent of its participation was needed as it is neither necessary nor feasible for the State to make large investments in areas that are best left to the initiative of the private sector.

The state can contribute through infrastructure development, the planning of broad development strategies, the provision of fiscal and monetary incentives to catalyse private sector investment and devise an effective regulatory and supervisory mechanism to protect the interests of the industry and the consumer. The acceptance of this view also led to the commencement of the process of disinvestment in 18 hotels of the India Tourism Development Corporation (ITDC) hotels.

The travel and tourism sector creates more jobs per million rupees of investment than any other sector of the economy and is capable of providing employment to a wide spectrum of job seekers from the unskilled to the specialised, even in the remote parts of the country.

The initiatives taken by the state so far have not yielded the desired result and India's tourism performance has failed to match its potential even as countries not blessed with its natural and cultural endowments have taken the lead in reaping the benefits of tourism development for their people. The reasons for this poor performance need to be speedily addressed to enable tourism to make an appropriate contribution to national development.

The Tenth Plan approach towards tourism signifies a distinct shift from the approach adopted in earlier Plans. Apart from acknowledging the wellaccepted advantages of developing tourism for the promotion of national integration, international understanding and earning foreign exchange, the Tenth Plan recognises the vast employment generating potential of tourism and the role it can play in furthering the socio-economic objectives of the Plan. In order to create a supportive environment for the promotion of tourism, the New Tourism Policy, 2002, that is to be implemented during the Tenth Plan, will generate awareness about the benefits of tourism for the host population.

It will mobilise state governments to use tourism as a means for achieving their socio-economic objectives, encourage the private sector to enhance investment in tourism and provide legislative and regulatory support for sustainable tourism and to protect the interests of the industry and the consumer. The policy envisages involving the rural sector in the promotion of rural, heritage, adventure and eco-tourism and will promote the development of competitive high quality products and destinations.

Most importantly, it will remove the barriers to growth and resolve contradictions in policy to achieve inter-sectoral convergence of activities that help the growth of tourism. The ITDC will have to redefine its role in the Tenth Plan. The State can also play an effective role in ensuring that tourism development does not harm the environment. The interaction between tourism and environmental pollution requires sensitive handling. There is complementarity, not conflict, between the high quality environmental requirements of tourism and the imperatives of maintaining the ecological balance.

## Global Status and Trends

Although global recession and the September 11, 2001, events are estimated to have resulted in a temporary decline in travel and tourism demand in 2001-02, international and domestic tourism is expected to boom over the next two decades. The World Travel and Tourism Council (WTTC) estimates a 4.5 per cent per annum increase in the total amount of travel and tourism economic activity between 2002 and 2012.

This is largely attributed to a rise in global wealth, liberalisation of international airspace, cheaper flights and the use of the Internet as a travel tool. The earnings from tourism have made it one of the world's largest industries and the fastest growing sectors of global trade accounting for 10.7 per cent of global gross domestic product (GDP), 12.8 percent of global exports, 8.2 per cent of global employment (or one in every 12.2 jobs), and 9.4 per cent of global capital investment.

Tourism in the least developed countries is growing faster than the world average, holding the promise of prosperity for many. International tourist arrivals worldwide reached 698 million in 2000, generating $ 595 billion revenues. International tourism flows are expected to reach 1.5 billion by 2020 and revenue estimated to cross $ 2000 billion. Today, only 3.5 per cent of the world population travels internationally but the number of Asian, particularly Chinese, tourists is predicted to grow enormously as the region becomes more integrated with the global economy.

The scale of world domestic tourism, on the other hand, exceeds world international tourism by a ratio of 10:1. In India, for every interna-tional tourist, there are 80 domestic tourists. Domestic tourism can form the basis of a viable and sustainable tourism industry in India.

### *Global Market Trends*

Consumer trends in tourism are gradually changing and require an appropriate response in terms of both policy formulation and investment. Current market trends indicate that:

— Long haul travel will grow faster than intra-regional travel. A growth of 24 per cent is expected by 2020.

— People with less time for leisure are likely to take more frequent but shorter trips nearer home, opening up opportunities for 'neighbouring country' tourism.

— The experienced traveller wants authentic, off-the-beaten-track vacations in remote and less well-known places as against luxurious five-star vacations, leading to an interest in rural and ethnic tourism.

— The increase in the number of people with lots of money but little leisure time has resulted in a growing emphasis on rest and relaxation, and 'wellness' and 'health' holidays.

— The elderly population in key tourismgenerating markets has shown a

— There is notable and increasing interest in spiritualism.

— The demand for eco-tourism and naturebased holidays is expected to double and even triple in the next 20 years.

— Sports and adventure holidays continue to be popular with the young.

The interest in cultural tourism, spiritualism, 'wellness' holidays, eco-tourism and rural tourism would tend to favour India, provided the country can avail of the opportunities offered to maximise its natural advantages in these areas. The development of new tourism products and destinations during the Tenth Plan must be based on market research and demand, keeping the source markets and the age groups of the tourists in mind. At the same time, the Government must develop new source markets nearer home and make India a safer destination for women tourists and family holidays.

### India's Place In World Tourism

The World Tourism Organisation forecast indicates an increasing tourism preference towards East Asia, the Pacific, West Asia and South Asia, although Europe and America still remain the world's foremost tourism destinations commanding 77 per cent of the global market. East Asia/Pacific achieved the highest rate of growth of 14.5 per cent in tourism and travel in 2000 followed by West Asia and South Asia.

With this gradual shift in focus, the outlook for the growth of tourism in the region is promising. In Asia, China has emerged as a leading tourist destination and is poised to become the world's top tourist destination by 2020. The WTTC has identified India as one of the world's foremost tourist growth centres in the coming decade. After Turkey, India is expected to achieve the fastest rate of growth of the total amount of economic activity likely to be generated by travel and tourism, at 9.7 per cent over the next 10 years.

Also, the largest employment creation after China is expected to take place in India over the same period. The growth in 'visitor exports' or spending by international tourists, is likely to be the fastest in India at 14.3 per cent per annum over the next decade. On the whole, the WTTC forecast for India is promising, subject to key policy issues that affect the growth of the sector being addressed.

If India is to realise its enormous potential in tourism it must provide exclusive world-class tourism products and destinations to compete successfully for a larger share of the Asian tourism market. Today, outbound tourism from India far exceeds visitor traffic to the country partly because there is a lack of world-class destinations within the country and partly because the domestic tourism policy has been largely directed towards those in the lower end of the spending spectrum. The high spender from India prefers to visit neighbouring countries as he gets better value for money.

The scope and reach of domestic tourism will have to be broadened in the Tenth Plan through the development of competitive destinations that match international standards in terms of price and quality and also satisfy the international traveller. India's international arrival figures have not been able to keep pace with neighbouring countries and have been exceeded by Thailand, Malaysia, Indonesia, Dubai and the Maldives. Since 1995, India's share of the world market has remained virtually stagnant at 0.38 per cent, while domestic tourism has grown at a phenomenal rate and India now accounts for 4.6 per cent share of domestic tourism worldwide.

In terms of tourism receipts, India has shown relative buoyancy because of the interest shown by visitors in traditional handicraft items and particularly in diamonds. The Tenth Plan visualises a mutually supportive role for tourism and handicrafts by encouraging haats and shilpgrams and recognising shopping as an integral part of the tourism experience to promote the 'Made in India' brand.

India receives the largest number of overseas tourists from the United Kingdom, which is its largest source market, followed by the United States, Sri Lanka, France, Germany, Canada, Japan, Australia and Singapore. Of the tourists coming to India, 27.5 per cent are in the age group of 35-44 years, 23.4 per cent in the age group of 25-35 years and 20.8 per cent in the age group of 45-54 years.

Women constitute only 30.5 per cent of India's total international arrivals. Repeat visitors account for 44.9 per cent of the overseas visitors. A substantial number of these may be non-resident Indians, as hotel reservations do not correspond to the number of international arrivals in the country. The average length of stay of foreign tourists in the country in 1998 was 31.2 days. Domestic tourism, on the other hand, is largely pilgrimage-oriented and requires improvement in travel facilities and pilgrim destinations.

Tourism in India has tended to be regarded as an elitist activity conducted primarily for the purpose of earning foreign exchange. Its vast potential as an engine of growth and employment generater has remained largely untapped. Although, with 25 million jobs, India ranks second in terms of number of persons employed in travel and tourism, yet the contribution of the sector as a percentage share of all employment is amongst the lowest in the world. The Tenth Plan objective is to integrate tourism with the socio-economic objectives of the Plan by creating 3.6 million jobs a year through the promotion of domestic and international tourism and to enhance India's share of international arrivals from 0.38 per cent to at least 0.62 per cent by 2007.

Being the nodal agency for the development of tourism in the country, the department of tourism needs to make greater efforts to co-ordinate and integrate the policies of central ministries that have an impact on the development of tourism and to mobilise state governments and the private sector to develop unique and competitive tourism products and destinations. Crucial decisions affecting tourism are taken by other ministries viz. the Ministries of Finance, Home, Civil Aviation, Surface Transport, Environment and Forests, Urban Development, Rural Development, Ocean Develop-ment etc.

The Department of Tourism has tended to concentrate largely on its role as the promoter of international tourism and generator of foreign exchange earnings while paying relatively less attention to inter-sectoral policy co-ordination and the all-important development of tourism infrastructure and product quality. In the Tenth Plan, the Department will redefine and expand its role and work towards intersectoral convergence and policy integration to remove the barriers to the growth of tourism.

There are several factors that are respon-sible for the inadequate growth of the tourism sector in India. These are: barriers related to approach, barriers that discourage private investment, factors that affect competitiveness and factors that affect the long-term sustainability of tourism. The effective and early removal of these barriers during the Tenth Plan is an essential determinant for the success of the New Tourism Policy.

The need for a national consensus on the role and level of tourism deve-lopment in the country has been voiced repeatedly but a concerted effort to achieve a consensus has not been made. Tourism should not be limited by state or regional boundaries if distortions in policies are to be avoided. It is important that a consensus among all states is evolved through the

National Development Council (NDC) and the barriers to the growth of tourism removed.

Tourism has been denied the priority it deserves over successive Plan periods because its potential as an engine of economic growth has not been appreciated. This is visible in the low allocation of resources. Allocation to tourism has averaged 0.16 per cent of the total Plan outlay from the Third Plan to the Ninth Plan. In the Tenth Plan, it is likely to receive an allocation of 0.72 per cent. According to the WTTC, India is one of the lowest spenders on tourism - 153rd out of 160 countries - while its neighbouring competitors and China invest far more: Malaysia (5.1 per cent), Nepal (5 per cent), Indonesia (8.4 per cent), Maldives (15.7 per cent), China (3.8 per cent).

The growing domestic and international demand, which is set to boom, reinforces the need for higher investment. Failure to measure up to additional investment demand for domestic tourism is likely to lead to the over-exploitation of existing facilities, discouraging foreign visitors while leading to an increase in the outflow of high-spending domestic tourists from the country.

Most State Governments give scant importance to tourism even though they virtually control the tourism product located within their boundaries. They are responsible, inter alia, for local infrastructure, transport systems, sanitation and hygiene, leisure and recreation, law and order, the upkeep of local monuments and the general well-being of the tourist. Their support and participation is essential for tourism to succeed and spread its benefits among the host population.

Their lack of interest has resulted in an unprofessional ad hoc approach that acts as a deterrent to the growth of tourism. The approach of the state governments needs to be focused, highly professional and result-oriented if India is to avail of the opportunity that the currently favourable market trends have to offer. Apart from the State Governments, the private sector plays a vital role in the growth and development of tourism. Although the Central Government and certain state governments have, from time to time, announced incentives to involve the private sector in tourism development, the results achieved have fallen short of expectations.

To provide a conducive environment for private sector investment, it is important to realise that the travel and tourism sector is adversely affected by the lack of synergy in inter-sectoral policies. The growth of the sector requires well-integrated and co-ordinated policies and stability in approach. Contradictions and arbitrary changes in policy send confused signals to the investor. Unless infirmities in policy are expeditiously removed well before the end of the Tenth Plan period, the New Tourism Policy is unlikely to succeed.

Being a long haul destination, India is more conveniently accessible by air and cannot be easily reached by rail or road. A restrictive air transport policy has a very deleterious effect on tourist traffic. There are insufficient connections to most tourism destinations. The situation could be eased if the large number of regional airports could open up as international airports. The existing international and national airports also require improvement. The price of aviation turbine fuel needs to be lowered to make air transport competitive and affordable. Today, it is cheaper to travel by air to neighbouring countries from India than to travel to certain parts of India itself.

A more liberal aviation bilaterals regime and a new aviation policy to benefit the economy of the country as a whole rather than the national carriers alone would greatly aid the development of tourism. Central and state governments need to evolve a taxation regime, which is revenue generating without being burdensome. Accommodation and transport taxes tend to be very heavy in certain states while the excise policy in others is extremely harsh. The land policy in some states makes the setting up of a hotel a formidable exercise and as many as 48 clearances are required for the construction and running of a hotel. Such policies deter private sector investment.

The importance of protecting private investment in tourism must also be appreciated and activities such as mining, unauthorised construction, encroachments and haphazard development around tourist resorts must be prevented through appropriate legislation and public support. As tourism is a highly competitive industry; the traveller has a wide range of choices and looks for good value for money. The lack of quality infrastructure, uncompetitive rates, indifferent or poor product quality, difficulty in getting access to information on travel and tourist destinations, untrained service providers, and above all, the lack of hygiene, have an enormously negative effect on the competitiveness of the tourism product.

A world class destination requires professional planning to prevent haphazard, uncontrolled growth, spatial and land use planning, strict architectural controls, sewerage infrastructure and water treatment plants. It requires improvement of entry points and appropriate facilitation services. The lack of a visaon-arrival regime on account of security considerations places India at a disadvantage vis-à-vis its competitors. It is necessary that India strikes a balance between security considerations and the need for tourism development and reviews its visa policy to permit tourists from its major source markets to obtain visas on arrival.

Equally important is the behaviour of the host population. Training programmes are required not only for hotel managers but also for tourist guides, taxi-drivers, staff at eating places, porters etc., as the manner in which they conduct themselves affects the tourist's experience of the country. Important do's and dont's in terms of a code of ethics need to be inculcated among the service providers. During the Tenth Plan, the Department of Tourism will organise capacitybuilding programmes for service providers through mobile training units.

A major impediment to the growth of tourism in India has been the lack of awareness about the benefits that it can bestow upon the host population. Unless the host population, both in the rural and urban areas, is supportive of tourism, it cannot become a vibrant economic force. The rural sector, in particular, has been largely ignored in tourism development and has consequently been deprived of the benefits of employment and income generation accruing from tourism.

The Tenth Plan will seek to rectify this, particularly in view of the world-wide interest in rural tourism. While an awareness campaign that elicits local support for travel and tourism is essential for the long-term growth of the sector, it is also important to create awareness about the environmental impact of tourism by generating respect for the carrying capacities of tourist destinations. This is imperative as excessive exposure of ecologically fragile areas to human interference can lead to irreparable environmental degradation.

As the demand for ecotourism is expected to grow enormously in the next decade, it is important to have regulations in place to prevent such damage. The local population must be convinced of the need to support such regulations in the interest of long-term sustainability. India's hill resorts have already suffered seriously from a lack of concern for their carrying capacities and the unchecked influx of tourists during the summer months. If India's forest sanctuaries and pristine beaches are not to suffer the same fate, attention will have to be paid during the Tenth Plan to obtaining regulatory and public support for sustainability concerns.

The Tenth Plan strategy is to work towards a national consensus on the role of tourism in national development and to focus on the removal of barriers that hamper its growth. To make public sector investment more effective, it is necessary to work towards the inter-sectoral convergence of policies and programmes that could benefit tourism. The New Tourism Policy envisages a framework, which is Government-led, private sector driven and oriented towards community welfare, with the Government creating the legislative framework and basic infrastructure for tourism development, the private sector providing the quality product and the community providing active support.

The overall vision of the development of tourism embodied in the new policy will be achieved through five key strategic objectives. These are:

— Positioning tourism as a national priority.

— Enhancing India's competitiveness as a tourist destination.

— Improving and expanding product development.

— Creation of world class infrastructure.

— Effective marketing plans and programmes.

### *Positioning Tourism*

A proposal to this effect has been circulated by the Department of Tourism to the state governments for comments and has also been discussed at a Chief

Ministers' conference and a majority of the states have agreed to the proposal. Other initiatives include the setting up of Tourism Advisory Council with key stakeholders functioning as a think tank and the constitution of a Group of Ministers on Tourism to improve policy integration and co-ordination. The adoption of a tourism satellite accounting system is underway to gauge more precisely the contribution of tourism to the national economy.

A national awareness campaign in order to create a popular movement in favour of tourism is being planned through a professionally managed communication strategy. Most importantly, the efficiency of public investment in tourism supporting activities will be improved through effective inter-sectoral coordination and prioritisation. As air capacity available to India is woefully short during the peak travel months, ranging from October to March, especially for the main tourism originating regions such as North America, Western Europe and South Asia, it is necessary to open India's skies to increase capacity and help enhance tourism.

Additional seat capacity from the major tourism generating destinations would significantly benefit the national economy and provide a major impetus to tourism. Improvement in the standard of facilities and services at the international and national airports will need to be speeded up by employing professional manage-ment agencies and by privatising and leasing out airports. To enhance India's competitiveness as a tourist destination, it is proposed to simplify the visa procedures and consider strategies for the speedy issue of visas including electronic visas and visas on arrival.

An attempt will be made, through a consensus, to reduce the heavy and multiple taxes that reduce the competitiveness of the Indian tourism product. Special tourism police will be deployed at major tourist destinations during the Tenth Plan to provide security to travellers and promote India as a safe destination.

**Expanding Product Development**

Product development strategy during the Tenth Plan will be related to the special interests of tourist target markets.

*Cultural and heritage tourism will be expanded*: India has a vast array of protected monuments with 22 world heritage sites, 16 of which are monuments. The integrated development of areas around these monuments provides an opportunity for the development of cultural tourism in India.

For the development of beach and coastal tourism, a number of sites on the west coast of India will be identified for the development as beach resorts by the private sector. The sites will be offered on long term lease at preferential terms. These sites will primarily be on the beaches of Goa, Kerala, and North Karnataka because of easier access by air.

During the Tenth Plan Kochi in Kerala and the Andaman and Nicobar Islands will be developed as international cruise destinations because of their proximity to international cruise routes and their exotic appeal.

— India's unmatched variety of cuisine is becoming increasingly popular in the world and will be developed as a special attraction. It is proposed to create a highly skilled workforce of culinary professionals through an innovative incentive scheme not only for India but also to promote Indian cuisine internationally.

— Village tourism will be promoted as the primary tourism product of India to spread tourism and its socio-economic benefits to rural areas.

— India's great wildlife variety has not been developed as a tourist attraction. Wildlife sanctuaries and national parks will become an integral part of the Indian tourism product. Priority will be given to the preparation of site and visitor management plans for key parks. The quality of tourist facilities available at the parks will be enhanced after a prioritisation of parks. Tentatively these will be: Corbett National Park, Kanha National Park, Bandhav Garh National Park, Kaziranga, Madhumali, Bharatpur, Periyar, Ranthambore, Little Rann of Kutch, Chilka, and the Sunderbans.

— India has the greatest adventure tourism assets in the world in the Himalayas and its rivers. Mountain-based adventure activities will be developed and promoted. Regulations and certification for adventure tourism operators will be introduced so that the minimum standards of safety and conservation are met.

— India receives only a minuscule proportion of the global meetings, conventions and exhibition market. It is important that India develops a world class international convention city not just for the sake of tourism development but also for international and domestic trade and commerce.

— India's most unique tourism product during the Tenth Plan will be holistic healing and rejuvenation packages. In focussing on this, it will capture the essence of Indian culture for international and Indian visitors alike.

— India's fairs and festivals, some of which are already well established such as the Pushkar mela, the Desert Festival at Jaisalmer, the Kumbh Mela etc. will be promoted as unique products of India. The Festivals of India programme will be re-introduced in the top 12 future markets for India - initially with an annual event in the United Kingdom and the United States, to be followed by triennial events in the other markets.

— Shopping will be recognised as an integral part of tourism. The development of dedicated shopping centres for traditional crafts designed along the lines of village haats such as Dilli Haat and Shilpgram will be encouraged and information on where to procure specific crafts made available through shopping guides.

— Delhi will be positioned as the cultural capital of India supported by an ongoing and vibrant calendar of cultural events. The development of such a niche-based special interest product mix will position India as a unique and competitive destination.

## World Class Infrastructure

The need for physical infrastructure for tourism ranges from ports of entry to modes of transport to destinations (airways, roadways, railways or waterways), to urban infrastructure such as access roads, power, water supply, sewerage and telecommunication. This underscores the need for inter-sectoral convergence of infrastructural schemes and programmes that could support tourist destinations.

The road network is vital for tourism as almost 70 per cent of passengers in India travel by road. Many tourist circuits are entirely dependent on roads. The current government plan for the road system in the country covering both inter-state highways and improvements to rural roads directly supports tourism development. There is urgent need to construct and improve highways linking the 22 world heritage sites and places of tourist significance. The Ministry of Road Transport and National Highways will collaborate with the Ministry of Tourism in this effort.

The Indian railway system can also become an enormous asset to the development of the tourism and hospitality industry in the country. The railways hold a special fascination for foreign tourists who wish to travel the country. For the vast majority of domestic tourists also, the railways is the most affordable means of travel linking the length and breadth of the country. Introduction of special tourist trains with pre-set itineraries and private sector participation will be encouraged.

The Indian Railways plan to establish 100 hotels at railway stations to serve specific tourist centres. The private sector will be given incentives to operate these hotels on long-term leases. These hotels will provide clean and inexpensive accommodation for budget tourists. The Indian Railways also owns a number of heritage structures, which, if effectively maintained and marketed, could serve, both as railway stations and places of tourist interest.

India has five hill railways, which compare with the best hill railway systems in the world. The enormous tourist potential of these products will be tapped during the Tenth Plan. As steam-hauled trains like the Royal Orient, Buddha Parikrama, Palace-On-Wheels and Fairy Queen are extremely popular with tourists, steam traction for special tourist segments will be continued. Trains like the Shatabdi and the Rajdhani with a special tourism and hospitality focus will be planned both for foreign and domestic tourists.

India's 7,000-km coastline and her mighty rivers will be tapped for the promotion of cruises. Care will be taken to develop world class tourism products. As the Ministry of Tourism's financial assistance to the states has not been able to have the desired impact in terms of creating of world class tourism infrastructure, the emphasis must shift to the development of specific travel circuits as internationally competitive destinations and the convergence of resources and expertise for these circuits.

The availability of trained manpower is essential to achieve excellence in the tourism sector. At present, there are 21 Institutes of Hotel Management and Catering Technology (IHM&TC) and 13 Food Craft Institutes in the country. In addition, a good number of accredited institutes also cater to the growing demand in the service sector. It is estimated that only 50 per cent of the requirement of the market is met by these institutes. Five new Institutes of hotel management would be set up in the Tenth Plan - three in the newly created states of Uttaranchal, Jharkhand and Chhattisgarh and two in the northeast.

In addition, 15 more Food Craft Institutes will be set up in the Tenth Plan, and efforts will be made to take culinary crafts and training to the rural areas through mobile training units. A new scheme on capacity building to train service providers in the unorganised sector such as small hotels, dhabas, restaurants and other eating joints is also proposed.

### *Effective Marketing*

As there is fierce competition for tourists from India's source markets, India needs to change its traditional marketing approach to one that is more competitive and modern. It needs to develop a unique market position, image and brand, which cannot be held by any other competitor. India's positioning statement will capture the essence of its tourism product to convey an 'image' of the product to a potential customer. This image will be related not only to its ancient Vedic civilisation with a cultural heritage that continues to thrive especially in its rural areas but also to its essentially secular nature.

In the Tenth Plan, an extensive market research programme will be launched in the target source markets and tourism products developed to cater to the interests of each source market. An effective and ongoing market representation presence will be established with the travel trade in each source market and an Internet portal set up in various languages to provide information, a description of the product and the product requirements of the target market segments.

The Internet has a great impact on the marketing of travel and tourism. It has already established itself as a channel through which tourism organisations can promote their destinations and products. Indian tourism will utilise both the Internet and other emerging interactive technologies to avail of the benefits to be gained.

# 10

# Scheduled Tribes

The Government has special concern and commitment for the well-being of the Scheduled Tribes who suffer as a Group due to their social and economic backwardness and relative isolation. According to the 1991 Census, they account for 67.76 million and represent 8.08 per cent of the country's total population. Of these, 1.32 million belong to the Primitive Tribal Groups (PTGs) whose conditions are even worse than those of the rest of the tribals.

## Constitutional Safeguards

Recognising the special needs of STs, the Constitution of India made certain special safeguards to protect these communities from all the possible exploitation and thus ensure social justice. While Article 14 confers equal rights and opportunities to all, Article 15 prohibits discrimination against any citizen on the grounds of sex, religion, race, caste etc; Article 15(4) enjoins upon the State to make special provisions for the advancement of any socially and educationally backward classes;

Article 16(4) empowers the State to make provisions for reservation in appointments or posts in favour of any backward class of citizens, which in the opinion of the State, is not adequately represented in the services under the State; Article 46 enjoins upon the State to promote with special care the educational and economic interests of the weaker sections of the people and, in particular, ... the STs and promises to protect them from social injustice and all forms of exploitation.

Further, while Article 275(1) promises grant-in-aid for promoting the welfare of STs and for raising the level of administration of the Scheduled Areas, Articles 330, 332 and 335 stipulate reservation of seats for STs in the Lok Sabha and in the State Legislative Assemblies and in services. Finally, the Constitution also empowers the State to appoint a Commission to investigate the conditions of the socially and educationally backward classes (Article 340) and to specify those Tribes or Tribal Communities deemed to be as STs (Article 342).

The Fifth Schedule to the Constitution lays down certain prescriptions about the Scheduled Areas as well as the Scheduled Tribes in states other than Assam, Meghalaya, Tripura and Mizoram by ensuring submission of Annual Reports by the Governors to the President of India regarding the Administration of the Scheduled Areas and setting up of Tribal Advisory Councils to advise on matters pertaining to the welfare and advancement of the STs (Article 244(1)).

Likewise, the Sixth Schedule to the Constitution also refers to the administration of Tribal Areas in the states of Assam, Meghalaya, Tripura and Mizoram by designating certain tribal areas as Autonomous Districts and Autonomous Regions and also by constituting District Councils and Regional Councils (Article 244(2)). To ensure effective participation of the tribals in the process of planning and decision-making, the 73rd and 74th Amendments of the Constitution are being extended to the Scheduled Areas through the Panchayats (Extension to the Scheduled Areas) Act, 1996.

## Welfare and Development Programmes of STs

The Constitutional commitments, prompted the policy-makers and the planners to accord high priority to the welfare and development of STs right from the beginning of country's developmental planning, launched in 1951. Accordingly, the First Plan (1951-56) clearly laid down the principle stating that 'the general development programmes should be so designed to cater adequately to the backward classes and special provisions should be used for securing additional and more intensified development for STs'. Unfortunately, the same could not take place.

The Second Plan (1956-61), which laid emphasis on economic development, gave a special focus on reducing economic inequalities in the society. Further, development programmes for STs have been planned for, based on respect and understanding of their culture and traditions and with an appreciation of their social, psychological and economic problems. In fact, the same was planned in tune with 'Panchsheel' - the philosophy of tribal development as enunciated by the first Prime Minister of the country.

An important landmark during the Second Plan was the opening of 43 Special Multi-purpose Tribal Blocks, later termed as Tribal Development Blocks (TDBs). Each TDB was planned for about 25,000 people as against 65,000 in a normal Block. The Third Plan (1961-66) continued with the very same principle of advocating reduction in inequalities through various policies and programmes to provide equality of opportunity to STs.

The Fourth Plan (1969-74) proclaimed that the 'basic goal was to realise a rapid increase in the standard of living of the people through measures which also promote equality and social justice'. An important step in this direction was setting up of six pilot projects in

Andhra Pradesh, Bihar, Madhya Pradesh and Orissa in 1971-72 with a separate Tribal Development Agency for each project.

The Fifth Plan (1974-78) marked a shift in approach as reflected in the launching of the Tribal Sub-Plan (TSP) for the direct benefit of the development of tribals. The TSP stipulated that funds of the centre and the states should be quantified on the population proportion basis with budgetary mechanisms to ensure accountability, non-divertability and utilisation for the welfare and development of STs.

The Sixth Plan (1980-85) sought to ensure a higher degree of devolution of funds so that at least 50 per cent of tribal families could be provided assistance to cross the poverty line. In the Seventh Plan (1985-90), there was substantial increase in the flow of funds for the development of STs resulting in the expansion of infrastructural facilities and enlargement of coverage. Emphasis was laid on the educational development of STs. For the economic development of STs, two national-level institutions were set up viz.

— Tribal Cooperative Marketing Development Federation (TRIFED) in 1987 as an apex body for State Tribal Development Cooperative Corporations, and

— National Scheduled Castes and Scheduled Tribes Finance and Development Corporation (NSFDC) in 1989.

The former was assigned to provide remunerative prices for the forest and agriculture produce of tribals, while the latter was intended to provide credit support for employment generation. In the Eighth Plan, (1992-97), efforts were intensified to bridge the gap between the levels of development of STs and the other sections of the society. The Plan not only emphasised elimination of exploitation, but also paid attention to the special problems of suppression of rights, land alienation, non-payment of minimum wages and restrictions on the right to collect minor forest produce etc.

However, attention on priority basis, was continued to be paid on the socio-economic upliftment of STs. The Ninth Plan (1997-2002) aimed to empower STs by creating an enabling environment conducive for them to exercise their rights freely, enjoy their privileges and lead a life of selfconfidence and dignity, on par with the rest of society. This process essentially encompassed three vital components, viz.

— Social Empowerment;

— Economic Empowerment; and

— Social Justice.

To this effect, while ST-related line Ministries/ Departments implement general development policies and programmes, the nodal Ministry of Tribal Affairs implements certain ST-specific innovative programmes, as per the details given below:

***Education and Literacy***

The special commitment of the National Policy on Education,1986 to improve the educational status of STs continues to be the major strength in launching special interventions and incentives to improve the accessibility for the tribals who live in the far-flung remote areas and remain isolated. Therefore, efforts for universalising primary education continued, especially through the programme of Sarva Shiksha Abhiyan.

One of the special features of this programme is the participation of ST parents/ guardians in the activities of schools, which ensures ownership of the programme, even by the most disadvantaged. The National Programme of Nutritional Support to Primary Education or the Mid-Day Meals acts as a support service to increase retention rates.

In the field of higher and technical education, special provisions such as reservation of seats, relaxation in minimum qualifying cut-off percentages, remedial coaching and scholarships were being extended by the Department of Secondary and Higher Education. Similar concessions were also given to ST students for improving their skills in the up-coming/modern trades which have better employability.

### *Health & Family Welfare*

The National Health Policy, 1983 (being revised), categorically emphasises the urgent need for improving the tribal health especially through detection and treatment of endemic and other diseases specific to tribals. In pursuance of the policy commitments, the Ministry of Health and Family Welfare continued to give focused attention to improve the health conditions of STs by implementing various health care programmes besides relaxing norms with a major objective to attend to the health needs of STs.

A separate Tribal Development Planning Cell has been functioning under the Ministry since 1981 to co-ordinate the policy, planning, monitoring and evaluation of the health care schemes for the welfare and development of STs. Keeping in view that most of the tribal habitations are concentrated in far-flung areas, forest land, hills and remote villages, the population coverage norms have been relaxed as -

— for a Sub-Centre, the average norm for Hilly/Tribal areas has been fixed at 3,000 as against 5,000 for plains;

— for Primary Health Centre (PHC) 20,000 coverage norm is fixed for Hill/Tribal areas as against 30,000 for plains; and

— the norm of Community Health Centres (CHCs) is fixed at 80,000 for Hilly/ Tribal areas as against 1,20,000 for plains.

Similarly, Multipurpose Workers are appointed for 3,000 population in tribal areas as against the norm of 5,000 population for general. Under the Minimum Needs Programme, 20,769 Sub-Centres, 3,286 PHCs and 541 Community Health Centres (CHCs) had been set up by June 1999 in tribal areas.

Also, the State Governments have been advised to introduce schemes for compulsory annual medical examination of ST population in rural areas. Under these schemes, Mobile Health Checkup Teams are deputed to villages according to a schedule drawn up annually. In case of a need for further investigation or treatment, tribal patients are entitled to avail of free facilities in Government/ Referral hospitals.

To reach the health-care services to STs especially those living in the most backward remote areas, 52 districts in 13 states (Andhra Pradesh-6, Bihar-6, Gujarat-3, Kerala-5, Madhya Pradesh-4, Maharashtra-6, Manipur-4, Orissa-8, Rajasthan-2, Tamil Nadu-2, Tripura-4, Uttar Pradesh-1 and West Bengal-1) were identified by the Central Planning Committee. The State Governments were also asked to take special steps to check deaths of children due to malnutrition, epidemics etc. in identified areas by the Central Planning Committee during summer/monsoon seasons by establishing adequate number of Sub-Centres, PHCs and CHCs as per the relaxed norms in tribal areas.

Besides, a focused attention was also paid to the deployment of medical and paramedical personnel in line with the recommended staffing pattern and regular field visits by them, stocking of essential medicines/drugs, provision of Mobile Health Units where feasible, spraying of DDT and chlorination of wells, etc. Along with the National Malaria Eradication Programme, the other programmes to control Filaria, Japanese Encephalitis and Kala-azar were also implemented by States/UTs with 50 per cent central assistance for spraying insecticides, supply of Anti-Malaria drugs etc. in tribal areas.

The 100 hard-core identified tribal districts in the states of Andhra Pradesh, Bihar, Gujarat, Madhya Pradesh, Maharashtra, Orissa and Rajasthan were also covered under the enhanced Malaria Control Project with World Bank support. In order to address the problem of high incidence of Leprosy amongst tribals, the National Leprosy Eradication Programme was implemented with 100 per cent central assistance for detection and treatment of leprosy cases especially covering the entire tribal population.

Similarly, the National Tuberculosis Control Programme was also implemented with 100 per cent central assistance for the supply of anti-TB drugs, equipment etc. in tribal areas. Amongst the tribals, PTGs and the nomadic groups are passing through the most fragile health conditions, when compared to the others. Therefore, a new Scheme called 'Medical care for Remote and Marginalised and Nomadic Communities' was launched during the Ninth Five Year Plan with an approved outlay of Rs.5 crore. Under this Scheme, the following projects were taken up towards -

— Prevention and control of Hepatitis 'B' infection amongst the PTGs of Andaman & Nicobar Islands;

— Intervention for hereditary common haemolytic disorders amongst tribals of Sundergarh district in Orissa;

— Intervention programme for Cholera and Parasiptism, Vitamin 'A' deficiency disorders among some PTGs of Orissa; and

— Intervention programme for Nutritional Anaemia and Haemoglobinopathies amongst primitive tribal population.

For the exclusive benefit of the backward tribal dominant districts of Orissa viz. Kalahandi, Bolangir and Koraput, a long term Action Plan was taken up rigorously with the aim of pooling the available resources and integrating them scientifically for speedy development. Health has been an important activity in this area and in order to provide immediate relief to tribals at the doorsteps, 53 mobile Health units have been functioning.

The programme of Reproductive and Child Health (RCH), which takes care of the maternal and child health needs, also made some special provisions for those living in remote areas, where the existing services at PHC level are under-utilised. A scheme for holding special camps was initiated during the year 2000-01. The scheme is being implemented in 102 districts in 8 states that are weak in implementation of RCH and 7 North Eastern states and some more districts will be added in the subsequent years.

### *Labour and Employment*

The Ministry of Labour implements special training programmes for upgradation of skills of STs, besides improving the working conditions of ST workers. The Scheme of 'Coaching-cum-Guidance Centres for Scheduled Castes and Scheduled Tribes' implemented through 22 Coaching-cum-Guidance Centres spread all over the country takes care of the special needs of educated ST job seekers. Of these, 13 Centres provide facilities for training in shorthand and typewriting.

These Centres provide occupational information as well as individual guidance and conduct confidence building programmes for the benefit of the ST job seekers. The applicants are provided guidance at the time of their registration with the Employment Exchanges and also when they are sponsored against notified vacancies. The Centres also keep a follow up with the employers for placement against vacancies reserved for ST candidates.

To facilitate recruitment of STs against reserved vacancies in various Central Government Ministries/ Departments, another scheme viz. 'Special Coaching Scheme' was implemented for ST job seekers registered with the employment exchanges to enable them to appear in Competitive Examinations/Selection Tests conducted for recruitment in Group C and equivalent posts.

### *Women and Child Development*

The National Nutrition Policy, 1993 recognises the problem of malnutrition and undernutrition prevalent amongst tribal women and children and strongly advocates the need for controlling the same. In pursuance of the commitments of the Policy, the Department of Women and Child Development through its nationwide programme of Integrated Child Development Services (ICDS) continued to provide the much needed nutritional and health inputs/services for the benefit of tribal children, adolescent girls and expectant and nursing mothers living in the remote tribal areas with relaxed norms.

Of the total 4,608 ICDS projects in action by the end of the Ninth Plan, 758 (13.4 per cent) were Tribal Projects through which a package of 6 services viz. health check-ups; immunisation, supplementary feeding; referral services; non-formal pre-school education and health and nutrition education were being extended to 4.77 million children and 0.96 million mothers. The concept of Mini-

Anganwadis introduced in the tribal areas was only to ensure that ICDS services reach the tribal women and children even in the remotest tribal areas.

*Rural Development*

As majority of tribals live in abject poverty, the Ministry of Rural Development plays a vital role in raising their status above the poverty line through implementation of various poverty alleviation programmes and providing them with financial and other support for taking up self-employment and income-generation activities. In addition to the poverty-alleviation programmes, this Ministry also provides basic amenities like housing, drinking water, etc.

Under the Integrated programme of Swarnajayanti Gram Swarozgar Yojana (SGSY), 50 per cent of benefits were earmarked for STs along with SCs. Under SGSY, 7.49 lakh STs swarozgaris, accounting for 13.2 per cent of the total number of swarozgaris, were benefited during the Ninth Plan. Under the Jawahar Gram Samriddhi Yojana (JGSY), which provides wage employment, 22.5 percent of Plan allocations were earmarked for STs/SCs. ]

During the Ninth Plan, 220 million man-days were provided for STs accounting for 15.9 per cent of total employment under this scheme. Under the Employment Assurance Scheme (EAS), which is open to all rural poor including STs, 308 million man-days were provided for STs, accounting for 20.8 per cent of the total employment under this scheme during the Ninth Plan. The two schemes of JGSY and EAS were brought under the purview of the mega scheme of Sampoorna Grameen Rozgar Yojana (SGRY) in September 2001.

The SGRY focuses on generation of wage employment, creation of durable rural assets and infrastructure and provision of food security to the rural poor including STs. Under the Indira Awas Yojana, about 60 per cent of the total allocation was earmarked for STs and SCs. During the Ninth Plan, a total of 7.68 lakh dwelling units were constructed for STs, which accounts for 20.3 per cent of the total houses constructed under the scheme. Similarly, under the Accelerated Rural Water Supply Programme, 10 per cent of total funds was earmarked for STs.

During the Ninth Plan a total population of around 11.9 million STs were benefited. Also, under the Central Rural Sanitation Programme, sanitary latrines are provided to rural population and 20 per cent of total funds are earmarked for providing subsidy to individual households of STs and SCs living below the Poverty Line. During the Ninth Plan, as many as 3.1 lakh (6.4 per cent) sanitary latrines were provided to STs.

Under the National Old Age Pension Scheme, 2.4 million STs were covered during the Ninth Plan, accounting for 7.4 per cent of the total beneficiaries. Similarly, while 1 lakh ST families were benefited under the National Family Benefit Scheme accounting for 10.2 per cent, 4 lakh ST women were benefited under the National Maternity Benefit Scheme (NMBS) accounting for 7.4 per cent of the total beneficiaries during the Ninth Plan.

***Urban Development***

Under the Urban Self-Employment Programme of Swarna Jayanti Shahari Rozgar Yojana, financial assistance is extended to STs to try various small-scale entrepreneurial ventures.

*Tribal Affairs*

The nodal Ministry of Tribal Affairs laid greater emphasis in the Ninth Plan on the educational and economic development of Scheduled Tribes. The scheme of 'Post-Matric Scholarships' (PMS) continued to be an important centrally sponsored scheme to promote higher education among STs. Under this, scholarships are extended to all the eligible ST students who pursue post-matriculation courses in recognised institutions within the Country.

The scheme was revised in 1997-98 for extending some additional benefits to persons with disabilities amongst STs and the ceiling of income limits of parents etc. The Ninth Plan saw an impressive increase in the allocation of funds for scholarships awarded to STs, when compared to the previous Plans. Under PMS, a total expenditure of Rs.176.56 crore was incurred to benefit around 5.31 lakh ST students.

The scheme of Book Banks facilitates easy access to the prescribed text-books to ST students who are pursuing professional/technical courses like medical, veterinary science, agriculture, polytechnic, engineering and bio-sciences, law, chartered accountancy, Master of Business Administration etc. and cannot afford to purchase costly professional books.

The scheme of 'Up-gradation of Merit of ST Students' extends special coaching to ST students of classes IX to XII. The other scheme of 'Coaching and Allied Scheme for STs' also extends special coaching to ST students to help them appear in competitive examinations. Progress in terms of both physical and financial achievements in respect of the above-mentioned 3 schemes viz.

Book Bank Scheme, Upgradation of Merit of ST Students and Coaching and Allied Scheme for STs has been included under the Chapter on 'Socially Disadvantaged Groups' as these schemes continued as combined schemes for both SCs and STs till 2000-01. The scheme of 'Hostels for ST Girls and Boys', being one of the major support services, aims to reduce the present high drop-out rates and increase the retention rates at the middle/ higher level education amongst STs. The pace of progress of this scheme has been very slow during the Ninth Plan as there was no encouraging response from the states/UTs due to the financial crisis.

Of the Ninth Plan outlay of Rs. 73.30 crore, an expenditure of Rs. 53.20 crore was incurred for the construction/ expansion of 289 hostels benefiting 10,649 ST girl students and Rs. 32.12 crore for 317 hostels to accommodate 13,958 ST boy students. The scheme of Ashram Schools, was launched in 1990-91, with an objective of extending educational facilities to ST boys and girls through residential schools with conducive environment to their learning.

A review of the functioning of the Ashram Schools has revealed that most of them are very badly maintained and do not have even the basic facilities. Against the Ninth Plan allocation of Rs. 44.86 crore for opening 250 Ashram Schools, the expenditure was Rs. 23.97 crore to construct 294 Ashram Schools to accommodate around 14,310 ST students. The scheme of Educational Complexes in low-literacy pockets has been launched with a specific objective of promoting education amongst ST girls.

The scheme imparts education to tribal girls, especially those belonging to primitive tribes, in 134 districts in 11 states where the literacy rate amongst the ST women is less than 10 per cent as per the 1991 Census. With an expenditure of Rs. 11.71 crore against an outlay of Rs. 23.20 crore, 306 complexes were established by the end of Ninth Plan. In addition, coaching facilities are being extended to ST students through Pre-Examination Training Centres to enable them to compete with others in various competitive examinations.

Vocational Training Centres (VTCs) is yet another scheme which aims to impart vocational training to ST students to increase their employability. Against the Ninth Plan outlay of Rs. 30.25 crore, an expenditure of Rs. 16.78 crore was incurred to establish 235 VTCs. (More details are available under Chapter on 'Socially Disadvantaged Groups').

In the sphere of economic development, NSFDC continued to function as a catalytic agent for financing, facilitating and mobilising funds from various sources for promoting economic development activities of STs living below 'double the poverty' line through 47 State Channelising Agencies, of which 19 were working exclusively for STs.

Financial assistance at concessional rate of interest is extended to STs for taking up technically feasible and financially viable income-generating self-employment activities. In order to give focused attention to STs, the NSFDC was bifurcated, to set up an exclusive Corporation for STs in April, 2001 with an authorised share capital of Rs. 500 crore. Through the combined NSFDC, a sum of Rs. 379.75 crore has been invested in 934 income-generation projects benefiting 38,436 STs.

The State ST Development Corporations (STDCs) function as channelising agencies in identifying eligible families and extending financial aid and other assistance to help undertake income-generation projects through credit support. TRIFED continues to offer remunerative prices for Minor Forest Produce (MFP) collected and the surplus agricultural items produced by the tribals, besides protecting them from exploitation by middlemen.

*Grant-in-Aid to State Tribal*: Development Cooperative Corporations (STDCCs) is provided for strengthening their share capital base. This would help increase the volume of procurement of MFP from tribals at remunerative prices, construction of warehouses/ godowns, establishing processing industries and research and development activities of the 16 STDCCs.

The scheme of Development of Primitive Tribal Groups (PTGs), launched in the Ninth Plan (1998-99), for the development of 75 PTGs spread over 15 States/UTs, aims at improving the lot of PTGs who are still leading a precarious and fragile life and some of whom are even on the verge of extinction due to hunger, diseases and ill health. Hundred per cent central assistance was given to States/UTs and to NGOs for implementing an integrated action plan incorporating supply of safe drinking water, food and nutrition security, health coverage, educational facilities etc.

The scheme had an in-built flexibility to cater to the specific needs of each tribe and its environment. Against the Ninth Plan allocation of Rs. 22 crore, an expenditure of Rs. 27.42 crore was incurred. For storage of foodgrains as a safety net against starvation deaths amongst STs and also for improving nutritional standards amongst the children of STs living in remote and backward tribal villages in the starvation prone belts, the Village Grain Banks have been established in tribal villages spread over 12 states in 1998.

Of the Ninth Plan allocation of Rs. 12.80 crore, an expenditure of Rs. 10.95 crore was incurred to set up 1,234 Grain Banks in tribal villages. In order to promote voluntary action in the tribal areas, especially in the remote and far-flung areas, 893 socio-economic development projects undertaken by the Voluntary Organisations were supported under Grant-in-Aid to NGOs for STs.

**TSP and SCA to TSP**

The Tribal Sub-Plan (TSP) for STs and the Special Central

Assistance (SCA) to TSP launched during the early 1970s, have proved to be the most effective strategies to ensure the additional flow of population-proportionate funds for STs from the other general development sectors. According to the information available, earmarking of funds under TSP is being followed by 25 Ministries/ Departments at the Centre, while at state level only 20 States/UTs are adhering to this.

The Tribal Sub-Plan strategy has been in effective operation in the country through 194 Integrated Tribal Development Projects, 259 pockets of tribal concentration (Modified Area Development Approach - MADA), 82 clusters and the Projects for 75 PTGs.

*Tale 1. Flow of Funds through TSP and SCA to TSP during the Ninth Plan (1997-2002)*

| Item | Outlay | Flow to TSP | Percentage Col.3 to Col.2 |
|---|---|---|---|
| (1) | (2) | (3) | (4) |
| Tribal Sub-Plan (TSP) —Flow fromCentral Plan (in respect of 25 Ministries/Departments) | 1,10,454.10 | 6,462.00 | 5.85 |
| —Flow from State Plan (in respect of 20 States/ Union Territories) | 2,96,911.20 | 22,314.22 | 7.52 |
| Special Central Assistance (SCA) to TSP | | | |
| —SCA to TSP (Outlay & Release) | 2,010.00 | 2,009.61 | 99.98 |

SCA to TSP is being extended as an additive to strengthen the efforts of the states by filling the critical gaps under the family-based income generation projects, catering to those living below poverty line. SCA was enhanced from Rs. 1,250 crore in the Eighth Plan to

Rs.2,010 crore in the Ninth Plan, indicating an increase of 60.8 per cent to benefit 6.75 million ST families living below the poverty line. Details of the flow of funds both at the central and state levels during the Ninth Plan, are given at Table 1.

As could be seen from Table 1, while the flow to TSP at the central level stood at 5.85 per cent with 25 contributing Ministries/Departments, it was 7.52 per cent at the state level with only 20 states contributing to it. Besides, the flow was also not in proportion to the population of STs (8.08 per cent). Though the releases of SCA to TSP was as high as 99.98 per cent of the earmarked outlay, yet what matters was its utilisation.

As the strategies of TSP for STs and SCP for SCs and SCA to TSP and SCP have been developed and are being implemented with a common philosophy, issues related thereto also happen to be more or less the same in nature. Therefore, issues and concerns that came up in answer to the enquiry made into the question - as to why earmarking of funds under TSP by the Central Ministries/Departments and by states/ UTs was not upto the expected level and what action was taken thereafter was already discussed in the previous Chapter on 'Socially Disadvantaged Groups'. The same is applicable to STs also.

*Article 275(1) of the Constitution*: Under the Article 275(1) of the Constitution, Grant-in-Aid (GIA) from the Consolidated Fund of India is extended annually to various State Governments having ST population. The major objective of the scheme is to raise the level of administration in the Scheduled Areas to that of the rest of the State, besides promoting the welfare of the STs living therein. The scheme covers all the TSP areas and also four tribal majority states in the country.

Grants to the extent of 100 per cent are released by the nodal Ministry of Tribal Affairs under the central sector scheme. With a view to providing accessibility to quality education to ST students, it was decided to establish 100 residential schools under this scheme on the pattern of Navodaya Schools with a non-recurring grant of Rs. 2.50 crore during the Ninth Plan period. Year-wise details of the allocations and releases during the Ninth Plan period, are given in Table 2

*Table 2. Year-wise Allocation and Releases under Article 275(1) of the Constitution during the Ninth Plan (1997-2002)*

| Year (1) | Allocation (2) | Grant-in-aid (Released) (3) |
|---|---|---|
| 1997-1998 | 75.00 | 75.00 |
| 1998-1999 | 75.00 | 75.00 |
| 1999-2000 | 100.00 | 100.00 |
| 2000-2001 | 200.00 | 191.29 |
| 2001-2002 | 300.00 | 225.56 |

Against the earlier practice of releasing lumpsum funds to individual states, from 2001-02, releases are being made against specific developmental works/ projects identified by State Governments. However, one of the major constraints in the implementation of this programme is that the State Governments do not release funds in time.

## Unresolved Issues

Tribal communities continue to be vulnerable even today, not because they are poor, asset-less and illiterate compared to the general population; but often their distinct vulnerability arises from their inability to negotiate and cope with the consequences of their integration with the mainstream economy, society, cultural and political systems, from all of which they were historically protected by their relative isolation. The requirements of planned development brought with them the dams, mines, industries and roads, all located on tribal lands.

With these came the concomitant processes of displacement followed by a conflict between development and protection of tribal rights and interests. Tribal institutions and practices were forced into uneasy co-existence, which paved the way to market or formal State institutions. Also, the tribals found themselves at a great disadvantage in the face of an influx of betterequipped outsiders into tribal areas. The repercussions for the already fragile socio-economic sustenance base of the tribals were devastating - ranging from the loss of livelihoods and land alienation on a vast scale to hereditary bondage.

As the tribals grapple with these tragic consequences, a small clutch of bureaucratic programmes could do little to resist the precipitous pauperisation, exploitation and disintegration of tribal communities. As a result of this, the tribals continue to suffer and bear with a number of 'Unresolved Issues' and 'Persisting Problems', which require immediate attention of the Government.

***Displacement of Tribals***

Displacement or forced/voluntary eviction of tribals from their land and their natural habitats and subsequent rehabilitation has been a serious problem that remains to be addressed by the Government. As per the information readily available, a population of 21.3 million have been displaced between 1951 and 1990 in the states of Andhra Pradesh, Bihar, Gujarat, Maharashtra, Madhya Pradesh, Rajasthan and Orissa.

Of whom, 8.54 million (40 per cent) are tribals and of those only 2.12 million (24.8 per cent) tribals could be resettled, so far. Displacement took place mainly on account of development projects, which include large irrigation dams, hydro-electric projects, opencast and underground coal mines, super-thermal power plants and mineral-based industrial units.

In large mining projects, tribals lose their land not only to the project authorities, but even to non-tribal outsiders who converge into these areas and corner both land and the new economic opportunities in commerce and petty industry. The incomplete rehabilitation of the displaced tribals has further compounded their woes as they are pushed into a vortex of increasing assetlessness, unemployment, debt bondage and destitution. Women and children as ever are the worst affected.

### *Tribal Land Alienation*

Land is not only the most important productive resource base for the tribals, but also occupies an important place in their psyche as the mainstay of their social and religious practices. Over a period of time, this resource base of the tribal communities has tended to get eroded not only through acquisition for public purposes but also through fraudulent transfers, forcible eviction, mortgages, leases and encroachments.

As per the information available with the Ministry of Rural Development, as many as 4.65 lakh cases of alienation of tribal land covering an area of 9.17 lakh acres were registered in the states of Andhra Pradesh, Assam, Bihar, Gujarat, Himachal Pradesh, Karnataka, Madhya Pradesh, Maharashtra, Orissa, Rajasthan and Tripura in January 1999. Against this, only 2 lakh cases were disposed of in favour of 1.56 lakh tribal families covering an area of 5.31 lakh acres.

Of these, the states affected by largescale tribal land alienation include Andhra Pradesh (2.79 lakh acres), Madhya Pradesh (1.58 lakh acres), Karnataka (1.30 lakh acres), and Gujarat (1.16 lakh acres). Various studies have pointed out that the lack of political and administrative will continues to be the cause for perpetuation of the problem of land alienation amongst the tribals as reflected in the reluctance to amend legal provisions and plug the existing loopholes and swift administrative action to identify alienated land, and restoring it to the tribals with delivery of possession.

### *Indebtedness*

The problem of indebtedness amongst tribals is not only an indication of their poverty but also reflects the wider economic malaise, i.e., lack of education, low purchasing/bargaining power and lack of resources for engaging in gainful activity and meeting emergent expenditure. Therefore, the problem continues to persist with increasing menace as the indebtedness pushes the tribals further into extreme conditions of poverty and forces them to dispense with their meagre resources, including the small bits and pieces of land to pay off the loans at exorbitant rates of interest.

The initiation of commercial vending of liquor in tribal areas has started impoverishing the tribal population, making them victims of indebtedness and exploitation. Although the States and UTs have broadly accepted the Guidelines (relating to the Excise Policy in Tribal Areas, 1975, issued by the Ministry of Social Welfare), effective follow-up action is not taken for their implementation.

Under the Fifth Schedule to the Constitution, the Governors of states with Scheduled Areas were given powers for making regulations and for placing restrictions on moneylending activities in the Scheduled Areas. Relevant Laws/Regulations exist in 16 TSP states/ UTs to regulate the business of money -lending and to give debt-relief. However, the legal measures to curb the activities of money-lenders and traders have failed to have much impact on the severity of the problem due to the ineffective enforcement machinery and lack of alternative sources of credit for meeting the tribals' consumption and productive needs.

Lack of a sound policy to support consumption credit to tribals has tended to make them dependent on usurious money-lenders, resulting in debt-bondage. The problem of tribal indebtedness often gets aggravated and compounded with the government subsidy-cumloan schemes which further lead the tribals into deep indebtedness.

### *Shifting Cultivation*

Shifting Cultivation, which is not ecologically sound, is still being practised by the tribals living on the higher slopes of hilly areas of the country. As estimated, more than 6 lakh tribal families in the North Eastern states, Orissa, Andhra Pradesh and Himachal Pradesh practise shifting cultivation on a continuous basis. This shifting cultivation is integrally linked to the tribal economy in the areas where it is practised and their social and economic activities and rituals are also centred around this practice.

The problem of shifting cultivation is a very complex one, involving economic, social and psychological aspects of the tribal communities. Although shifting cultivation is one of the prime sources of living for the tribals, yet the same has been severely restricted. The Ministry of Agriculture has been implementing a scheme for control and transformation of Shifting

Cultivation in the North Eastern states, but the pace of its implementation has been very slow.

### *Forest Rights*

Forests and Tribals share a symbiotic relationship. Tribals continue to live in forest areas, though in isolation, yet in harmony with environment. Recognising this dependency, the National Forest Policy, 1988, stipulated that all agencies responsible for forest management should ensure that the tribal people are closely associated with the regeneration, plantation, development and harvesting of forests so as to provide them gainful employment.

Despite these special safeguards, tribals continue to struggle for mere survival as they face formidable problems and displacement due to development of national parks and wild-life sanctuaries and other environmental restoration projects, lack of development in forest villages etc. The protection of rights of tribals in forests is key to the amelioration of their conditions.

While the 'Un-resolved Issues' need to be attended to on a priority basis, the on-going efforts along with new initiatives for empowering the tribals will continue simultaneously with added thrust so as to mitigate the 'Persisting Problems' in the critical areas of education, health, livelihood, poverty, vulnerability, violence, unrest etc. so as to accelerate the process of empowering STs towards accomplishing the task of raising their status on par with rest of the society. Prominent amongst such Persisting Problems requiring the most concerted and time-bound efforts.

### *Low Literacy and High Drop-out Rates*

Despite the programme of Universalisation of Primary Education, which has been in effective operation since

1986, the literacy rate of STs remained as low as 29.6 per cent, while the general literacy rate reached 52.2 per cent in 1991. Similarly, the female literacy rate of STs stood at 18.2 per cent which is also much lower in comparison with 39.3 per cent in respect of general category. As the 1991 Census data reveals, there are tribal districts like Koraput in Orissa where the literacy rate of STs is as low as 8.9 per cent,while there are districts like Aizawl in Mizoram with as high as 88.8 percent.

Similarly, there are districts like Jalor in Rajasthan with as low as 0.6 per cent of ST female literacy rate, while Aizawl in Mizoram has female literacy rate as high as 85.7 per cent. Further, the gap between the general population and that of STs was also found to have widened from 19.9 per cent to 22.6 per cent between 1981 and 1991, as discussed earlier. Adding to this are the problems of intra and inter-state/district and intercommunity variations in the literacy rates of STs.

Although, the drop-out rates have been showing a declining trend amongst STs in Classes I to VIII from 78.6 percent in 1990-91 to 72.8 per cent in 1998-99, yet the same is still very high, when compared to 60.9 per cent and 56.82 per cent of general categories, respectively for the same years indicating a gap of 17.7 and 16.6 per cent.

### *Inadequate and Inaccessible Health Services*

Although the National Health Policy, 1983 accords high priority to extending organised services to those residing in the tribal, hilly and backward areas as well as to the detection and treatment of endemic diseases affecting tribals, yet the tribals continue to be one of the fragile population, mainly due to their poor health and nutritional status. Tribal health is one of the important areas for action in the health sector.

The major contributors to the increased disease risk amongst tribal communities include -

— poverty and consequent under-nutrition;

— poor environmental sanitation, poor hygiene and lack of safe drinking water leading to increased morbidity from water and vector-borne infections;

— lack of access to health care facilities resulting in the increased severity and duration of illnesses;

— social barriers and taboos preventing utilisation of available health care services;

— vulnerability to specific diseases like G-6 PD deficiency, Yaws, and other endemic diseases like malaria etc.

Also, the tribal population, being heterogeneous, there are wide variations in their health status, access to and utilisation of health services.

### *Nutritional Deficiencies and Diseases*

Malnutrition is fairly common amongst the tribals, especially their children and women, debilitating their physical condition and lowering their resistance to disease, leading at times even to permanent brain impairment. As most tribal women suffer from anaemia which lowers resistance to fatigue, this affects their working capacity and increases susceptibility to disease particularly for those having closely-spaced frequent pregnancies.

The nutritional status of tribal women directly influences their reproductive performances and the birth weight of their children, which is crucial to the infant's chances of survival, growth and development. Almost all the tribals in the country do not have a satisfactory dietary pattern as their diets are frequently deficient in calcium, Vitamin A, Vitamin C, Riboflavin and animal protein. The tribals are thus caught in a vicious cycle of malnutrition and ill-health.

### *Lack of Adequate Irrigation Facilities*

Tribals in India primarily depend upon agriculture for their subsistence, which constitutes their mainstay. According to the 1991 Census, 42 per cent of the ST population are Main Workers. Of these, 54.5 per cent are cultivators and 32.7 per cent agricultural labourers. Thus, more than 87 per cent of the tribal main workers are dependent on agriculture.

Further, while 42.9 per cent of the operational holdings of tribals belong to the category of marginal farmers with less than 1 hectare, 24.1 percent are of small farmers category with 1 to 2 hectares; and only 2.2 per cent STs have large operational holdings with more than 10 hectares. The tribals generally live in most in-hospitable terrain and practise shifting cultivation on higher slopes and dry-land cultivation in plains and lower slopes where productivity and output are very low.

Lack of proper irrigation facilities, decline in soil fertility, and risks and uncertainties involving damages caused by the wild animals, pests, cyclones, droughts etc. have further deteriorated the agricultural yield. The growing tribal population and the declining agricultural productivity have become a serious threat to the subsistence base of the tribal communities, endangering their self-supporting food security system.

### *Abject Poverty*

The impact of various poverty alleviation programmes put into action during the last two developmental decades has, no doubt, brought down the poverty levels among STs from 51.94 per cent in 1993-94 to 45.86 per cent in 1999-2000 in rural areas and from 41.14 per cent to 34.75 per cent in urban areas over the same period. But, it is much higher when compared to 27.09 per cent in rural and 23.62 per cent in urban areas in respect of general categories during 1999-2000.

Therefore, there has been an increasing unrest amongst the tribals and also in tribal areas in the recent past. Radical/Extremist movements are already operating in some parts of the country; the root cause for all these is the perceived dissatisfaction with the existing conditions and failure to receive benefits and facilities promised to them. Therefore, there is an urgent need to critically review the approach adopted so far for tribal protection and development, and reorient the same, wherever needed, so as to ensure flow of development benefits within a definite time-frame and restore the faith of the tribals in the capability of the government to deliver.

### *Intellectual Rights*

Having lived closely with forests and also interacting constantly with various flora and fauna, the tribals have developed invaluable indigenous knowledge. This indigenous knowledge amongst the tribal communities is passed on from generation to generation through the medium of oral tradition, folklore and practice, which find a place in various life-cycle events including treatment of diseases/ ailments, without any codified text or rights to accredit their legitimate ownership.

As tribal communities have a very close dependence on biological resources, their livelihood and life-style often depend upon and are shaped by these resources. Therefore, their survival and sustenance is closely linked to conservation and utilisation of these resources.

Corporate protectionism in terms of patents and Intellectual Property Rights arising out of various international treaties/instruments on trade and common property resources such as the Trade Related Aspects of Intellectual Property Rights (TRIPS) under the World Trade Organisation (WTO) represents a real threat to economic livelihood of these communities.

They are also a source of potential exploitation of the tribal resource base as bio-diversity expressed in life forms and knowledge is sought to be converted into private property and treated as an open access system for free exploitation by those who want to privatise and patent it. There is an urgent need to provide appropriate legal and institutional arrangements for recognising and acknowledging the rights of tribal communities to such resources and knowledge.

### *Atrocities against STs*

As per the National Crimes Record Bureau, New Delhi, the number of crimes against STs indicated a decline from 4,644 in 1997 to 4,450 in 1999. However, although the share of crimes committed against STs remained the same in 1997 and 1998 at 0.07 per cent, yet, it showed a contrary trend with an increase to 0.09 per cent in 1999. The number of crimes attracting the provisions of Special Legislations of the Protection of Civil Rights (PCR) Act, 1955 and the Scheduled Castes and the Scheduled Tribes (Prevention of Atrocities) (POA) Act, 1989 has shown an increase from 731 in 1997 to 759 in 1998 and a decline to 619 in 1999.

Further, though there was a decline in the number of crimes committed against STs in 1999, the number of violent crimes viz., murder, rape, hurt, dacoity, robbery, arson etc. have registered a steady increase from 491 in 1997 to 511 in 1998 and to 577 in 1999. The increase in the number of crimes against STs has been continuing, despite effective enforcement of Special Legislations and existence of 118 Special Courts in 12 states to deal with the cases exclusively related to STs.

### *Neglect of Rural Villages*

As the 5,000 identified Forest Villages are located in the remote interiors, and are declared revenue villages, the 2.5 lakh families who inhabit these villages are deprived of even the basic minimum services available to residents of Revenue Villages. While the forest resource base, on which inhabitants traditionally depended, is fast eroding and adversely affecting the very survival of the tribals, alternative sources of income extended through the implementation of various social forestry activities by the Department of Forests are also not ensured throughout the year.

Some of the major problems faced by the Forest Villages include lack of infrastructure facilities viz. approach roads, electricity, drinking water, schools, hospitals, and irrigation tanks; lack of fair price/food-grain shops; lack of stable land tenure system; and lack of proper credit facilities and bank loans as the villagers do not have the papers related to the land which are necessary in getting the loans sanctioned.

This is due to the fact that the land has the status of Reserved Forests attracting the Indian Forest Act, 1927 and especially the Forest (Conservation) Act, 1980; and the departmental rivalry between the Forest and Revenue Departments resulting in the exploitation and negligence of Forest Villages.

### *Primitive Tribal Groups*

The Government of India identified 75 tribal communities as Primitive Tribal Groups (PTGs) with a total estimated population of 1.32 million in 1991 spread over 15 States/ UTs. There is a marked difference between the conditions of the relatively advanced tribal groups and the PTGs. As they live in the most interior and inaccessible forests, they are subjected to extreme backwardness, when compared to the other tribals.

A decline in their sustenance base and the resultant food insecurity, malnutrition and ill-health force them to live in the most fragile living conditions and some of them are even under the threat of getting extinct. The Bay-Islanders like the Great Andamanese, Shompens, Jarawas, Sentinelese of the Andaman & Nicobar Islands. Even some of the mainland groups which can be cited in this context like the Bondos of Orissa, Cholanaickans of Kerala, the Abujhmarias of Chhattisgarh, the Birhors of Jharkhand are also dwindling.

As adequate information on the demographic, educational, health and economic aspects of individual primitive tribes is not available, immediate steps need to be taken for building up a comprehensive information/ data base on PTGs and wherever necessary to conduct intensive studies and prepare detailed Status Reports. There is no doubt that the 73rd and 74t h Constitutional Amendments of 1993 followed by their extension to Scheduled Areas through the Panchayats (Extension to the Scheduled Areas) PESA Act, 1996, are landmark achievements in conferring powers and authority to the Panchayats and Gram Sabhas.

But, unfortunately, the same are not being enforced in the right spirit, as the PRIs are yet to stabilise on a firm footing. The State Governments should, therefore, take appropriate measures immediately to translate the legislation into reality so that tribals will have full say in their own affairs.

### *Routinised Mechanism of TSP*

The special strategy of Tribal Sub-Plan (TSP) has been under implementation since 1975 both at the central and state levels with the objective of ensuring that the benefits from various developmental sectors do not by-pass STs and accordingly funds, in population proportion, are earmarked for the development of STs. Only 25 Central Ministries/Departments and 20 States/UTs, have been earmarking funds for TSP.

Despite repeated suggestions to the State Governments to adopt the Maharashtra Model of resource allocations and utilisation, not many states have done so far. In Maharashtra, funds under TSP are pooled under the administrative control of the nodal state department in-charge of tribal development and utilised in the identified/needy areas. The strategy of TSP, as is implemented, has also become very much routinised. Thus, its impact on improving the conditions of STs is not being felt.

# 11

# Science and Technology in Rural Development

There is an urgent need to make all-out efforts to ensure that appropriate research outputs, which can be put to use for the benefit of society, are generated and reach the people. It is, therefore, essential to evolve a mechanism and identify programmes for application of S&T for improving the quality of life of the people, particularly the weaker sections and women, for the development of rural areas to reduce regional imbalances and for inculcating scientific awareness among the masses.

During the Tenth Plan, a mechanism would need to be instituted through which the scientific institutions/departments take stock each year of the industrial products developed and the impact of these on improvement in the quality of life in the rural areas, in terms of health and nutritional status, purchasing power potential and increasing knowledge and empowerment.

The S&T interventions must aim at providing simple, affordable scientific solutions, which help the individual save time and energy and augment income. The kind of technologies to be provided should be what people want rather than what someone else wants them to adopt. This approach would not only ensure acceptability of the technological innovations but would also help in inculcating a scientific temper amongst the masses. Technologies that aim at value addition in the products of cottage/small scale industry can play a vital role in improving their competitiveness.

Broadly speaking, S&T can play important role in reaching IT to the remotest parts of the country by emphasising on computer literacy, making it accessible even to those not having formal education. The 'problem population' can thus be converted into a valuable 'human resource' through activity-oriented training and skill improvement, helping to develop entrepreneurship and facilitating self-employment by using new technologies.

For this, it is important to involve people by working on scientific and research-based solutions for their long-term problems like drought, epidemics, drinking water shortage, nutrition, sanitation, health, housing etc. and other day to day problems including shift towards non-conventional energy sources and product packaging.

Special emphasis would be given to identifying, promoting and supporting grass root innovations, adding value to them and disseminating them to ensure that the impact of such innovations is reflected in improved prospects of livelihood of a large number of people. Efforts would be made to scout for advanced time and energy-saving tools/ machineries and equipment available in other countries, their adaptation, motivation of entrepreneurs to take up their manufacture and also encourage the innovators of advanced tools and equipments.

### Human Resource Development

Although there has been a phenomenal growth in the number of universities and colleges imparting science education, there has been a consistent decline in the percentage of school students opting for science after passing the higher secondary examinations, from 32 per cent in 1950 to 15 per cent now. There has also been a marked change in the profile of students taking up the science stream.

Today, high school students opting for science are often those with low scores while in the past, those with high scores would opt for science. Even the majority of the meritorious 150 students selected for the mathematics, physics, chemistry and biology Olympiads do not opt for careers in the sciences. The drop-out rate among the research fellows qualifying the National Entrance Test (NET) is also a fairly high 35 per cent.

Human resource/manpower development assumes a special significance in the process of developing technological innovations as well as implementation of new technologies and finding solutions to problems arising during the process of modernisation. It is also a measure of the strength of the country as it contributes to socio-economic development. Development of S&T manpower depends on the quality of higher education in science and technology.

Considerable strengthening of the scientific and technical manpower will be needed with the liberalisation of the economy and the thrust on science and technology programmes. This would be done by selectively nurturing excellence in S&T education; identifying talented students and motivating them to take up science and technology as a career; providing avenues and opportunities for those engaged in the science and technology field to update and enhance their knowledge and skills; devising strategies to retain the best talents in active scientific work and involve the corporate sector in science education and R&D.

All this will be achieved through setting up of specialised science institutes as centres of excellence on par with the Indian Institutes of Technology (IITs) and Indian Institutes of Management (IIMs); adoption of at least one school and one undergraduate college by each national laboratory; attracting talented students to R&D through an assured career opportunity scheme; and upgrading the knowledge base of teachers through the concept of floating academics on a regional basis in new emerging areas like genomics, bio-informatics, conducting polymers etc.

### *Department of Science and Technology*

Some of the major R&D programmes supported by the Department include: sub-Himalayan cenozoic sediment studies; macromolecular crystallography; bio-organic chemistry; Raman spectroscopy study on strongly correlated systems; laser application in high resolution molecular spectroscopy; non-accelerated particle physics; etc. A programme on drug development was initiated for promoting collaborative R&D in drugs and pharmaceuticals involving national laboratories, industry and academic institutions.

Thirty research projects relating to new chemical entities/formulations to treat diseases like cancer, arthiritis, diarrhoea, gastritis, pancreatitis, tuberculosis, Hepatitis-B, rabies etc. were funded. Four national facilities for identification of the immuno-modulating potential of herbal products and extracts of natural origin, pharmacological testing, characterisation of crystals and medium throughput screening in different national laboratories were established.

Technology development programmes have been pursued through the Technology Development Board, Technology Information Forecasting Assessment Council (TIFAC), New Delhi, and Advanced Research Centre, Hyderabad. The Technology Vision 2020 Reports published by TIFAC have, for the first time, documented new areas of S&T covering various science disciplines. Besides, it also released 31 reports on frontier technologies like transgenic seeds, recombinant DNA products, bio-degradable plastics etc. TIFAC also facilitated networking of seven engineering/ research institutions with high performance computing facilities for taking up selected technology demonstration projects.

Keeping in view the importance of protection of intellectual property rights in the globalised world, a Patent Facilitating Centre (PFC) was set up in 1995 which has helped in generating patent awareness. Under the Technopreneur Promotion Programme (TePP) started jointly by the DST, Department of Scientific and Industrial Research (DSIR), and TIFAC, several projects relating to zeolite-based catalytic converter, next generation membrane oxygenerator etc. were supported.

Through the IS-STAC mechanism, 12 joint technology projects have been taken up in the areas of column flotation technology for ore benefaction and pilot plant for enrichment of helium from hydrothermal sources etc. As a means of promoting S&T for socio-economic development, Rural Technology Parks have been set up in the northeastern region. A number of need-based S&T projects were supported in several places including hilly regions in the farm and non-farm sector.

These covered areas like: inland aquaculture, sustainable agriculture, solar/bio-mass-based energy devices/ systems, post harvest technologies, land-based activities, women's health, rural engineering etc. Three women's technology parks were also set up at Dehradun, Manipal and Barmer. A major breakthrough was achieved with the launching of a project on food security by installing a fish aggregation device in Andaman Island for the primitive tribal group.

Project-mode support to tackle statespecific problems was provided to the State S&T Councils. These projects related to: the problem of high mortality of broiler birds at Namakkal, Tamil Nadu; drying of large cardamom in Sikkim; documentation of medicinal plants in the Thar region of Rajasthan and in Madhya Pradesh; documentation of traditional fishing crafts and gears in Manipur; cultivation of ginseng by tissue culture technique in Manipur; use of hydrams for irrigation purpose in Himachal Pradesh; demonstration plants for cupola furnace in Bihar and solar passive housing technology in Manipur.

Under the S&T Communication and Popularisation Programme, four National Children's Science Congress (NCSC) were organised. A television serial Kudratnama on science and technology was also telecast and video programmes on different scientific topics exhibited. Under the NRDMS programmes, 15 GIS database centres were set up, Planning Atlas for some districts of Gujarat was prepared and coordinated programmes for ground water modeling, coastal zone management and conservation, and bio-geo database and ecological modeling were taken up. Since the DST is a nodal department for international S&T cooperation, several programmes were undertaken in this area.

These include: setting up of an Indo-US S&T Forum; launching of the Department of Science and Technology-National Science Foundation (DST-NSF) programme from 1999; supporting technology-oriented projects on surface engineering of components; steel for automobiles; special plastics processing and pharmaceuticals development under an Indo-German programme; and DST-DAAD projectbased Personnel exchange Programme.

Thirteen DST-aided autonomous institutions continued their research activities and transfer of technologies to industries. Significant achievement of these institutions include: development of a folion spray beneficial to crop yield; development of laboratory-scale process for microbial detoxification of cyanide and metalcyanide complexes; nano-structured semiconductor and CMR materials and devices; and establishment of the world's highest observatory for optical astronomy in the Himalayas. Professional science academies continued their efforts in promoting scientific activities such as publication and communication programmes in S&T and promotion of engineering education and research.

In order to achieve the goals envisaged for the Tenth Plan, efforts would be made to build upon the strengths of the country's S&T system and address its weaknesses. While the S&T system is robust and has a graded organisational structure, lack of linkages with industry has resulted in R&D being largely academic in nature, with very few applications and very little commercialisation and patenting. Although the S&T infrastructure facilities in strategic areas as well as areas of basic sciences have been strengthened significantly over the years, it is not robust enough to take on the national challenges in some of the key areas.

India has also demonstrated its strength in several areas of R&D which has led to the country achieving self-sufficiency in food grain production; eradication of communicable diseases like small pox and plague, substantial decrease in the infant mortality rate and increase in life expectancy; and the development of indigenous technologies and their commercialisation particularly in health, engineering, drugs, agriculture, electrical systems; etc.

In the strategic sectors, India has demonstrated its capability to build and operate nuclear reactors, including FBRs, build and launch satellites including cryogenic technology for GSLV, and application of space technology for resource management, meteorological services etc. India has also emerged as a significant basic research power, with worldclass scientists in almost all areas of basic research, a fact that is reflected in the quality and number of publications.

Our scientists have built world-class facilities like Giant Metre Wave Radio Telescope (GMRT), Variable Energy Cyclotron, Synchrotron Radiation Sources etc. and are also in the process of building superconducting cyclotron and a superconducting steady state Tokamak.

At the international level, India is now participating as an equal partner in several front-ranking experiments like the compact mono solenoid (CMS) experiment and a large ion collider experiment (ALICE) experiment at European Organisation for Nuclear research, CERN, Geneva, experiments at Fermilab in the United States and RIKEN and KEK in Japan etc. However, India's strength in R&D has not translated into commensurate benefits for society due to lack of a sufficient number of competent scientists working in the areas of technological innovation and commercialisation.

Barring some landmarks like GMRT and developments in the strategic sectors, the instrumentation activities, particularly machineries and equipment, have been declining. India's failure to compete technologically with the developed world has resulted in outright import of machineries and equipment. Further, the Government has so far been the main source of funding S&T activities in the country. This needs to be significantly supplemented by the industry.

Therefore, the focus during the Tenth Plan would be on important areas of basic research, technology development, demonstration and dissemination including strengthening and creation of infrastructural facilities, development of skilled and trained manpower and providing technology for societal benefits in the fields of space sciences, nuclear sciences, ocean sciences, biotechnology, scientific and industrial research and science and technology.

With the broad vision of developing India as a leader in space technologies, the overall direction of the Space Programme, formulated within the framework of a Ten Year Profile (2001-2010), will be to consolidate the gains and build upon the achievements of the Ninth Plan.

The major goals set by the Department of Space for the Tenth Plan are: to acquire new capabilities for space communications by positioning indian satellite systems - GRAMSAT and INSAT networks - for operational services; to maintain leadership in earth observations by positioning earth observation infrastructure to meet the national imaging demands and supporting the NNRMS and Disaster Management Support (DMS).

The other areas of action will be developmental activities and improved weather and ocean state forecasting; major thrust for space transportation by regular production of PSLV, operationalising GSLV, upgrading launch capabilities and undertaking major R&D leading to future generation vehicles; to encourage space science enterprise by mobilising high quality scientific groups for advanced space science endeavours; to encourage spin-offs in human resource development and with industry and international partnerships.

Within the framework of the long-term vision, the Indian Earth Observation Programme will continue to serve as the mainstay of the NNRMS. A disaster management support programme drawn up by the Indian Space Research Organisation (ISRO)/Department of Space will be implemented during the Tenth Plan. The programme, with special focus on the northeastern region involves: mapping and monitoring support; creation of thematic and cartographic information database for flood-prone and cyclone-prone areas and ortho-photomaps of earthquake-prone areas; demonstration of the applicability of GIS-based decision support system for disaster management; infrastructure, including networking facilities; R&D support etc.

Based on the launch vehicle requirement scenario and the long-term vision of the space transportation system, programmatic targets have been set. PSLV would remain the workhorse vehicle for earth observation and space science and meteorology satellites. The development flights and operationalisation of GSLV (Mk I and II) with indigenous cryo stage and the establishment of second launch pad at Sriharikota Range (SHAR) will be completed .The development of GSLV Mk III will be an important thrust area. It is also proposed to develop the critical technology base related to the Recoverable Launch Vehicle (RLV) and realisation of the proto unit of RLV technology demonstrator.

While bilateral and multilateral efforts to pursue international cooperation will continue, the major thrust will be on: space mission operations, meteorology, environment and humanitarian services such as Megha Tropiques; a cooperative satellite mission with Synthetic Aperture Radar; international charter on Space Disaster Management Support, Global Observing Strategy, Global Precipitation Mission etc.

Another thrust area would be organisational development and human resources. These would relate to: consolidation of core competences and enhanced outsourcing; reorientation of administrative systems and efficiency improvement; motivation, improving morale and maintaining organisational health; succession planning through induction and retention of talent; learning and knowledge management etc.

The major identified mission mode programmes would include: operationalisation of NNRMS, technology development for future generation launch vehicle, development of allweather remote sensing technology, and application of space technology in education and health.

*Nuclear Science*

Nuclear science involves a chain of activities viz. research, development, demonstration and deployment of technologies, which has been a crucial factor in building a self-reliant capability in all aspects of the nuclear fuel cycle. Concerted efforts have been made in the field of nuclear science to carry forward the developments in advanced technologies in order to insulate the country from technology denial regimes. Since energy security is important for economic as well as strategic reasons, thorium-based nuclear energy systems will have to be a major component of the Indian energy mix in the longterm.

Realising that India has to be in the lead in the development and deployment of thorium utilisation technologies, the future policy of the Department of Atomic Energy will be to build a strong indigenous R&D infrastructure as well as to marshal the trained scientific and engineering manpower in their future programmes. India is pursuing a three-stage nuclear power programme which has been formulated to provide long-term energy security based on indigenous nuclear fuel resources.

The programme envisages a closed fuel cycle involving reprocessing of the spent fuel to separate the fissile fuel for recycling. The focus would be on R&D to ensure that the technology does not become obsolete, the safety and economic competitiveness of nuclear power is continually improved, and capacity utilisation is maximised. Technology for the fuel cycle needs to be pursued along with the nuclear reactor technology with the objectives of: improvement in the existing technology for the enhancement in process performance; development of cross-cut technologies to merge nuclear reprocessing and waste management; development of new process and technologies to cater to the programmes involving FBR and AHWR fuel cycles etc.

In addition, health, safety and environment programmes form an integral component of the entire spectrum of activities in the nuclear fuel cycle. The Tenth Plan objectives in the field of nuclear sciences include: utilisation of thorium as fuel on a commercial scale; large-scale deployment of nuclear power; improving cost-efficiency as compared to alternate options for energy generation; attaining higher levels of safety through utilisation of inherent and passive safety features; utilising the proliferation resistant potential of the thorium fuel cycle to the fullest extent.

It will also attempt to provide for adaptability to non-electrical applications, particularly desalination and high temperature processing applications, including those for generation of non-fossil fluid fuels.. Emphasis would also be laid on basic research in nuclear sciences and allied areas. This would cover frontier areas in physics; in chemistry; in biology (molecular biology, radiation biology, genetics, cancer research); in agricultural sciences and food technology; and in mathematical and computer sciences.

The radiation technology applications programme will continue to develop research reactors, accelerators and lasers and other advanced technologies. Important mission mode programmes would be identified in some of these areas. Recognising the long-term strategic necessity of ensuring the availability of adequate and quality human resource , emphasis would be laid on research-education linkages and evolving a mechanism to facilitate large-scale deployment of applications, especially in agriculture.

The second stage started with the FBR Programme at Indira Gandhi Centre for Atomic Research (IGCAR), Kalpakkam utilising plutoniumbased fuel. Improvements and upgradation in the technology will be an important part of the programme in the coming years. For irradiation of fuel and structural materials to be used in the fast reactors, various projects are to be pursued in the areas of physics and shielding, chemistry, materials, thermal hydraulics, structural mechanics, component development, fuel development, inservice-inspection, instrumentation and control and fuel cycle.

The third stage pertains to designing and developing advanced nuclear power systems that will utilise the plutonium resources in an optimum way to maximise conversion of thorium to 233U, extract power in-situ from the thorium fuel, and recycle the bred 233U in future reactors. Keeping the objectives and the current international trends in nuclear technology in view, a roadmap has been drawn up for the third stage of the nuclear power programme. This involves four steps viz., development of AHWR for utilising thorium for commercial power generation; design and development of high temperature reactor-based power packs, mainly for process heat and non grid-based electricity generation applications.

Accelerator Driven Sub-critical Systems (ADS) to produce several times more electrical energy than that required to run the accelerator; and acceleratordriven system with a fast reactor sub-critical core, together with a mainly thorium-fuelled thermal core somewhat similar to that present in the AHWR. Under the radiation technology application programme, one of the major activities to be initiated is the setting up of a research reactor for isotope production and associated isotope processing facilities at a new campus to be set up for BARC.

Development of technologies for desalination will be given further impetus. Efforts to develop technologies for the production of strategic materials in the country will be intensified. The DAE will also initiate projects around all its installations for the deployment of technologies. Some examples are: farming for the production of breeder seeds using mutants developed by BARC; setting up of laboratory facilities for the production of saplings by tissue culture techniques for distribution to farmers in the area; any other technology which could provide improved means of livelihood to the people.

For this purpose, land around nuclear installations will be utilised with the farmers and the DAE scientists working together. Under the Polymetallic Nodules Programme, survey and exploration, environment impact assessment, mining and allied technology development, and metallurgy will be continued. Bay of Bengal Fan (BENFAN) programme will also be taken up with emphasis on long coring of the sediments at selected locations. Comprehensive systematic EEZ topographic surveys using stateof-the-art multi-beam systems will be initiated to identifying areas for future detailed surveys for the non-living resources exploration. A strategy would then be evolved for comprehensive assessment of resource potential of the Indian EEZ including gas hydrates, cobalt crust, etc.

The existing stations for collection of nearshore samples identified under the Coastal Ocean Monitoring and Prediction System (COMAPS) programme will be more carefully planned to reflect the pollution load occurring close to the shore. The activities under Integrated Coastal and Marine Area Management (ICMAM) capacity building programmes funded by the

World Bank, training to coastal states on the use of GIS and on critical habitat information system using GIS, and zoning of coastal waters will continue. As a pre-requisite for the preparation of ICMAM plans in selected areas, eco-system modelling studies which can be used for management of the shoreline land, particularly to control erosion and accretion, will be conducted.

Other R&D activities in this area include: decision support system for management of small to large habitats, migratory patterns of turtles, longterm monitoring of pollutants, development of online pollutant detection system using sensors for hotspot areas etc. Under the Ocean Observation Systems, the number of moored buoys would be increased to 40 with indigenisation of its prototypes. The number of drifting buoys would be increased to about 150, tide gauges to 34, besides 150 Array of Real Time Geostrophic Oceanography (ARGO) floats.

Extended Bathy Thermograph (XBT) line would also be added. Development of algorithms, models etc. will continue to make full use of the newly planned Indian and foreign satellite missions such as Megha Tropiques, Oceansat-II etc. Consolidation of the ongoing efforts under the Indian Ocean Modeling and Dynamics (INDOMOD) for operational applications will be continued on a priority basis.

Under the ocean energy programme, modification of the 1 MW OTEC plant to function as a land-based or shelf-mounted plant for islands would be taken up. Deep sea technology activities include development of technologies for direct applications to shallow and deepwater mining and technology base for deepwater applications. The technology and necessary expertise for the exploration and recovery of gas hydrates will also be developed.

National Institute of Ocean Technology (NIOT), Chennai would endeavor to have institutional cooperation/collaboration for technology development with reputed national and international research laboratories, academic institutions, international organisations and private R&D institutions. New initiatives include: development of wave-powered data buoys for offshore applications and establishment of a marine meteorology cell, and marine instrumentation and sensors calibration cell.

India is well poised to embark upon biotechnology-based national development. The underlying assumption of the policy framework is that the developments in the field of biotechnology will have the greatest impact on food, nutrition, health, environment and livelihood security. The recent advances in many areas of biological research, notably genomics, cell biology, structural biology and molecular approaches to biological function hold great promise for future developments in biotechnology.

Long-term support would be provided for basic biology research in areas related to infectious diseases, metabolic engineering, biomaterials, stem cell research, chemical ecology etc. by providing the necessary infrastructure and instrumentation facilities. Some important areas for research would be food and nutritional security; optimal utilisation of biological resources through biotechnological interventions; genomics; costeffective, easy-to-administer and affordable healthcare regime, especially molecular medicine; biotechnological solutions for environmental issues like biodiversity conservation, and waste recycling and pollution abatement.

Conversion of indigenous research leads into biotech products and processes would continue to be a major endeavour. This will be facilitated by instituting new academia-industry and private-public partnerships. Human resources needed for biology research and biotech development would be generated through specific programmes. The Department of Biotechnology's mission is to develop biotechnology as an intellectual enterprise, to provide the impetus to help utilise this knowledge for the benefit of mankind and to launch well-directed efforts for harnessing biotechnological tools for generation of products, processes and technologies that will enhance the efficiency and productivity of agriculture and forestry improve nutritional security, development of molecular medicine and environmentally safe technologies for pollution abatement, biodiversity conservation and bio-industrial development and creation of a strong infrastructure both for research and commercialisation of bio-products, bioprocesses and biotechnologies.

Concerted and long-term support would have to be provided to basic research in the new areas of modern biology and biotechnology and mechanisms to identify creative talents among the youth need to be established. Commercialisation of the knowledge base should be facilitated through simplification of some procedures and policies. These include: single window clearance mechanism for the biotech industry, especially based on recombinant DNA technology; venture capital funding to encourage large-scale production of biotech products, incubators or pilot plants through the joint efforts of the public and private sectors and tax holidays to publicly supported indigenous R&D.

Bioscience enterprises will be identified and encouraged in three major areas: agriculture, health-care and the environment. The commercialisation of bio-products will be encouraged by developing innovative policies in conjunction with other government departments and agencies. Besides the ongoing programmes on genetic counseling, emphasis would also be placed on genomics of humans, animals, plants and microbes, human genome diversity studies, molecular epidemiology; setting up of network facilities in at least four to five centres for high throughput screening, functional genomics, microarray and structural genomics, etc. The major funding for this would come from industry, with the Government providing only a nominal support.

Major mission mode programmes would be initiated in the areas of genomics, new drugs and molecules from important medicinal plants, bio-resources characterisation, bio-fuels, new generation vaccines, food and nutritional security. In the field of agriculture, biotechnology research will be used mainly in crop improvements for high export-value products through genetic modification of other crops or through in-vitro techniques. Other approaches in this field are: fine mapping of genome regions harbouring useful genes; developing transgenic biofertilisers; creating an awareness among farmers on the benefits of bio-pesticides and integrated pest management (IPM) technologies etc.

Research on plant biotechnology would be directed towards molecular and genetic phenomena associated with the process of infection, progression of disease (infectious and systemic) and the underlying pathology; metabolic engineering using recombinant DNA technology; characterisation of enzymes involved in carbon and nitrogen assimilation; plant tissue culture; bio-prospecting of wild plants; generation of a network programme on bioengineering of crops for Bio-fuels and Bioenergy; development of medicinal and aromatic plant crops with value addition in terms of proteins, minerals, vitamins and bio-molecules of therapeutic value and industrial use, genomics of selected medicinal and aromatic plants etc.

In animal biotechnology, the focus will be on large animals and employment of newer techniques like cloning and stem cell derived animals (transformed and non-transformed). In the area of aquaculture and marine biotechnology, a Marine Biotechnology Centre would be set up for research on novel enzymes, bioremediation, extremophilic organisms, bio-medicals, genomics and proteomics of various marine organisms.

The areas of focus for medical biotechnology research are: tuberculosis, HIV, malaria, cholera, Japanese encephalitis, edible vaccines, helicobactor pylori, rabies, cancer and drug delivery systems. The programmes will be prioritised taking into consideration criteria like disease burden, cost effectiveness of technologies and the potential utility of these technologies for community needs.

Broad areas of activity identified for genomics (human, animal, plant and microbial) are: computational genomics and genome-sequence data analysis, micro-array technology, structural genomics of humans and microbes, singlenucleotide polymorphism (SNP) analysis and pharmaco-genomics.

In the field of environment and biodiversity, the projects to be initiated relate to: collection, conservation and sustainable use of bio-diversity; bio-remediation, waste recycling and wasteland reclamation; development of biosensors, bioindicators; phyto-remediation; and engineering of microbes for pesticide degradation, production of industrial and specialty chemicals, resource recovery and waste recycling etc.

Major new initiatives are also planned in the expanding area of bioinformatics. These include: dedicated high speed network for the BTIS net to achieve near-instantaneous access to the biological databases; setting up of teraflop supercomputer facilities for bioinformatics; establishment of a National Bioinformatics Institute for carrying out various activities like policy making; establishment of a Centre for Genome Informatics for carrying out research related to genomics and proteomics that include database mining, computational gene discovery, sequence similarity searching, gene expression analysis, etc.

Besides continuing the existing biotech facilities and repositories at various places, the new facilities to be set up pertain to: high field nuclear magnetic resonance (NMR) imaging facility, mass spectrometry and microarray facilities at two to three centres; pilot plant facilities and biotech incubators for diagnostics; good manufacturing practices (GMP), facilities in collaboration with private industry participation etc. Biotechnology parks and biotechnology incubators will be set up in a few states in collaboration with the concerned State Governments.

A few centres of excellence will also be set up in emerging areas such as: marine biology, high altitude biology, medical molecular biology, molecular ecology, invertebrate neurobiology and computational biology. To address biotechnologyrelated intellectual property rights (IPR) issues in a holistic manner, a Biotechnology-IPR Centre will be set up as an autonomous society under the DBT for organising training programmes and setting up of a Patent Information Networking System.

In the area of human resource development, support would be provided to 20 additional institutions and between 100 and 150 fellowships, besides instituting distinguished biotechnology professorships, biotechnology chairs and national bio-sciences career awards. Popularisation of biotechnology will be intensified through the mass media and co-curricular programmes. In order to attract a large number of small and medium scale biotech entrepreneurs, a Biotech Venture Capital Fund will be initiated in collaboration with organisations like the Small Industries Development Board (SIDBI), Industrial Development Bank of India (IDBI) etc.

While the existing programmes of international collaborations will continue, the focus for the initiatives will be on basic research in new biology for understanding molecular and genetic phenomena of pathogenesis in plants, animals and human beings; plant molecular biology; biosensor development; metabolic and tissue engineering; and product and process-oriented research involving scale up/ field trials and validations through technology transfer of both techniques and materials.

**Scientific and Industrial Research**

The plans and programmes relating to scientific and industrial research are implemented by the DSIR and CSIR. The DSIR is concerned with the promotion of industrial R&D, development of new technologies and processes, acquisition, management and export of technology and development of consultancy capabilities.

The objectives/activities of the various programmes of DSIR covers financial support for SIROs, fellowship, traineeship and international R&D collaborations; support to new technology development projects; support to grass roots decentralised projects; support for technology innovations and resource centres and chairs in technology and innovation management; support for technology trade facilitation centres, technology counselors in developing countries and product design centres.

The NRDC will continue to undertake the projects under two programmes - Invention Promotion Programme (IPP) and Technology Promotion Programme (TPP). In addition to awards, assistance to investors, publications etc, some new programmes have been proposed for IPP like organisation of Inventors' Clubs and exhibitions and revamping their publications to cater to the needs of the small-scale industry.

Under the TPP, for the development and promotion of rural technologies, a demonstration-cum-operating centre will be set up near Delhi for demonstration of rural and household technologies. In order to promote the export of technologies, the NRDC will participate in international exhibitions/seminars/trade fairs and prepare multimedia compact disc presentations of technologies.

Other measures under the TPP relate to:setting up a technology information-related portal covering information on indigenous and foreign technologies, IPR, R&D institutes and awards, training programmes etc.; interactive multimedia package on IPR; funding of technology development programmes in the areas of gene delivery systems, digital fountain clock, slow release spray of pesticides etc.; and providing loan/equity/ convertible loan/grant to licensees of NRDC technologies, etc.

CEL will continue to work on technologies relating to 250 micron thick silicon wafers for manufacturing solar cells, and manufacture of 125 mm and 150 mm pseudosquare multicrystalline solar cells. CEL would also initiate R&D work on thin film solar cells; photovoltaic products for use as building materials; strategic electronic equipments and systems so as to make this area of operation contribute to about 20 per cent to 30 per cent of the turnover; digital axle counter and other signalling and safety systems for Indian Railways and export; and hybrid remotelyoperated PV systems for microwave repeater stations, and applications of piezo electric elements for defence and automobiles.

**Council of Scientific And Industrial Research (CSIR)**

CSIR seeks to foster the values of excellence in science; global competitiveness in technology based on high science; local relevance in tune with socio-cultural and economic ethos of the people and innovation in all the spheres of activities ranging from science to technology management to financing. These principles, coupled with the results of a SWOT analysis carried out in CSIR laboratories, were taken into consideration in drawing up the opportunities for CSIR technologies in the market place.

Accordingly, CSIR will seek to form strategic partnerships with Indian industry for innovative research; application and development of technology; commercialisation of technology; technology transfer, especially to SMEs and helping certain weak industrial sectors to regain their growth rates and become competitive globally. Other factors which influenced the formulation of CSIR programmes for the Tenth Plan are: responsibilities arising out of the international IPR arena; continuous training and retraining of CSIR staff; advancement of knowledge through enlarging the scope of fellowships to transdisciplinary areas and supporting basic research; and extension of S&T to the masses by involving the NGOs.

The focus of the CSIR would be to provide scientific industrial research and development that maximises the economic, environmental and societal benefits. The major thrust of the programmes would be on needs of and the opportunities in the market place; partnerships with industry for innovative R&D; development, application and technology transfer in areas that promote global competitiveness; technology based on high science and finding holistic and optimal solutions to the pressing problems of the nation.

The core programmes include: high science and technology for national aerospace programmes; medicinal plant chemotypes for enhanced marker and value-added compounds; globally competitive chemical processes and products; development of speciality polymers; industrial waste minimisation and clean up; coal preparation for quality enhancement; biomolecules; infectious diseases handling; design analysis and health assessment of special structures etc.

The activities in the area of leather processing technology, leather product technology, leather environment technology, biotechnology in leather would be strengthened. Mission mode programmes would be launched in the areas of leather technology, carcass utilisation technology, design and development of civil aircraft, documentation of traditional knowledge, exploration and exploitation of the nation's microbial wealth, molecular biology of selected pathogen, evolving pollution monitoring system/devices for air /water / solid waste, microwave tube technology and rural technology.

The Tenth Plan programmes of the national laboratories have been formulated under 14 heads. These are: aerospace, biology and biotechnology, chemicals, earth resources and natural hazards mitigation, ecology and environment; electronics and instrumentation, energy, food and food processing, health-care and drugs and pharmaceuticals; housing and construction, information dissemination and products like leather, materials, minerals and metals and manufacturing.

In addition, a 'training and motivation' programme will be initiated for selected science teachers. In order to attract youth to science and to promote interest, excitement and excellence in science education at the school and undergraduate levels, each CSIR laboratory will adopt at least one school and one college in its area. It will not only offer its facilities for project work and experimentation but also carry out student guidance and motivational programmes.

Fellowships will be offered to researchers in trans-disciplinary areas and a spirit of entrepreneurship will be inculcated among research scholars through appropriate motivation, skills development and venture financing so they may establish their own R&D enterprises. The IPR regime is presently in a state of flux and there are major unresolved issues with respect to 'traditional knowledge', 'genomic sequences', 'copyright on the Net' etc.

National Institute of Science, Technology and Development Studies (NISTADS), New Delhi in CSIR has been mandated to coordinate this activity through enhancing the portfolio of foreign patents from 500 to 2,500 by the end of the Tenth Plan; identifying potential threats to and opportunities in the IPR regime; creating electronic/digital database on CSIR's intellectual property and knowledge- base holdings; developing educational programmes on intellectual property and technology management, etc.

During the Tenth Plan, CSIR has envisaged the establishment of an organisational Human Resources Development Centre at Ghaziabad as a follow up to the recommendations of the CSIR Review Committee in 1986. The Centre is expected to train around 600 senior personnel annually. Other activities under R&D management support include: partnerships that could add value to R&D activities in the national laboratories; popularisation of CSIR activities among masses through various media; and continuing support to the Unit for R&D in Information Products to catalyse and mobilise packaging of information products based on CSIR databases in order to make it selfsustaining.

The objective of the New Millenium India Technology Leadership Initiative (NMITLI) scheme, initiated in February 2000, is to help India capture the global leadership position in a few selected technology areas. In the first year of its operation, CSIR initiated nine 'proof of concept projects'. On completion, five of these projects will qualify for the next stage of specific product/process/application/ development and upscaling.

Around 20 per cent of the funding for these projects will come from external sources. This scheme will enable India to acquire global leadership/monopoly position in at least three niche technology domains. Programmes under infrastructure renovation and refurbishment include: internet connectivity to all laboratories through a national level Internet service provider (ISP) including Virtual Private Network (VPN) solutions to establish a CUG (Closed User Group) and refurbishing of the antiquated physical infrastructure which was built or acquired more than thirty years ago.

Some of the laboratories like the Central Drug Research Institute (CDRI), Lucknow, Central Food Technology Research Institute (CFTRI) Mysore, Central Salt and Marine Chemicals Research Institute (CSMCRI), Bhavnagar etc. are housed in centuries-old palaces which were converted into laboratories by carrying out minor renovations.

Most of the CSIR laboratories are not suited for modern day R&D especially in terms of good laboratory practices (GLP), International Standards Organisation (ISO), National Accreditation Board for Testing Laboratories (NABL) requirements for accreditation and certification. Also many buildings are dilapidated and unsafe and need renovation.

# Bibliography


Adams, J. 'Female Wage Labor in Rural Zimbabwe'. *World Development 19(2/3) (1991): 163–177.*

*Agnihotri, S. Sex Ratio Patterns in the Indian Population: A Fresh Exploration.* New Delhi: Sage Publications, 2000.

Amis, P. "Indian Urban Poverty: Labour markets, gender and shocks". *Journal of International Development* 6(5) (1994): 635–42.

Baden, S. "Gender Issues in Agricultural Liberalization". *Bridge briefings on development and gender, Report 41.* Brighton: Institute of Development Studies, 1998.

Bardhan, K. "Women's Work, Welfare and Status: Forces of tradition and change in India". *Economic and Political Weekly* XX (50 and 51) (1985).

Bennett, L. "Women, Poverty and Productivity in India". *World Bank EDI seminar paper 43.* Washington, DC: World Bank, 1992.

Boserup, E., *Woman's Role in Economic Development.* New York: St. Martin's Press, 1970.

Chambers, R. "Participatory Rural Appraisal (PRA): Analysis of experience". *World Development* 22(9) (1994): 1253–68.

Chant, S. *Women-Headed Households: Diversity and Dynamics in the Developing World.* New York: St Martin's Press, 1997.

Davin, D. "The Impact of Export-Oriented Manufacturing on Chinese Women Workers". *UNRISD Project on Globalization, Export Oriented Employment for Women and Social Policy.* Geneva: UNRISD, 2001.

Demery, L. and Walton, M. "Are the Poverty and Social Goals for the 21st Century Attainable?" *IDS Bulletin* 30(2) (1999).

Dollar, D. and Gatti, R., "Gender Inequity, Income, and Growth: Are good times good for women?" *Background paper for Engendering Development.* Washington, DC: World Bank, 1999

Lloyd, C. and Blanc, A., "Children's Schooling in Sub-Saharan Africa: The role of fathers, mothers, and others". *Population Council Research Division Working Paper* 78 1995.

Miller, B. D. "Social Class, Gender and Intrahousehold Food Allocations to Children in South Asia'. *Social Science and Medicine* 44(11) (1997): 1685–1695.

Norton, A. and Elson, D. *What's Behind the Budget? Politics, Rights and Accountability in the Budget Process.* London: Overseas Development Institute, 2002.

*Sen, A. Collective Choice and Social Welfare.* San Francisco: Holden Day, 1970.

*Sen, A. Poverty and Famines: An Essay on Entitlement and Deprivation.* Oxford: Clarendon Press, 1981.

United Nations Development Programme (UNDP), *Human Development Report 1990.* New York: Oxford University Press, 1990.

# Index